T0168286

Perspectives of
Black Popular Culture

Edited by
Harry B. Shaw

Bowling Green State University Popular Press
Bowling Green, Ohio 43403

Perspectives of
Black Popular Culture

Contents

Introduction

The normal distinction between popular and high culture is based largely on how esoteric the art, skill, or concept is that characterizes and reflects a given people at a given time. In Western high culture, the knowledge and "consumption" of classical and traditional music, literature, painting, and drama, for instance, are enjoyed by a relatively exclusive minority of the people. There is also some claim that the defining and categorizing strictures applied by society along with the degree of sophistication of the art forms and habits in high culture, often acquired through formal training, further set it apart from Western popular culture. More important is the fact that the access to high culture is rather limited. Like its associate, etiquette, high culture has an aura of exclusiveness guarded by the rigorous dogma of correctness—sometimes tacit but often blatant; sometimes authentic but often artificial in its strictness. For example, the dress code and general decorum of the more genteel sports of tennis and golf are but more overt and visible manifestations of the same kinds of distancing strictures used in other aspects of high culture. The descendants of the ribald pit dwellers who adorned the Elizabethan stage have long since lost touch with the receding—or ascending—art form, forsaking it for more hospitable and more contemporary forms. Popular Culture, on the other hand, is broadly and affectionately embraced by common people because it is produced, reflected, and consumed by them in the course of their everyday lives.

Black popular culture in America holds a peculiar status in that, unlike Western popular culture in general, it has no counterpart in Black high culture. In other words, Black culture is to a great extent Black popular culture, for there is no identifiable Black culture that can not be or is not readily embraced by the wide spectrum of Black society. Black culture is popular culture partly because it continually looks toward the roots of the common Black experience and draws from those roots for its creativity. Black artists continue to create new modes that replace older ones which in their decadent stages are abandoned and drift slowly away as they are customarily usurped and then adopted by the larger American community. Jazz, swing, and even more recently rock music, for example, have gone this route.

In America this particular kind of decadence creates a curious dialectic where the creators reject their own creations once the creators' identification is weakened or blurred by Americanization or assimilation. The dynamics of this particular dialectic contain an insidious irony in that an unequivocal self-identification is made essential precisely because of the special and

1

pandemic resistance to the assimilation of Blacks into the mainstream of American life. Willing joint ownership of such cultural commodities, therefore, is understandably not the strong suit of people whose identity depends on fine and definite distinctions. The lyrics of popular songs, like those of blues and spirituals, provide Blacks the needed symbolic posture of opposition to or at least separateness from white society. While ostensibly concerned about the relationship of a man and woman or of man and God, the lyrics often convey a subliminal symbolic message about the relationships of Blacks to whites. This may explain why themes are often accusatory or assertive of manhood and why, for example, "you done me wrong" and "I am a man" are prevalent blues themes.

The identification is more stable, it seems, closer to the roots. The blues, for instance, emanates from the people to be consumed by the people. Likewise, gospel and spirituals, dance, folk poetry, folkways, and lifestyles among Blacks are popular because they come from, are presented for, and consumed by everyday Black people. When Jimmy Reed sings "Big Boss Man," he is singing out of the direct or indirect experience of most Black people. The shared common heritage of slavery, freedom, field work, house service, subservience, defiance, squandering, sacrifice, shame, pride, joy, sorrow, industry, sloth, cunning, stupidity, forthrightness, duplicity, and others have all been part of the collective experiential background for Black people. This heritage often evinces itself in their art in a symbolic declaration of cultural independence and recognition.

For whites, it is often only incidental and therefore esoteric for poetry and art in general to protest man's inhumanity to man, especially the white man's treatment of Blacks. When people read this protest in or into the works of Twain, Whitman, Melville, etc.—if it is there at all—it is incidental and therefore, esoteric and rightly placed in high culture. The very act of hide-and-seek that the author and the audience indulge in is the essence of the high culture literary convention. By contrast the "find-the-art-in-the protest" or "hide-the-protest-in-the-art" approach by Black artists is so basic to black thought that it is necessarily popular culture. Blacks' popular songs, sermons, dances, paintings, poems, and stories are nearly all protests or affected by protest—a culturally collective "hurling one's body, one's being, one's soul as an armor or as a weapon" against the evils of the surrounding and enveloping system.

The accomplishment, the marvel would be black art without protest or a self-conscious celebration of Blackness as suggested by Countee Cullen's "Yet do I marvel at this curious thing:/To make a poet black and bid him sing!" Whether a laughing to keep from crying or a genuine celebration, the topics of Black popular culture are many and varied. Black literature often carries common popular themes. Blacks of all levels socially, educationally, and economically have a strong cultural kinship and that kinship is a popular one. Fittingly then, it is the people's Soul Train, it is the people's Dance Troupe of Harlem, the people's Wall of Respect in Chicago, the people's OBAC workshop. Furthermore the distinctive Blackness of each of these is gained through the basic Black culture in churches, taverns, and homes.

But being a Black artist is not enough to make one's art Black popular culture. When, for instance, Winston Marsalis performs Mozart's "Concerto in D Major for Trumpet and Orchestra" he is not producing nor reproducing Black popular culture. When, however, he plays the blues, he is. The same distinction can be said of Leontyne's renderings of an Aria from *Aida* and "Swing Low Sweet Chariot," even when done in the same setting. Similar distinctions can be made in other arts as, for example, the novels of Frank Yerby belong to high culture or at least to American popular culture, but decidedly not to Black popular culture. The novels of Zora Neale Hurston, on the other hand, record the same kinds of peculiar insights of Black life through literature that Marsalis does with his blues. One could conclude that if the art is distinctly Black, then it will be distinctly popular. Furthermore, if the art is distinctly Black and popular, it is also distinctly American.

The distinctive American contents and form in an American setting has made Black popular culture, especially music and dance, extremely influential throughout the world. Black popular culture is a hotbed of America's popular culture, especially in the music, dance, and language. Through Black Americans, African-derived music and rhythms permeate the world's popular music, making Marshall McLuhan in *The Gutenberg Galaxy* very prophetic.[1] Indeed the world is a global village with the auditorally highly sophisticated Blacks dominating some of the popular cultural directions. Blacks obversely, have plainly been greatly influenced by the general American popular culture. Cultural influence has clearly flowed both ways. Leroi Jones in *Blues People* says that the combination of the retention of cultural Africanisms and "the *weight* of the step culture produced the American Negro. A new race...a *new* music...."[2] However, one can extrapolate from Marshall McLuhan's discussion of "The Global Village" that Blacks who are more aurally-oriented than visually-oriented are more sophisticated with sounds than are their more visually-oriented white counterparts. The African-American sound, for which the Black taverns and the Black churches are sources of creativity, dominates American and world popular music and dance. The electronic interdependence which recreates the world in the image of a global village helps to explain why the Blacks who are more sophisticated in popular sounds, have their music and their sound becoming dominant in Copenhagen and in Sydney and even in Hong Kong as they already are in Detroit and Chicago. That happy combination of the tribal folk element and being in a technologically advanced culture that can transport this sophistication around the world, like Black cultural spores borne by an electronic wind, is a graphic example of the global village which itself parallels the spread of Christianity through the vehicle of the Roman Empire or the dissemination of ideas through the Gutenberg press phenomenon itself.

The very technology that has helped to spread this particular popular culture results in a kind of global "slumming" which has become indirect and second-hand. Now when whites emulate whites in popular music, they often emulate whites who first emulated Blacks. The full impact of Black popular culture is forever muddled by the dynamics of the melting pot and the disinclination of many to acknowledge Black beginnings. For example, for a short period in American history efforts were made to deny that even the Negro spirituals were actually created by Blacks. More insidious but nonetheless real is the gradual disassociation of an artistic creation with its Black origins. White Americans in the 1920s were unaware that the "Charleston" had its origins as a West African (Ashanti) ancestor dance.[3] Katherine Dunham and her comparative study of Black dancing of the new world revealed a high retention of Africanism in dance style. This rhythm out of Africa is both exotic and familiar. Although most Black Americans might have been just as ignorant about the African origin, they would never doubt that Blacks had created the dance. Blacks may also generally be unaware that slave work songs and spirituals had their origins in West Africa or that the blues is an outgrowth of the slave songs, and that it, in turn, spawned jazz, swing, rhythm and blues, rock and roll, soul and other major popular music forms. Nevertheless, through its basic forms and their derivatives, Black popular music and dance culture have remained on the cutting edge of popular culture creativity throughout most of America's history.

While Blacks have made perhaps their most obvious and substantial contributions to Western popular culture through music and dance, they have developed a rich popular culture in a number of other areas, including the visual arts, mass media, health practices, recreation, and literature. Contrasting the distinctiveness and prevalence of Black music and dance, the other areas, though tenacious in their survival, remain largely outside the sphere of general familiarity in Western or even American popular culture. These three areas of Black popular culture share the common characteristic of involving efforts to relate appropriately to the unpleasant aspects of this society and to bring mental, spiritual, and physical health to the individual. The visual arts reflect the lives, the trials, triumphs, joys, and sorrows that comprise the fabric of Black popular culture. Black visual arts and mass media have, like other areas of Black culture, had to contend with a prevailing negative relationship of the visual arts and mass media of general Western culture to the images of Black America. Stereotyping aimed at vilifying or ridiculing Blacks in popular visual arts, especially in advertisements of all kinds, and in the mass media such as radio and film has been gratuitous and continuous. It significantly influences the posture of the Black visual artists and those in mass media to be in varying degrees defensive, apologetic, or defiant. For example, the Aunt Jemima and Uncle Tom images spawned efforts by Black artists to "correct" the image or at least to provide balance. Similar efforts occurred in radio in reaction to depictions like Amos and Andy and in film to Stepin Fetchit. Black popular culture, then, played a significant role in creating a wholesome environment for the survival of a positive Black self-image. Carving out a wholesome, healthful environment has also been the endeavor of that part of Black popular culture associated with health practices. Popular health practices in the Black community reflect and preserve the beliefs and identity of the group with a direct effect on the physical and psychological health of the community. In much the same way Black recreation has provided an escape from not only the pressures of the work-a-day world but also the reality that historically segregation has most often barred Blacks from the outlets of fun and frivolity open to the general public. Hence, among other Black avenues of escape, the development and growth of Black resorts such as that at Idlewild, Michigan appealed especially to middle class Blacks looking to replace the burdens of ghetto life with respites of fun-filled leisure.

Among the less traveled areas of Black popular culture, literature presents the greatest difficulty in categorization. Literature, except for that vast and nebulous category referred to as popular literature, is usually thought of as high culture. While whites often seek their aristocratic beginnings and relationships as points of reference in literature, the fiction of Faulkner, Eudora Welty, and Erskine Caldwell are examples of white writers whose works reflect the experiences of the folk element and thus may be construed as treating or reflecting popular culture. In the case of Black literature the significance of the folk and popular element even in the works of the most acclaimed Black writers makes the association with popular culture rather natural. *Invisible Man, Native Son, Go Tell It on the Mountain, Their Eyes Were Watching God,* and *The Color Purple* all lend themselves well to a discussion of the Black folk or of the popular elements they contain. This attention in Black literature to common Black folk is not only a glorification of them but also a reminder that in Black society the common man plays a much more prevalent role numerically and ideologically than he does in society in general. For the most part even the rich and famous Blacks have relatives, recent memories, and roots among the poor. Indeed, the common denominator for most Blacks is the background of the common man.

Because literature captures so many aspects of Black culture, it becomes a perfect medium to begin the study of Black popular culture. The common roots are sought by the artists who regularly present situations that are grounded in the essential qualities of Black life hence, the popular element of Black culture. For literature there is the reflection of the life styles which produce, modify, retain, appreciate, and even try to escape these basic elements of Africanisms which culminate in Black popular culture. Whether the author is Toomer, Wright, Baldwin, Ellison, Morrison, Walker, or Brooks, the depiction of Black folk are indeed at the folk or the popular level. The women most assuredly are not coming and going speaking of Michelangelo. *Go Tell It on the Mountain,* for example, modifies, expands, and captures the popular culture surrounding the Black urban store-front churches—a culture not out of the reach nor the interest of the common Black person, who is not always likely to read the Black literature once it is produced but certainly participates in its creation. Even in *Invisible Man* the folk element is always close as exemplified by the protagonist's unpretentious declaration, "I yam what I am!"[4]

Just as blues, jazz, and spirituals are directly attached to the popular elements, so the literature is dependent upon and reflective of the Black popular culture. Dress, rapping, styling, scatting, bebop—all forms heavily laden with folk essence—make their way into other forms, or expressions of art imitating nature.

To look at Black popular culture as expressed or presented through any medium is to get a glimpse of the essential Blackness. It is the DNA that affects all Black—and to a great extent American—artistic achievements and helps to explain the hearty retentions of those things identifiable as African or Black culture. Anything that is not popular culture among Blacks will almost assuredly have its roots in other parts of Western culture. Only Black popular culture has retained identifiable Africanisms and Black culture traits in a culturally competitive environment while making innumerable significant contributions to American and Western Culture.

Notes

[1]Marshall McLuhan, *The Gutenberg Galaxy*, Toronto: University of Toronto Press, 1962, pp. 8, 27.

[2]LeRoi Jones, *Blues People*, New York: William Morrow and Company, 1963, pp. 7-8.

[3]Jones, p. 17.

[4]Ralph Ellison, *Invisible Man*.

University of Florida   Harry B. Shaw

The Black Tavern in the Making of A Jazz Musician: Bird, Mingus, and Stan Hope

Harry A. Reed

Introduction

Young black musicians have always served a considerable period of their apprenticeship in black bars. There the young player learned acceptable professional standards. He worked to improve his technique, expand his repertory, extend the range of his instrument, and to internalize a positive attitude toward improvisation. Additionally, the bar was the place to experiment with new ideas. If the novice's competence did not match his confidence the negative response usually spurred him to greater effort and sometimes final achievement. Among other things the bar provided a site where companionships could be made and maintained. As the musician moved through the stages of novice, imitator, innovator, and finally cult leader the bar functioned as an institution in which behavior was modified. In this setting a new language was learned, a new type of dress was adopted, and, new social modes were accepted. In short the teenage musician and his lifestyle separated him from his contemporaries who pursued more normal pre-adult pastimes.

This paper will discuss the above themes as they relate to three musicians during the period 1935-1955: Charlie Parker, Charlie Mingus and Stan Hope. Parker and Mingus are obvious choices because of their centrality to the new musical forms of that era. Stan Hope, however, requires brief explanation. He represents the legion of jazz musicians who were talented and dedicated but never made the name, the money, or the recording dates although they travelled the same avenues.[1] Hope's career does validate the black bars position in the socialization of black musicians.

Review of Literature

Two recent writings have reaffirmed my idea that the black bar served as a laboratory to aspiring young musicians. Neither incident takes place in a black bar but this only serves to strengthen the paradigm. In the first encounter[2] we are told how Bird stays in his dressing room at Billy Berg's while the rest of the quintet warms up the house. At precisely the moment of dramatic impact Bird leaves his dressing room alto in hand, wailing "Cherokee." The place, the audience, the time, belongs to Bird. It is a supreme example of macho, musicianship and a man at the top of his creative abilities.

7

The scene at Billy Berg's represents finished product, a show-casing of the years of struggle. Yet Berg's could not have provided that atmosphere where Bird and others like him molded their craft and their personality. Berg's place was in Hollywood, far from the Black Belt's honky tonks, jam rooms, and corner bars where Bird learned, or more precisely refined, his gift. Too, the place was establishment: only the top acts played Bergs, and no loose policy of sessions, sit-ins or jams prevailed there.

The second scene, brief and fictional, with an indeterminate racial setting but a definite black ambience is closer to the shaping influence on the young musician.[3] Hideo Yamaguchi, from Tokoyo, Japan, a stellar new trombonist challenges and ultimately loses a cutting session to Hokie Mokie, the king of jazz. It's all there: a sense of camaraderie with an underlying deadly seriousness; the tensions in the audience as the young man early gains the upper hand; the respect Hideo holds for Hokie even in the midst of the challenge; the sly confidence game of Hokie as he steals the show while the young player fronts the group; and, the admission by Hideo that he not only lost but indeed had "many years of work and study before [him] still.[4]

The above incidents convey the essence of jazz and jazz musicians at work. And they almost stand alone in reporting the atmosphere where the musician does his thing—in a bar, night club, or tavern. The body of literature in the sociology of jazz is incredibly thin on the relationship of musician to work site. Instead researchers have concentrated on jazz as social deviance,[5] protest,[6] cultural conflict[7] and a number of equally negative paradigms. For example Cameron stated that "Jazzman are not only non-literate but nonverbal as well."[8] It must be remembered that the jazz musician was/ is a creator, not an academic. His principle responsibility is to play and experience the music not to dissect and explain it. He is neither non-literate nor non-verbal. I believe he understands most clearly that the music must be appreciated initially as an emotional not an intellectual experience. And therefore, has little patience with academic types wishing to chronicle his deviance, rebelliousness, isolation, protest, tolerance, and etc. Finally the researchers seem hardly interested in value free research. Moreover it would be apparent to most musicians that the biases of most early academics were to a large degree anti-jazz musician.

More recently, however, the literature has been more positive in tone and findings. This new academic interest has produced a large and varied literature, the bulk of which focuses on matters of origin, structure, acceptance, and community among jazz musicians.

Almost all of the monographs on jazz address themselves to the question of when various musical styles came into being. Be bop is no exception: its birthdate given as the period 1939-42, in such places as Minton's Playhouse and Monroe's Uptown House.[9] Essential in the origins of this new black music were Charlie Parker, Dizzy Gillespie, Bud Powell, Kenny Clarke, Max Roach, *et al.* Along with these individuals were the institutions in which be bop grew: the Deuces, the Downbeat, the Onyx. None of the chroniclers of jazz have failed to note the centrality of the bar, nightclub or tavern to the musics growth. But they have failed to develop fully this relationship.

Those writers primarily concerned with the structure of the music have often failed to give central place to the jazz laboratory: the bar.[10] Here the research is principally toward the end of making the music more understandable to the laity. Attention is given to notation, chord structures, rhythmic patterns, improvisations, etc. Of this group of writers only Patrick has included brief mention of the club or cabarets.[11]

Perhaps the greatest research concentration within the sociology of music has been concerned with the acceptance of jazz as an art form and concomitant matters such as evaluating the word jazz.[12] The findings in this area range from the West African origin of the word jazz to its total rejection by a small number of contemporary black musicians. Much of the acceptance or non-acceptance of the music has definite race and class overtones. The appreciation of the music has definitely been slowed by the fact that its originators have been blacks and that the music itself was for long associated with lower class pursuits. The music was featured in drinking establishments rather than the concert stage. Secondly, the music seemed surrounded by an unhealthy aura of narcotics, loose morals, and vice.

Finally those researchers who treat the growth of community among musicians do acknowledge the existence of the bar as important in the jazzman's life. More appropriately they, however, focus on institution building among the musicians for control and perpetuation of their occupation and life style.[13] It is instructive, however, to note as in the case of Stebbins that three of the five core institutions utilized by jazz musicians are either directly or indirectly associated with the bar: jazz jobs, jam sessions and after-hours social life.[14] He mentions but does not develop fully how the community socializes its new adherents.

The young jazz musician typically comes to the jazz community as a late teenager, already socialized by the wider community. As a jazz musician he is resocialized: This involves a partial defection from his earliest set of values and an acquisition of a partially new set from a new set of significant others.[15]

This writer will argue that Stebbins is correct as far as he goes. He has, however, failed to look specifically at the black bar where the young musician learns his craft. Moreover he reveals a slight bias when stating that "ecologically, there is a tendency for jam sessions to occur in or near the transitional areas of the city."[16] Black residents would not call the areas where they reside or pursue their entertainment transitional.

In addition to overlooking the importance of the black bar most of the written work on jazz suffers to a greater or lesser extent from one fundamental fault. They tend to view jazz in the absence of its emotional dimension. Since this is the most essential element in jazz and conversely the most difficult to commit to paper or analysis much of the present literature is wide of the mark when it attempts to assess the socialization of the black jazz musician.

The Black Bar

Most of the work sites of black jazz musicians that have made it into print are the established institutions of the jazz world. These may euphemistically described as cabarets, clubs or nightclubs.[17] There the policy of name acts prevails and the young musician is usually restricted to learning by listening. While Birdland, the Village Vanguard, Watts Club Mozambique and the Five Spot are a step up from Herman's Bar, the Brown Jug, the It Club, and the Californian they were essentially the same: establishments dispensing alcoholic drinks and featuring live entertainment. With the latter an essential difference existed. The format more closely approximated working conditions in the 1935 to 1940 Kansas City jazz joints.[18] Herman's and the Brown Jug did not always feature jazz but did maintain a jam session policy. On those nights usually a rhythm section which was also subject to changes would play for visiting hornmen. Since Atlantic City was midway between New York and Philadelphia it was a magnet for aspiring black musicians. Simultaneously, the larger clubs, both black and white, and the Steel Pier booked big bands and more well-known groups to attract the tourist trade. In the years 1948 through 1955 a typical week might have the Count Basie band, Tadd Dameron's Orchestra, Earl Bostic,[19] and Chris Powell's Five Blue Flames featuring Clifford Brown, all playing in town. Additionally smaller big name groups would be booked into the smaller clubs: Dizzy Gillespie, Milt Jackson, Lester Young, Jimmie Smith, and Sonny Stitt. Lesser known musicians from the New York State and Pennsylvania area would augment this talent supply. Preeminent among this latter group would be Morris Lane, Billy Butler, and Coatsville Harris. Finally, local musicians such as Stan Hope, drummer Sid Trusty, bassist Donald Watkins and others would fill out the musical talent pool. In short a ready supply of musicians and bars existed to provide the laboratory for exploring musical ideas.

Herman's, at the corner of Maryland and Arctic avenues, basically a neighborhood bar was multileveled and featured two circular bars. The front bar, the larger of the two had a small bandstand with piano and sound equipment that could accommodate about eight musicians comfortably. While jam sessions and jazz were only part of Herman's program, such sessions were usually well attended by musicians and listeners. At this establishment sessions were usually scheduled during the summer months on Sunday afternoons. The remainder of the year Herman's reverted to its neighborhood bar status. Even so, the short period of activity provided an atmosphere where new skills were learned and new habits adopted. Coatsville Harris' Quintet was one of the first groups to use the fender bass. In 1952, after an initial period of reserve, young bassists in Atlantic City began discussing the merits of the instrument. Although none moved to the new instrument, it caught the imagination of all the young bassists who heard

Coatsville Harris' group. Saxophonists had the most immediate and far-reaching effects. Clarence Sharp, Morris Lane and Sonny Stitt would be part of the young musicians' conversations for weeks. A few of the local jazzmen began to use Stitt's solo marching pattern. Or weeks would be spent dissecting, practicing Stitt's solo on "Teapot" or "Elora" or his long slow bluesy "Smoke Gets in Your Eyes."

More important to the novice was another bar one block east of Herman's. The Delaware Inn had no policy of live music. Instead its magnet was cheaper drinks, a clientele more seriously into be bop, a very contemporary jukebox, and a small room where two or three musicians could warm up without being disturbed. Conversely, so long as the musicians didn't act as if they were going to play to the bar they could remain. The Inn had a policy of keeping the most contemporary sounds on the jukebox. It was possible to listen endlessly to Bud Powells' "Un Poco Loco" or Bird's "Ko Ko" and discuss how to duplicate them[20] or to use them as bridges to new ideas.

The Brown Jug, different from either Herman's or the Inn, represented big time jam sessions. The locals watched and listened while Basie's sidemen fired up in the traditional breakfast jam session. Starting time was usually 6 am Sunday morning and frequently sets ran until noon or even 2 pm. These sets belonged to the established stars and only occasionally did the city's aspiring stars brave the battles. Those who did like Sid Trusty and Donald Watkins received double benefits. Even if they failed miserably the ridicule they got from their peers had overtones of awe. Moreover, the courage they exhibited at the Brown Jug gave them a new reputation, one that caused stars like Joe Benjamin and Doug Watkins (no relation) to share their expertise with Donald. Don would then play new bass lines and figures at Herman's and other places. All this of course improved his own playing and the exchange was learning process for all concerned. Since the Brown Jug was located in a neighborhood that had rooming houses which catered to traveling musicians, it was, more than Herman's, a musician bar. On any given afternoon you might find Billy Butler, Sarah McLawler and others running changes and rehearsing with the young locals. The Jug had one other inestimable feature: it was located only a few short blocks from Kentucky Avenue, the heart of the Black entertainment district. It was possible then for players during their breaks to make it over to the Brown Jug for a few quick solos. This peripatetic existence was enthusiastically appreciated by local players and listeners.

In the years 1955 through 1957 the two California bars were different from their earlier East Coast counterparts. First, the It Club, then located at 42nd., and Avalon and the Californian at St. Andrews and Santa Barbara had house bands which permitted sitting in. Second, the house groups were led by people at the top of their musical powers who had for one reason or another settled in Los Angeles. The It Club group was fronted by two former members of the ill-fated Max Roach Quintet which featured Clifford Brown and Richie Powell.[21] Harold Land, tenor and George Morrow, bass, led the group that also had Jimmy Robinson a talented pugnacious trumpeter of the Clifford Brown school. The Californian Club band was led by pianist/ vocalist Ernie Andrews. Like Land and Morrow at the It, Andrews' prior recording and working experience attracted a number of young musicians to the regular Monday night jams. A third differentiation from the East Coast scene was the frequent inclusion of a small number of white musicians as participants at these sessions. Significantly the white players were not those who held lucrative studio gigs but more the talented and itinerant young white players. Among these were Rolf Ericson, Swedish trumpet player resident at the time in Los Angeles; Jack Sheldon another trumpeter who later had a nationally syndicated television comedy "Run Buddy Run;"[22] and two altomen, the late Joe Maini and Tony Ortega.

The It Club's policy of open sessions could be attributed directly to Land, Morrow and Robinson. In the case of Land and Morrow, two superior musicians, professional experience and mastery of their instruments put them in an unassailable status. Robinson, on the other hand, a brash, young and talented player defied anyone to cut him. And he/they did not lack challengers. On any given night the audience contained such jazz luminaries as Hampton Hawes, Phineas Newborn, Elmo Hope, Sonny Criss, Billy Higgins, LeRoy Vinegar, Walt Dickerson, Matthew Gee, and Kenny Drew. Such talented but lesser known musicians as Wilber Brown, James Clay, Frank Butler, and Frank Morgan would also be waiting. The mix produced nights of pure musical excitement.

Bird and Mingus

Bird, born Charles Christopher Parker, Jr., on 29 August 1920, came early to the overwhelming influence of the bar. He began, it seems, at about fourteen years of age to frequent Kansas City's many jazz spots. Once his mother, Mrs. Addie Parker, had taken the streetcar to her all night cleaning job at Western Union, Bird started his rounds. He quickly developed rapport with several older musicians who would smuggle him into clubs and also give him pointers about the music and the stars. Just which individual taught Bird what has become so entangled with legend that it is virtually impossible to disentangle.[23] Frequently mentioned as friends, confidantes or mentors, are Gene Ramey, Buster Smith, Jessie Price, John Jackson, and others. The primacy of the bar in his training is attested by the facts that he learned more in his nightly sojourns than he did playing in the band of his high school peers.

The black bars of Kansas City were white-owned. The management and clientele, however, was almost solidly black. In the period 1928 to 1939 only the Reno owned by "Papa" Sol Epstein at 12th Street between Cherry and Locust had a mixed policy on audiences.[24] Yet even at the Reno prevailing racial attitudes discouraged mixing. And black and white customers were separated by means of a wooden partition. Perhaps the most famous of the old K.C. bars was the Sunset Club owned by white operator Felix Payne but managed by black Piney Brown. Payne seems to have interfered little with the day to day running of the club. Being located in the Afro-American district with a popular black manager, a singing bartender, Big Joe Turner, and a favorable attitude toward black musicians made the Sunset, for all intent and purposes, a black bar. In addition Kansas City's own Pete Johnson a former drummer turned pianoman was the regular piano player during jams. With Brown, Turner and Johnson in attendance young black musicians must have found the Sunset comfortable, challenging and inviting.

> During the early and middle thirties the Sunset was the site of more major jam sessions than any other place in town. Night after night its bandstand would be packed with musicians waiting to solo. On gala nights still others would stand at the bar, instrument cases in hand, waiting for the chance to climb on the bandstand.[25]

Thus the club became one of the places to jam and also one of the most popular.

Since the Sunset was especially favored by saxophonists it offered an excellent lab for Bird. A brash but impressionable youngster, he had many players to observe and learn from. Lester Young, Hershel Evans, Buster Smith, Ben Webster, Dick Wilson, and Buddy Tate were regular sitters. Once Bird had had his baptism of fire he too became a regular at the Sunset's sessions.

Most sessions were open to beginners and inexperienced players. It was hoped by the older musicians that common sense would act as a restraint on the younger group. This was not always so and even Bird paid the price of embarrassment on at least two occasions. In the first of these disasters Bird, only fourteen, described later, the results of his precocity:

> I knew a little of 'Lazy River' and 'Honeysuckle Rose' and played what I could. I was doing all right until I tried doing double tempo on 'Body and Soul.' Everybody fell out laughing. I went home and cried and didn't play again for three months.[26]

Nevertheless, within a year Bird again was ready to test his mettle. This time he chose to sit in at the Reno with some of Basie's sidemen. With Jo Jones setting a torrid pace Bird would have been better off playing only the ensemble riffs. But he decided to solo. After a chorus or two he faltered and finally stopped playing completely. The ensuing silence was broken by Jones' crashing cymbal which he had disgustedly thrown at Parker's feet.[27] Charlie left the stand amid catcalls and hoots. This time, however, there were no tears just determination to return and according to Gene Ramey to avenge himself.[28] Toward this end he left for the Ozarks with the George Lee band to work and woodshed.

A few years later upon his return to Kansas City Bird was ready. From about 1937 through 1939 he took his place in the front rank of Kansas City's formidable hornmen. The jam session format was still the same: long improvisations while still producing imaginative solos. The lessons Bird internalized became musical staples during the be bop period.[29] An arrangement consisted of opening and closing "heads" or riffs played in unison. The major emphasis was placed on the improvised solo and during jam sessions these could run 20 or 30 minutes until the soloist had run out of ideas. Bird excelled at improvisation because among other factors, he and Lester Young were "the most persistent and indefatigable cabaret hoppers and sitters-in."[30]

The character of Kansas City's Afro-American entertainment section, in addition to Bird's talent and his proclivities to session, contributed overwhelmingly to the mastery of his horn. The district abounded with clubs that turned a profit catering to the musicians. The Reno, Sunset, Cherry Blossom, Subway, Hi Hat, Lucille's Band Box, College Inn, Mayfair, and Elmer Bean's provided the necessary laboratory in which to nurture new musical ideas. And the recorded Bird was a product of this environment.

Charlie Parker was the last of a breed of jazzmen apprenticed at an early age, styled in emulation of the great master players, tempered in the rough-and-tumble school of the jam session, a master of his craft by the end of his teens, disciplined to the exacting requirements of the big swing bands, and, eventually the maverick who turned his back on the big bands to create, almost single-handedly, the musical revolution of the forties.[31]

In 1939 Bird left K.C. as the leader of the saxophone section in the Jay McShann Orchestra. He was, however, not finished in his apprenticeship. For, in 1942, when he left McShann in New York City, World War II had started. War conditions brought not only a shortage of recording materials, but a recording ban as well. Bird went back to the streets, to that stimulating atmosphere that had nurtured his playing in Kansas City. He found it in New York's clubs such as Monroe's, Minton's, The Famous Door, Jimmy's Chicken Shack, and Kelly's.

Unlike the amiable ambiance of early K.C. where most musical styles were fairly accepted, Bird's new development toward be bop created conflict.[32] The older musicians generally tried, in vain, to dismiss the boppers. In the midst of all this conflict Bird found companions ready to follow his lead: Dizzy Gillespie, Max Roach, Little Benny Harris, Curley Russell, Bud Powell, and others. In between working the Fifty Second Street scene he did brief stints with the big bands of Earl Hines, Noble Sissle, and Billy Eckstine. The New York City scene completed the process; for by the mid-forties Bird emerged as a fully mature artist and cult leader.[33]

Chronicling Mingus' apprenticeship in black bars presents more difficulties than with Bird or Hope. Comparatively less has been written about Mingus than about Parker. That which is printed seems more concerned with depicting Mingus' inner turmoil and genius than how he made it to that point. His own autobiography[34] is not any more instructive. When Mingus tells his own story he concentrates overwhelmingly on sexual prowess or frustrations. No doubt these are part of the man, part of the artist but it tells little about how he learned his music. Of course he talks about acquiring ideas from Britt Woodman, Buddy Collette, Red Callender and for a brief period Art Tatum. But much of his jamming, unlike Bird and Hope seems to have been done during the daylight hours at musician's pads.

In many ways *Underdog* is not about music but about the man behind the music. Other writings concerning Mingus also focus on his struggles to become an integrated human being.[35] While this point of view produces some brilliant insights it scarcely lends itself to the study herein attempted.

Yet, some speculations can be advanced about Mingus' association with bars. If the community paradigm is valid than Mingus like all jazz musicians was influenced by the core institutions that make up that structure. Stebbins posits that five factors constitute the core institutions in the jazz community: jazz jobs, jam sessions, after-hours social life, musicians' union, and cliques.[36] As has been demonstrated in the analysis of Bird's formative years three of the above factors directly relate to bars, clubs or taverns. It would have been exceptional indeed had Mingus avoided that learning process. Even in the cases of jazz musicians attending venerable institutions like Julliard, attendance came after a lengthy maturation period on the streets.[37]

Actually Mingus does hint broadly at the process of cabaret hopping which characterized Bird's early musical training. He described on one occasion practicing to solve all the problems involved with the bass so he could scare all the other musicians. One night an opportunity to cut Oscar Pettiford materialized. Pettiford, because of illness did not show but Charles played and experienced a breakthrough on his instrument. He discovered he said "It was suddenly me; it wasn't the bass anymore [playing the music].[38] Leaving aside his revelations; the eagerness with which he sought out the challenge suggests that he was no occasional visitor to the jazz clubs. Moreover, the extent to which he became a virtuoso[39] on the bass indicates not only his heavy attendance but also that he learned his instrument.

Superlatives seldom cease when critics on musicians speak of Mingus' talent. Thus he has been called the best pizzicato player the instrument has had.[40] Even after a self-imposed ten year absence from music his playing was greeted enthusiastically. On 4 February 1972 he was welcomed back in by an all-star performance recorded as "Charles Mingus and Friends in Concert." Mort Goode summed up the evening:

It all added up to a night of musical history, moments, memories. Those of us who had come to hear were served so magnificently.[41]

Like Bird, Charlie Mingus is a jazz giant. Unlike Bird, Mingus has had a longer, more rewarding creative life and more actively has been involved with the training of younger musicians.

Stan Hope

Sadly, Stan Hope never found a Mingus to assist him through the maturation process. Hope, a very good young pianoman, never achieved fame or fortune and only limited recognition for his talent. He was one of the musicians that this writer watched closely in the fertile Atlantic City atmosphere. As teenagers we frequented sessions at Herman's Daddy Lou's and Mac's Tavern where Stan quickly developed a well deserved local reputation as a swinging two-handed player. Largely self-taught he admired but did not copy the Bud Powell style.

Prior to his consuming interest in playing jazz Stan Hope had been a mildly interested high school student. Most of his energies were concentrated on basketball. For several years he was the play-making backcourt man for Artic Avenue YMCA, the black branch of that institution. In 1952, before the proliferation of scholarships and lucrative professional contracts for black ballplayers a high caliber of play could be seen in the "Y." Usually other black teams and an infrequent white one from new York, Pennsylvania, or New Jersey would play Friday and Saturday night series with the Artic Y. As idols Hope and his contemporaries admired the New York Rens more than the Harlem Globetrotters. Their style of play was more serious than the "Trotters." The Rens, organized during the late 1920s Harlem Renaissance period, represented the best in black basketball. With an attack built around the legendary Charlie (Tarzan) Cooper an appearance by the Rens was a gala affair.

Until around 1951 Hope's life was dominated by sports. At that time he and another basketball player, turned drummer, Jake Toulson began to frequent the sessions and hold sets of their own in some of the neighborhood bars. The passion that they had formerly reserved for basketball was turned to jazz. Ironically when they could not find a bar to play in, they would play at an elementary school playground between pick-up games. In the schoolyard sessions Stan played guitar modeled on the style of Johnny Moore. As they became more deeply involved in the music, basketball was left farther and farther behind. Ultimately, Jake's loyalties remained divided between basketball and the drums. But Stan shifted away from sports completely.

As he moved into the music world, Stan's attendance at bars increased accordingly. That he became a habitue was not in the least unusual. He and most of his contemporaries had begun attending sessions in their early teens. This was possible because Atlantic City was a small tightly-knit community. We were all known to the barmaids and bartenders who cautioned us to stand by the juke box away from the paying customers and not to try to order any drinks. Although our attendance might be construed as lax parental control actually the reverse was true. If any misconduct were reported by the bar personnel, none of us would have defied our parent's orders to stay away. To have done so would have exposed us to triple jeopardy: parents, bartenders and police. In short as 17 or 18 Stan's visit to bars did not separate him from his contemporaries. We all had been attending sets from the time we were 15 or 16.

What began to differentiate Stan from the others was his desire to be a musician. He first began to talk about technical aspects of the music in a way we never could. During the Herman's sessions Hope was no longer a spectator but a participant. Where we stood slightly in awe of the musicians there, he was talking to them. J.J. Johnson would jokingly tell us to bring our older cousins and uncles to the next set. With Stan the conversation probably concerned eighth notes, block chords, "comping," on what to do with the left hand. Language thus became a differentiating not alienating factor. Anyone who was interested in the music would get the musicians' attention. Simultaneously, those who expressed hostility usually got hostility in return. Certainly there were lots of put-ons[42] but put-ons were part of street culture and had no greater significance because the perpetrator was a musician.

Obviously musicians like any human grouping are interested in protecting their sense of community. Closure is the general term for the institutional arrangements which give cohesion and protection to the community.[43] If, indeed language is a device used for the purpose of community survival, the fact that "jive talk" is utilized by jazz musicians should not be construed as it has so often been as social deviance.[44] We would not so label conversations of businessmen and/or politicians even when their language would shut out most laymen and possibly mask criminal intent.[45]

In addition to developing a new technical and social language, Stan Hope also internalized aspects of the music that were beyond our capabilities. His sense of timing and pitch while humming or whistling a tune was more acute than ours. Like Bus Jackson another contemporary who was learning the alto, Stan could anticipate the changes a soloist was likely to make. Finally they could build more coherent extensions of the music we listened to.

As Stan moved more into his identity as jazz musician, his style of dress changed. His contemporaries usually wore jeans, warm-up jackets, and sneakers. Our dress suited a life-style that could not pass up a pick-up basketball or football game. Stan, on the other hand, totally discarded our style for hats, topcoats, suitpants, and dress shirts. His identification with the music moved him more rapidly into the adult world.

Whatever happened to Stan Hope and his talent is impossible to say. In 1952, at age seventeen this writer left Atlantic City and had no more contact with Stan Hope. What is interesting, however, is that on subsequent visits a new young generation of musicians represented mostly by Gary Graft, Clint Edwards, and Barry Bair were into the cabaret-hopping and trying to learn their craft as had Bird, Mingus, and Stan Hope.

In summary, although the literature on jazz is expanding rapidly it still suffers from a number of faults. Most researchers seem still slightly reluctant to put a positive social valuation on jazz. In this they appear to be victims of an attitude toward jazz that is still current in the larger society. Perhaps the latest reflection of this view is contained in a current television ad for general tires.... "Back in the days before jazz was respectable enough for the concert stage...." Moreover historians have hardly touched the subject of jazz at all. Thus no historian has done for jazz what Lawrence Levine, Sterling Stuckey, and James Weldon Johnson have done for spirituals.

Simultaneously, even the sociologists of music who have pioneered the new attitude concerning jazz are restricted by their own built-in biases. Although admitting that a sense of community exists among jazz musicians, they still find the motivations for the community and its parameters socially suspect. Although the bar seems central to the core institutions of the community, it has received only partial attention from researchers. This writer has suggested that the analysis of the musicians lifestyle can be carried farther. And, more importantly, that the black bar has contributed overwhelmingly and positively to the professional and personal maturation of young musicians.

Notes

[1]A.B. Spellman, "Herbie Nichols," *Black Music: Four Lives*, New York: Schocken Books, 1971, pp. 151-78.

[2]Ross Russell, *Bird Lives: The High Life and Hard Times of Charlie (Yard bird) Parker*, New York: Charterhouse, 1973, pp. 18-25.

[3]Donald Barthelme, "The King of Jazz," *The New Yorker*, February

[4]*Ibid.*, p. 32.

[5]William Bruce Cameron, "Sociological Notes on the Jam Session," *Social Forces*, 33, (December, 1954).

[6]Norman M. Margolis, "A Theory on the Psychology of Jazz," The *American Imago*, XI. (Fall, 1954).

[7]Aaron H. Esman, "Jazz—A Study in Cultural Conflict: *The American Imago.*" VIII, (June, 1951).

[8]Cameron, 179-180.

[9]See Ira Gitler, *Jazz Masters of the Forties*, New York: The Macmillan Company, 1966; Nat Shapiro and Nat Hentoff, eds., *Hear Me Talkin' To Ya: The Story of Jazz as Told by the Men Who Made It*, New York: Dover Publications, Inc., 1955; Marshall Stearns, *The Story of Jazz*, London: Oxford University Press, 1971, and George Hoefer, "The First Bop Combo," *Down Beat*, (June 20, 1963).

[10]Irving Lewis Horowitz, "Authenticity and Originality in Jazz: Toward A Paradigm in the Sociology of Music," *Journal of Jazz Studies I* (October, 1973); Lawrence O. Kotch. "Ornithology: A Study of Charlie Parker's Music," Part I, *Journal of Jazz Studies*, 2, 1, (December, 1974), 61-87 and Part II, *Journal of Jazz Studies*, 2, 2, (June, 1975), 61-85; and James Patrick "Charlie Parker and Harmonic Sources of BeBop Composition: Thoughts on the repertory of New Jazz in the 1940s," *Journal of Jazz Studies*, 2, 2, (June, 1975), 3-23.

[11]Patrick, *Ibid.*, p. 6.

[12]Morroe Berger, "Jazz: Resistance to the Diffusion of a Culture Pattern," *Journal of Negro History*, XXXII, (October, 1947), 461-94; Max Roach, "What 'Jazz' Means to me," *The Black Scholar*, 3, (Summer, 1972) 3; and Ortiz Walton, *Music: Black, White and Blue*, New York: William Morrow and Com., 1972.

[13]Alan P. Merriam and Raymond W. Mack, "The Jazz Community," Social Forces, 38, 3, (March, 1960), 211-222; Robert A. Stebbins, "A Theory of the Jazz Community," *The Sociological Quarterly*, 9, 3. (Summer, 1968), 318-331, and "Class, Status and Power Among Jazz and Commercial Musicians," *The Sociological Quarterly*, 7, 2, (Spring, 1966), 197-213.

[14]Stebbins, "A Theory of the Jazz Community," *The Sociological Quarterly*, 320.

[15]Stebbins, *Ibid.*, 328-29.

[16]Stebbins, *Ibid.*, 322.

[17]Frank Bach, "Music's Still Strong and the Nights are Still Long at Detroit's Black-owned Clubs," *Detroit the Free Press*, (Sunday, 6 February 1977), 16-22.

[18]Ross Russell, *Jazz Style in Kansas City* and the Southwest, Berkeley: University of California Press, 1971, 11-24.

[19]Earl Bostic and Eddie "Cleanhead" Vinson were not jazzmen in this writer's use of the term but their sidemen frequented the jam sessions. For tributes to these two musicians' abilities see J.C.   , Chasin' the Trane, Garden City, New York: Doubleday and Company, 1975-37-42, 58-60.

[20]Some musicians were interested in reproducing the classic solos in order to understand the essence of the music.

[21]Early in the morning of 26 June 1956 Clifford Brown and Richie Powell died when Clifford's automobile skidded off the highway. Both were in their middle twenties.

[22]This situation comedy (c. 1967) was loosely modeled on a more dramatic series "The Fugitive." Sheldon starred as a young musician who had inadvertently crossed the mob and the plot revolved around his continuing efforts to escape their clutches. He is now under contract to Disney Productions and most recently appeared in "Freaky Friday."

[23]Ross Russell, *Bird Lives: The High Life and Hard Times of Charlie (Yardbird) Parker*, New York: Charterhouse, 1973, is now the definitive biography of Bird. Other biographical materials include: Robert George Reisner, *Bird: The Legend of Charlie Parker*, New York: The Citadel Press, 1962; Orrin Keepnews, "Charlie Parker," Nat Shapiro and Nat Hentoff, eds., *The Jazz Makers* New York: Rhinehart and Company, Inc., 1957, 202-217; a thinly disguised fictional work by John A. Williams, *Night Song*, New York: Farrar, Straus and Cudahy, 1961.

[24]Russell, *Jazz Style in Kansas City*, p. 22.

[25]Russell, *Ibid.*, 17.

[26]Gitler, *Jazz Masters of the Forties*, 18.

[27]Russell, *Ibid.*, 28.

[28]Ibid. Some dispute surrounds this incident. Russell states it took place when Bird was 15. Gitler on the other contends that it took place in 1937. The other specific details are the same. This writer has used the Russell citation because Russell handles chronology with more confidence and because he has done the most substantive work on Bird's life.

[29]Patrick, "Charlie Parker and Harmonic Sources on Bebop Composition," *JJS*, 5.

[30]Russell, *Jazz Style in Kansas City*, 20.

[31]Russell, *Bird Lives*, 34.

[32]Barry Ulanov, *A History of Jazz in America*, New York: The Viking Press, 1952, 272-73.

[33]Gitler, *Jazz Masters of the Forties*, 20.

[34]Charles Mingus, *Beneath the Underdog*, New York: Alfred A. Knopf, 1971.

[35]Nat Hentoff, *The Jazz Life*, New York: The Dial Press, 1961, 162-65.

[36]Stebbins, "Theory," *SQ*, 320.

[37]Hentoff, *Ibid.*, 45.

[38]*Ibid.*, 164.

[39]Whitney Balliett, "Mingus," *Dinosaurs in the Morning: 41 Pieces on Jazz*, London: Phoenix House, 1952, 99.

[40]*Ibid.*

[41]Mort Goode, liner notes, "Charles Mingus and friends in Concert," (Columbia, KG 31614).

[42]Hentoff, *The Jazz Life*, 19.

[43]Stebbins, "Theory," *SQ*, 330.

[44]Cameron, "Sociological Notes on the Jam Sessions," *SF*, 180-81.

[45]Watergate and Lockheed are simply the most recent examples of this conduct. And while there have been prosecutions one should note that most of those involved received sentences less than the general population would have gotten. Indeed, several have capitalized on their criminal acts. See, Michael C. Jensen, "Watergate Donors Still Riding High," *The New York Times*, (Sunday 24 August 1970) John W. Dean, *Blind Ambition: The White House Years*, New York: Simon and Schuster, 1976, and Charles Colson, *Born Again*, Old Tappen, New Jersey: Chosen Books, 1976.

Works Cited

Bach, Frank, 1977, "Music's Still Strong and the Nights are Still Long at Detroit's Black-Owned Clubs" *Detroit Free Press* (Sunday, 6 February), 16-22.

Barthelme, Donald, 1977, "The King of Jazz" *The New Yorker*, 7 February, 31-32.

Berger, Morroe, 1947, "Jazz: Resistance to the Diffusion of a Cultural Pattern" *Journal of Negro History*, XXII, October, 461-94.

Cameron, William Bruce, 1954, "Sociological Notes on the Jam Session," *Social Forces*, 33, 2, December, 177-82.

Esman, Aaron, H., 1951, "Jazz—A Study in Cultural Conflict," *American Imago*, VIII, June.

Goode, Mort, Liner notes "Charles Mingus and Friends in Concert," (Columbia), KG 31614.

Hoefer, George, 1963, "The First Bop Combo," *Down Beat* (20 June).

Horowitz, Irving, Lewis, 1973, "Authenticity and Originality in Jazz: Toward A Paradigm in the Sociology of Music," *Journal of Jazz Studies* I (October).

Koch, Lawrence O., 1974 "Ornithology: A Study of Charlie Parker's Music" Part I *Journal of Jazz Studies*, 2, 1, (December).

———— 1975, "Ornithology: A Study of Charlie Parker's Music," Part II, *Journal of Jazz Studies*, 2,2, (June).

Margolis, Norman M., 1954, "A Theory of the Psychology of Jazz," *American Imago* XI, Fall.

Merriam, Alan P. and Mack, Raymond W., 1960, "The Jazz Community," *Social Forces*, 38, 3, (March) 211-222.

Patrick, James, 1975, "Charles Parker and Harmonic Sources of Be Bop Composition: Thoughts on the Repertory of New Jazz of the 1940s," *Journal of Jazz Studies*, 2, 2, (June) 3-23.

Roach, Max, 1972, "What 'Jazz' Means to Me," *The Black Scholar*, 3, (Summer).

Stebbins, Robert A., 1966, "Class, Status and Power among jazz and Commercial Musicians," *The Sociological Quarterly*, 7, 2, (Spring) 197-213.

———— 1968, "A Theory of the Jazz Community," *The Sociological Quarterly*, 9, 3 (Summer) 318-

Books
Balliett, Whitney, 1962, *Dinosaurs in the Morning: 41 Pieces of Jazz*, London: Phoenix House.

Colson, Charles, 1976, *Born Again*, Old Tappen, New Jersey: Chosen Books.

Dean, John Wesley, 1976, *Blind Ambition: The White House Years*, New York: Simon and Schuster.

Gitler, Ira, 1966, *Jazz Masters of the Forties*, New York: The MacMillan Company.

Hentoff, Nat, 1961, *The Jazz Life*, New York: The Dial Press.

Mingus, Charles, 1971, *Beneath the Underdog*, New York: Alfred A. Knopf.

Reisner, Robert George, 1962, *Bird: The Legend of Charlie Parker*, New York: The Citadel Press.

Russell, Ross, 1972, *Jazz Style in Kansas City and the Southwest*, Berkeley: University of California Press.

_____ 1973, *Bird Lives: The High Life and Hard Times of Charlie (Yardbird) Parker*, New York: Charterhouse.

Shapiro, Nat and Hentoff, Nat, ed., 1955, *Hear me Talkin' to Ya: The Story of Jazz as Told by the Men Who Made It*, New York: Dover Publications, Inc.

Simpkins, Cuthbert Ormond, 1975, Coltrane: A Biography, New York: Herndon House Publishers.

Spellman, A.B., 1971 *Black Music: Four Lives*, New York: Schocken Books.

Stearns, Marshall, 1971, *The Story of Jazz*, London: Oxford University Press.

Thomas, J.C., 1975, *Chasin' The Trane*, Garden City, New York: Doubleday and Company.

Ulanov, Barry, 1952, *A History of Jazz in America*, New York: The Viking Press.

Williams, John A., 1961, *Night Song*, New York: Farrar and Straus and Cudahy.

Williams, Martin, 1970, *The Jazz Tradition*, New York: Oxford University Press.

The Curse of Capitalism in the Caribbean:
Purpose and Theme in Lindsay Barrett's *Song for Mumu*

Philip M. Royster

In the end, nobody hears more out of things, including books, than he knows already. For that to which one lacks access from experience, one has no ears. Let us then imagine an extreme case: that a book speaks of all sort of experiences which lie utterly beyond any possibility of frequent, or even rare, experiences—that it represents the first language for a new sequence of experiences. In that case, simply nothing is heard; and people have the acoustic illusion that where nothing is heard there is nothing.

This has been my usual experience and, if you will, the originality of my experience. Whoever thought that he had understood something of me had merely construed out of me, after his own image. Not infrequently, it was an antithesis of me....(Nietzsche)

A reviewer of Lindsay Barrett's *Song for Mumu* (1967, Washington, D.C.: Howard UP, 1974) does not perceive the continuity of the abstract level of this Black Jamaican's first novel, that explores the world view of the Black Caribbean peasant:

...there is not enough philosophical connections to hold the book's random bits and pieces together. This is a pity because the novel is otherwise sustained by a lyrical momentum that is worthy of attention. Attention is diffused however by a maze of unrelated happenings including homicide, infanticide, dismemberment and human sacrifice. (Levin 40)

This comment attacks both the concrete as well as the abstract levels of the unity or integrity of the novel. It signifies that fitting relationships do not adhere among the novel's characters, episodes, and scenery, on the concrete level; and, on the abstract level, that there is no clear or discernible purpose or intention uniting the ideas, values and attitudes of the novel. Rather than speculate why this particular critic attributes his responses to the novel to flaws in the author's craft, a reader might hold the book's pieces together should he bring to bear on the structure of the narrative the Afro-Caribbean culture it expresses and what Barrett says of his artistic intentions. Such applications suggest that the purpose of the novel is to show how earthly pleasure and pain stimulate the human search for paradise and the divine. The episodes of the narrative adhere in two ways: First, the form of the narrative voice is an elegiac song lamenting the death and celebrating the life of the protagonist, Mumu, the chief character in search of the divine. Her life is celebrated because of the sanctity and poignancy of her search. Second, the structure of the narrative line is determined by the myth of the Garden of Eden and the fall of humankind. This Edenic imagery reflects and alludes to illusory impressions held by many people, especially Western tourists, concerning the geography and climate of the Caribbean. If there is a Garden, there is also a curse that destroys human innocence: Euro-American capitalistic imperialism which has vitiated and corrupted the lives of both rural and urban Caribbean people. To clarify the relationships between author, work and audience, it is important to explore the cultural underpinnings of the techniques that unify the novel.

A short summary of the novel may be helpful to the reader.[1] The novel begins at the chronological end of the narrative: At the funeral of Mumu, her grandfather Papa Peda stabs her mother Meela while the latter attempts to jump into her daughter's grave. Both are then buried together. Playing on the reader's emotional involvement with this tragic prologue, the plot of the rest of the novel is the story of how this tragedy comes about. In book one, the first chapter begins with accounts of how Mumu's parents—Meela and Scully—met, became lovers, became outcasts of Meela's parents, and birthed and named their child. Before the chapter closes, Scully—who has been kicked in the head by his rich white employer's wild horse—is taken to an insane asylum after he blinds his father-in-law Papa Peda and kills one of his new-born twins. In chapter two Meela, who has returned to the farm of her parents, attempts to maintain her marriage with a crazed Scully in the asylum until he commits suicide. The rich man whose horse kicked Scully senseless is then punished by the community for his part in this tragedy and for the fact that he has been appropriating the land of the farmers. In chapter three Mumu—the fearless, natural, adolescent girl now tutored by Mother River—takes Joker for a lover while her mother Meela becomes the lover of Junji, Joker's father. The two couples participate in a ritual of marriage before departure to sea, but Joker and his father are killed in an accident at sea. The grieving mother and daughter leave the country for the city. In chapter four, the mother and daughter—searching for fulfillment and an understanding of their past—work, take on various suitors as lovers, and make various acquaintances while they search for peace in the "evil" city. Meela convinces one of her lovers named Preacher to return to the country with her, while Mumu falls in love with Oboe, one of Meela's former lovers. Oboe too is killed, and Mumu grieves his loss while also memories of Scully haunt her. In book two Mumu mourns her many looses and takes on two new lovers, first Sidnisweet who is jailed for an attempted burglary and then Poet, a sadist. Upon Sid's release the two suitors duel over Mumu before an audience of birds, and Poet wins. Poet is sent to an asylum for murdering Sid; there he hangs himself, as did Scully. Mumu slips off the edge of sanity, and Dilly, a prostitute and former lover of Scully, sends a note to the country for Meela and Preacher to come rescue Mumu. The couple comes, but Mumu wants to die. In a ritual sacrifice Preacher repeatedly plunges a knife into her heart. The River Women complete the ritual by purifying Mumu's body in the river.

The song form that shapes the narrative voice is derived from the oral folk traditions of Blacks in the Americas and West Africa. Barrett's vocalization of the narrative line with the techniques of song expresses an African aesthetic value that vitally informs the world view of Black Caribbean peasant culture. Barrett has said that he sees himself as someone who "withdraws from the common thrust of the crowd to savour with a more leisurely and analytic touch the source of the nation's natural music" (Barrett; *State* 27). This statement reflects Barrett's intentional use of song technique to express his culture. He reveals the extent of his identification with his culture when he says that his "soul quivers with the pulsation of a land's peculiar rhythm" (Barrett, *State* 27). Barrett is a child of the African aesthetic tradition in which music and song express the nature and the vitality of human existence. When the Poet, lonely and hungry, first spies Mumu with Dilly enjoying a picnic by the ocean, he thinks that "food is a great song" (Barrett, *Song* 127). His association of song with food reflects the nurturing, sustaining qualities of song.

The Poet's thoughts concerning Mumu further develop the symbolic properties of song: "And then a flash of black fire among the blue and silver of the violent ocean raging in its peace and calm beneath the sun, a flash of black, a young girl's body is the shape of her sweet song...is a song a young girl's body" (127). Song is not merely a nurturing force for Black existence; song is Black existence itself.
The Poet

saw songs...thousands of songs crisscross the sky each day...you call them clouds. He was alone. In a crowd. Horse's hooves. A sweet song. Horse feet give out good sounds so is singing...horses' hooves are voices against stones. Oh yes. And then delirium. Young girls' cries make music always, in grass, bed, or meadow. Ho. Like waves like water, greatest singer of them all. (126-27)

The Poet, who reflects the aesthetic consciousness and values of Barrett, sees nature (the clouds moving in patterns) as song, and the actions of nature (the sound of horse hooves) as song. Song is the existential form of life; it is irreducible. Song expresses the ecstasy of sexual intercourse. Water is the greatest singer because it is the mother of life. This interpretation is consonant with the characterization of Mother River, who is a priestess of water. The Poet's dedication is to song: "Sweat and sadness go together and a song is all that's ever wanted, needed...a song is the heart soul and bone frame of it all. He said often he remained lonely for a song was all he knew" (126).

Barrett's portrayal of the Caribbean peasant's priority of song is a survival of a West African aesthetic value. In his autobiographical narrative, the Ibo, Olaudah Equiano, says: "We are almost a nation of dancers, musicians, and poets. Thus every great event, such as a triumphant return from battle or other cause of public rejoicing, is celebrated in public dances, which are accompanied with songs and music suited for the occasion" (Equiano 9). In the West African tradition, music serves a spiritual purpose whether or not it is explicitly religious, for it organizes, socializes, and unifies the people with their environment and their past. Barrett's narrative song form is his communion.

In an autobiographical essay written while he was living in London, Barrett (who is an artist as well as a writer) complains of his desire to "paint a picture of the communion of the souls...." But

[n]othing comes to me even in answer to my imagination's most urgent calls, I think futile desire has helped me to know a little more than I knew about my own identity. I know I am no cloud. My sojourn in this alien heaven won't offer me the breath of union that I crave for. After all the vital vapour that I want is the breath of another kind of dream, a distant climate, and exists nowhere here. (*State* 40)

The function of song is to capture the communion of soul of his Jamaican people "whose desires he intends to tap and satisfy" (*State* 27). (Barrett uses Mumu, his protagonist, to express both this search for identity and breath of union.) He says that when "a man is far away from his most favorite and familiar home all desire is a longing in him. He is never alone inside then, and is pursued if not by shadow shapes inside his head by voices all his own and yet outside of his own centre" (*State* 25). The vocalization of the song form expresses these voices haunting the writer. The voices themselves are a medium between his inward self and the community of speakers from the island. The voices express his personal world view as well as that of his people.

As a writer, Barrett identifies with the role of the voices as a medium:

I have grown into myself discovering the essence of my history in the need to love the memories of the desire and pleasures of my youth, in my land, and this love needs no hate to hide the aches of my alien habitation for it transports me to an island lying lonely in the vast endless ocean of my soul. (*State* 41)

The growing into himself expresses not only his introspection but also, and more significantly, his self realization. His history is both Jamaican and African. The essence of that history is an inexorable awareness of both his past and his present. The memory selects desire and pleasure, but the critic knows that it is more inclusive since fear and pain are inseparable from these attachments. Barrett aches from homesickness. Present also is his visionary communion with his own omnipresent soul in which he finds the spiritual expression of his island home, Jamaica. The cultural past becomes the spiritual present through a meditative awareness of self.

Barrett achieves the song form in his narrative line by employing the subjectivity and the sensuousness of the lyric; by assuming the tonal tensions of the long elegy; by employing stylistic flourishes such as ellipsis, dissonance, dislocation, transposition, surrealism, evocation, incantation; and by incorporating the oral tradition of story telling and poetry with its dense and distilled cultural allusions, internal monologue, dialogue, and vision. Technically, the narrative line should be compared and contrasted with those of two other experimenters in the African folk tradition in the Americas—that of Jean Toomer's *Cane* (1923) and that of Amiri Baraka's *The System of Dante's Hell* (1965), but such comparisons are beyond the range of this essay.[2]

The elegiac character and mood of the novel mourns the death and praises the life of Mumu, the protagonist, who is in search of knowledge of her identity and her father. During that search, she discovers the anguish as well as the beauty of what it is to live, and she discovers that only in the divine will her search end. But Mumu is a child who is buried by her mother and her maternal grandparents, and during the funeral Meela, Mumu's mother, is killed and buried by her own father. Thus the death of the child is the seminal conflict out of which the energy and pace of the narrative flows.

The Caribbean peasant has inherited his priority of concern for this problem from his West African ancestors. Two contemporary West African novelists, Chinua Achebe and Wole Soyinka, describe episodes which reveal the traditional world view concerning the death of children. Ezeulu, the chief priest of the Ibo village of Umuaro and the protagonist of Achebe's *Arrow of God*, prays to the deity, Ulu: "May children put their fathers into the earth and not fathers their children" (7). Ezeulu outlives his favorite son, Obika, as part of the price he must pay for his inordinate pride. In a contrasting parallel that supports the same world view, Soyinka's Bandele of *The Interpreters* utters a primal curse upon the Nigerian petit-bourgeoisie: "I hope you all live to bury your daughters" (273).[3] Bandele's powerful curse reinforces the value of children surviving parents as well as it points to the significance of curses themselves within the African cultural sensibility, that is grounded in a religious and spiritual world view that believes in the creative power of the word—Nommo. A curse has causal properties. *Song For Mumu* is the story of children who die not only before their parents but also by the curse and the hand of their parents. Barrett has chosen to explore what is at once the intentional destruction, the realization, and the transcendence of this most primal and passionate of human relationships—parenting.

There are three other concerns in this section on cultural underpinnings that will inform the audience's approach to this novel. First, the world view of traditional West African cultures and of their descendent cultures in the Americas is characterized by a religious and spiritual focus. "Focus" is a concept used by anthropologists that "posits that each culture has a distinguishing style or characteristic: it may be sun-centered or acephalous, ceremonial or casual, materialistic or contemplative. And everyone agrees that the focus of African culture in the Caribbean was religious" (Braithwaite, "African Presence" 73). This cultural focus influences every aspect of existence, and thereby smears the distinction between the sacred and the profane. Thus, Mumu's search for her identity and that of her father's is a mask for her search for her God. The meditator Krishnamurti asserts that whether or not one is aware of it, all human desires, searches, and striving are for God (Krishnamurti 226). Joseph Campbell's stunning construction of the monomythic journey of heroes in myth and literature corroborates the testimony of the mystic (*The Hero With A Thousand Faces*).

Second, it is important to understand the influence of slavery and its aftermath on Afro-American communities. Slavery was an oppressive system because it attacked both individual autonomy and social cohesion. Slavery was racist because Europeans and Americans decided that most of their slaves would be Black people. The aftermath of slavery is that the essentially oppressive character of the institution has not faded but remains stamped, seemingly indelibly for now, on the hearts, minds, and institutions of every human being who lives in this so-called new world. Some of us are tools of such oppression; some of us strive to escape it; and some of us are committed to bringing it to an end. The heart of the oppressive situation, whether it adheres between individuals or groups, is the threat of death from the persecutor to the victim, and the fear of death by the victim. Violence, the threat of death, is used to control the life of the victim, that is, to intimidate him into relinquishing control to the persecutor. The most trenchant irony of oppression is that the persecutor and the victim are essentially psychological and social reflections of each other. Thus, the violence within the Black communities of the Americas is a reflection of the violence of dominant, oppressive, white cultures. Barrett is deeply sensitive to this issue of violence:

Our life governed by black has been so far a chronicle of understressed violence since the outer government of our actions has been dictated by something explainably white and yet irrationally selfish in its hold on our existence and possession of the commodities that are necessary for the simple and necessary business of survival. (*State* 10-11)

Levin's critical response, cited at the beginning of this essay, of what he calls diffused attention to the "maze of unrelated happenings including homicide, infanticide, dismemberment and human sacrifice" *understresses* (to use Barrett's concept) the violence in the novel by seeking justification for his own inattention and the resulting failure to see the relationships among the events.

Finally, it is important to understand that *Song for Mumu* is written out of what Braithwaite calls a "belly-centered bawdy" world view that reflects the peasant consciousness and the African tradition rather than a "heady" intellectualism that the Jamaican middle class inherited from the British (Braithwaite, "Jazz" 40). The aesthetics of the "belly-centered" tradition demand that life be not explained away with rational comment and analysis, a mode that dominates the narrative form of a Huxley or Lawrence novel. Rather, existence should be expressed directly and tangibly in the narrative, and it should be experienced holistically with all of one's being. Thus, Barrett does not explain away the meaning of his novel in some convenient paragraph. He sings the song of Mumu's life with the expectation that his audience will experience that life as it might the beat of a drum. It is important to add that traditional Black cultures are not non-rational; nor do they suffer from any intellectual inferiority in comparison to other cultures. They simply do not believe that reasoning is the most important human behavior, not do they believe, therefore, that human beings should or can govern their lives by mere reasoning. Reasoning is an indirect filtering process that is employed to solve problems or to adjust (adapt) when human attention cannot sustain more direct experiences of existence such as intuitive knowledge, emotional feeling, meditative awareness, and communication with ancestors. The expressive techniques of Barrett's narrative voice appeal to Afro-American audiences that have maintained this cultural priority for direct experiences.

The structure of the narrative line of *Song for Mumu* is determined by the curse on human existence sustained during the Garden of Eden episode of Genesis. The novel is an allegory of that episode to demonstrate that human existence stimulates a search for the divine, the novel's purpose. With this understanding of purpose and structure, the abstract level of the novel is clearly discernible: Human beings are born into a seeming paradise, and although they appear to be personally innocent, they are actually cursed by their ancestors and the world their ancestors have created. There are three essential responses to the cursed paradise of the world—one may blindly become an instrument of the curse; he may fearfully choose to seek the pleasure and to avoid the pain; and he may seek to know the nature of his identity, his ancestors, and the world. This last response, the search for knowledge, is ultimately the search for the divine. The novel celebrates this search because the path to knowledge is the most difficult and the most rewarding to both the social order and the individual. These relationships among the major ideas of the novel's abstract level constitute the theme.

The problem of the curse is the most important abstraction because it controls the narrative line as well as provides a backbone for the thematic structure of the ideas. The Garden is Papa Peda's farm; Meela and Scully are Adam and Eve. The curse begins after Papa Peda beats Scully, whom he believes to be carrying a venereal disease, for participating in sexual love with Meela. When Scully angrily insists on leaving after his recovery, "...Papa Peda...growled his anger at them saying yes if they wished to leave they should. And how the devil will caress them...drive them into the evil corners of the world for they are evil" (25-26). The power of his curse arises out of the Nommo (the power of language to create reality), the energy of his anger, and his projection of that galvanized energy by attributing evil to the lovers in both their identity and outcome.

Both lovers and their offspring, Mumu, are the victims of Papa Peda's persecuting power. In Preacher's song for Mumu he says, "She was no evil woman/But all her youth was misfortune" (3). His verse could be uttered for her parents also. One of the novel's reviewers noted that "Mumu and her mother are pursued by malevolent fates as surely as are the characters of Greek tragedy" (Levin 40). A Hebreaic or Christian figure of speech would have been more appropriate to the novel's symbolism, for the evidence indicates that a major source of evil in the novel is the character and behavior of Papa Peda himself, who is described with demonic imagery: "With his whip hanging loose a silent snake docile by his side...a storm cloud hung on his face...driven to harsh unlovely anger...He was a dark confrontation, a demon or a devil in their path. Scully saw...[t]he presence of his ancient violence" (26). Papa Peda seems to be unaware of the diabolic significance the narrator assigns to his personality (his whip is the snake of the Garden); instead, the peasant farmer projects his diabolic characteristics onto Scully: "you be too much of a devil in my life boy for me to harbour you under mah roof no longer" (27). Papa Peda scapegoats Scully and casts him out by banishing him from the Eden-like farm. When Meela chooses to join Scully in his banishment, Papa Peda's anger strikes out again:

A tear that will not fall. Her father's voice following them. If that's what you want you got it, don' either one o' you set you' foot on my lan' again, don't you ever call my house our home. The crack of his whip. Pounding of his feet. The dam of anger bursts. Breezed on by blind demons he chases after them. ...Confused by the calmness of their retreat Papa Peda halts. Breathes fire. Stamps his feet. Cracks the dim evening open with his whip. Screams heated curses at their darkening shapes. Splits the night air with his whip and begins to cry, suddenly to cry. (27)

More than the dim evening is cracked open by Papa Peda's whip: the lives of the lovers and their offspring, allegorically Adam, Eve, and humanity cursed by original sin. It is Papa Peda's pride that causes him to suppress his sensitivity and display his anger with curses for which his tears are too late. His sorrow is his payoff in this very unpleasant transaction, for now he has cast out his daughter as well as her lover, his informally adopted son.

Scully first observed Papa Peda's demonic anger the morning after he arrived on the farm: "His eyes blaze. A green flame flying from them. Scully was to see this light in Papa Peda's stare at other times but this morning was his first sight of it and it scared and bewildered him. What brings such demons from those depths?" (12) For himself, Scully never does find the answer, but the narrator, addressing the audience, indicates the importance for the reader to answer Scully's question concerning the source of Papa Peda's anger. I believe that his anger is related to his identity as a peasant farmer. He displays an unswerving and ruthless attachment to his land, an attachment which the narrative brilliantly exposes during his first encounter with Scully, when he uses his whip to force Scully to retrieve a cigarette butt from the river. He is attached also to the members of his family, and he assumes the personality or role of a big-daddy who is responsible for providing for their support. But if he provides he also wants to control, and it is the cultivation of his land that is the chief means by which he can provide for and control his wife and daughter:

> If he loved the river Papa Peda loved his wife Olida and his daughter Meela more. To feed two lovely mouths, he used to say, when The Farmers wailed keen laughter from Fat Polly's dark bar at him beating a path to his field in the bright hot sun, to feed two such lovely mouths a man must break the soil and ply his axe and hoe all year in rain or in sunshine. (6)

The inordinate strength of his personal pride and of his attachment to his family is a direct result of the inordinate energy he must use to successfully cultivate his land, for he is the only farmer of his community who has been able to maintain his independence in the face of the ruthless competition of the white, rich estate owner. At Fat Polly's, Papa Peda chastises the other farmers:

> You all sure is a bunch of prideless wrastels yes. For why would yuh want to make the Rich Man enslave you rather than work your own land?...Scully boy tell these good for nothin's hello, though there ain' a man among 'em worth a quarter of your salt...bow you' head to they age anyhow 'cause I can remember the time when we all was we own man together. Since Rich Man come here it ain' been the same. (19-20)

In his legitimate efforts to avoid one master Papa Peda has become the victim of another, his pride.

This pride and attachment are reinforced socially by the admiration and jealousy of the other peasant farmers, who consider Papa Peda the best farmer and family man of the district: At Fat Polly's Bar, Lazzirus, the oldest of the farmers says,

> Listen to me Peda, we all does laugh at you when you goes off in the morning to your fields...ain' 'cause we want to laugh Peda, is more cause every last man of we here wish we was like you...did have our pride together like you do and when we laugh is 'cause we want to cry. So we want to thank you for the little strength we can receive from you even though we ain' got the big strength like you got.... (20)

Thus, Papa Peda's social relationships parallel his family relationships in reinforcing his pride. His pride in his own power and accomplishments becomes so much a part of his identity that he feels easily threatened during his interactions with people. He works so hard for security that he is insecure. So he feels as threatened when Scully flips a cigarette butt into the river as when he discovers that Scully and Meela are sexually intimate.

Papa Peda's responses to these perceived threats are inordinate anger and violence, inordinate because they are directed towards vulnerable scapegoat victims—his daughter and adopted son—rather than towards the condition that really manipulates and exploits his identity—the Rich man who controls the economy that forces Papa Peda into an inhuman struggle with the land. Papa Peda's anger and scapegoating behavior reveal that he carries the consciousness of the oppressed. Primarily and ultimately a victim himself, he forces others, even more vulnerable than himself, to bear the consequences of his anguish. He is psychologically blind to the forces and relationships controlling his identity and outcome. This psychological blindness is ignorance that echoes the retributive physical blindness he suffers at the hands of Scully. The narrator laments Papa Peda's ignorance with regards to the issue of the venereal disease:

Papa Peda never understood then how it was that Scully's illness had left him...how his urge to see the green again had come when he had purged all the city grey...the ash harsh violence of his bone and blood had raged and rushed out of him taking all symptoms, signs and insects with it. When the green hand claimed him a clean soul had reclaimed him and his body was pure and whole again. Papa Peda had not understood. (26)

At the deepest and simplest level this ignorance, chained to his pride and strength—is the cause of his anger. Ridden by such anger, he tramples the cleansed soul and pure and whole body of the adopted son he loves.

Moreover, Papa Peda's anger is willful and stubborn, for he rejects Scully's clarification of the truth: "Now is always too late. The old man has his pride. He thrives on pride. Meela, come on home my daughter. City man tongue is sugar but his heart ain' nothing but gall" (27). Papa Peda's pride aggravates his intransigence and blinds him to his own hard heartedness and the true nature of others.

Scully's identity is one of the central questions of the novel. It begins to unfold in an Eden-like episode when the angry Papa Peda sends Scully to retrieve his recalcitrant daughter, Meela. To thwart her father and entice Scully, she climbs a tree and teases:

And such a pretty little tongue slipped between teeth and lips to make mockery of his serious plea. Where'd you get such a silly name, Scully, Scully, Scully, I bet its 'cause yo head's so big, all skull, Skully, Skully, ha ha ha...

Skully continued pleading. But then she threw a plum at him. Her aim was superb. Square in the middle of the top of the skull. His temper blew itself. Goddammit gal I goin' show you who is who heah today. He had always been superb at climbing trees but as he hooked his right leg over the first branch at the crook of the tree where the trunk split into limbs she gave the branch such a violent shake he saw the ground rising in double time to kiss him, Smack! so hard the wind left him completely. I am dead, he thought in a moment. And lay there face down. (13)

Meela's tongue is described as a snake's to suggest Eve's alliance with the snake of the garden. Her recognition that his name is a homophone for "skull" leads the reader to associate Skully's identity with death. The "plum" suggests the fruit of the tree of knowledge. Scully's curse reinforces the significance of death. His assertion that he will show Meela "who is who heah today" is a bit of dramatic irony that renders the identity issue unavoidable for the reader. Scully's fall and his mental utterance "I am dead" clinch his identity as an Adam-like figure. Like the mythical first man, Scully is a symbol for all men, lovers who die striving for perfection in an imperfect world. Scully's garden of the world is Papa Peda's farm; and Peda, who embodies both creative and destructive potentials, is the devil who rings his curse upon the head of mankind.

To demonstrate that mankind has inherited this curse is an essential argument of the novel, especially of Mumu's characterization. To this end, a variation of this tree episode between Skully and Meela occurs between Mumu and her first lover, Joker:

She sees him laughing among the leaves. Faster than he can know it she is up the tree trunk among the leaves and birds and branches pummelling him screaming nasties at him, fearless, so has to hold hard and fast to the closest limb for love and life his feet swinging far over the ground, afraid he'd fall, and hear her screaming. You mother hoppin' arsehole what's the matter with you...what'd you wanna mess my nice dress up for? I'm gonna kill you, kill you...Junji's son Joker saw the rocks below, he didn't want to fall. (54)

As a means of getting acquainted with Mumu, Joker, sitting in a tree, drops a fruit upon her while she is walking through the "deep forest." Joker's joke turns against him, as he becomes the victim holding on for love and life. The image of his feet swinging and his fear of falling underscore his victimization. Her curses, pummelling, and her ominous threat emphasize her role as a persecutor, like Eve. The episode itself foreshadows Joker's death and traces an ironic edge to Mumu's queries, guilt, and remorse concerning the death of the men in her life.

The true nature of the paradise-like earthly Eden soon becomes apparent to the characters. Forced to compete directly with the Rich Man after Papa Peda cast them out, Meela, with Scully, found that her "last months gone from heaven to hell" (p. 29). But even before this, Papa Peda's world, at least for Scully, was populated with demons. After Scully got drunk at Fat Polly's bar, he perceived a demonic quality in the faces of the farmers:

Demon faces burn red together blaze up there and hang grinning up there swaying in a wind that ain't even there.... As the night grew older Scully remarked the lantern faces were growing more demonic and the blood red gaze they held growing redder. ...Each new drink intensifies the kiss of the flame inside the red blight of the demon eyes above his head. (21)

As the unfolding narrative later reveals, ironically, Scully believes that he has escaped the sullied city, that his return to the country and his adoption by Papa Peda are signs that he has been cleansed of the corruption of the city. Actually, he has fallen into the devil's maw.

When Papa Peda hears that Scully got a job grooming the Rich Man's wild white horse, Peda bears down with his curse, "I told you didn't I no good could come from it...none at all, no good" (29). Even after Papa Peda's reconciliation with the lovers, when he uses his snake-like whip to protect Scully from the Man in the White Coat, this new victim of Papa Peda's anger "leapt into his ambulance and wheeled screaming out of the village back to the city convinced he had fallen into hell or another place like his own house of insanity" (32)

Barrett's vision of the world and world view of the Caribbean peasant contrasts sharply with the image of paradise that dominates the notions of the tourist set and of even some Caribbeans, such as the Jamaican poet and novelist, Claude McKay (his early immigration to the United States contributed to his nostalgically romantic memories of the Caribbean). Beneath the surface of pristine nature lies a hellish world where the people's lives are cursed because they are exploited and manipulated by Euro-American capitalistic imperialism. Papa Peda's abusive anger, pride, and curses are responses to the assault from the Rich Man's systematic domination of the country, a domination that has stripped away the integrity and dignity of the rest of the farmers. The more he strives to avoid the Rich Man's exploitation, the more he becomes a tool of that exploitation. Although Scully hangs himself with the whip Papa Peda gave him, the River Women assert without hesitation that the Rich Man killed Scully (45). The curse of modern man is a ruthless economic system. Papa Peda's retribution is a justice ameliorated with mercy; he is blinded by his victim who uses the very whip with which he has flogged that victim. But for the Rich Man there is no mercy.

And just as capitalistic imperialism is the force that scourges the lives of the peasants, giving rise to Papa Peda's curse, that same exploitive system corrupts the lives of the people of the city, including Megmarie, who is convinced that she destroyed Scully (86). Megmarie is just as much a victim as Papa Peda, for her values and attitudes arise from a capitalistic and imperialistic consciousness. She is the tool of a materialistic system, and her function is to exploit and persecute, which is what she does to Scully. The gluttonous gut of the city grasped her life and destroyed her:

...I was such a stubborn young gal, you know I laughed and said I wasn't no country bumpkin and all the beg he beg me I would not go with him and so he say he wouldn't go without me...I tell him I ain't interested in all his big talk 'bout cool green places and be better don' come by no more till he get some city sense and begin to hustle so we can live comfortable like in a house and all or I will go right out an' fin' me a sensible man who can get me the riches I want .... (106)

Deluded by the corrupt materialism of rich white people, such as Mrs. Steven Lasso—the pandering woman who solicited Mumu for the man who was both her brother-in-law and her lover—Megmarie spurns Scully and sends him packing. She casts him out just as Papa Peda does. The narrator reinforces the paralleled situations by having Mumu compare her fantasy of Mr. Lasso's living body with her memory of the Rich Man's dismembered body floating down the River (105).

Technology plays the same oppressive and exploitative role in the city as the Rich Man's tenant farming system did within the country. For Meela the automobile is a symbol of that technology:

She could not know more than the insistent scream in her head, I've seen blind murder, blind, a green car crushed a man like nothing, crushed him as a mountain would have crushed a paper doll...if a mountain falls upon a paper doll. Blind murder. This is a monster's home. This city. She began to hope for a quick release in that bright moment. (83)

The monster image echoes that of the Rich Man's white horse that kicks Scully's brains senseless. This episode foreshadows the death of Oboe—the cartman and lover, who is killed by a small truck while chasing his cart (101).

The material wealth, power, and corruption of both the Rich Man's country and Steven Lasso's city are the profits and heritage of Euro-American slavery. Significantly, the narrator portrays the triumph of the peasants over their oppressors. The River Women judge, condemn, and dismember the Rich White Man, and then along with the farmers, they take over his estate. Papa Peda calls back his children to nurture and love them. In the city, Mumu rejects Mrs. Lasso's enticement and continues her search for her identity and her source. Megmarie redeems her soul by nurturing Scully's child as well as by repudiating cynical, Western materialism.

With the characterization of Mumu, the narrator portrays the steps of an innocent human being, especially a woman but also any human being born into an oppressive world, who is curious concerning her identity and who needs love. Both these concerns for identity and love lead Mumu to look for the identity of her father, Scully.

On the way she becomes the victim of incomplete or inadequate lovers—Joker, Chino, Oboe, Sidnisweet, and Poet, men striving for the perfection of love despite their identities as victims of oppression. From Megmarie and Meela, Mumu discovers her father's identity. Unprotected after Megmarie's death, Mumu's mind becomes deranged. In this condition she accepts the Preacher's answer, offering herself to JaJa in ritual suicide that will enable her, according to Preacher, to return to the Father who loves her. Thus through her search for her worldly father, she discovers her spiritual Father, the divine author of all, JaJa.

Barrett sings of Mumu's search for her father as the means by which to delineate the oldest human journey—the cursed in search of the divine. Her journey is an adventure through a seeming paradise that is actually a world that has been corrupted by a vicious economic system that alienates human beings from themselves and each other.

Notes

[1]For a more detailed description and analysis of the plot see Royster, "Narrative Line."

[2]In *Cane* Toomer collects poems and/or stories in three parts that tell the profoundly ironic stories of speakers or characters who (although for the most part they are inadequate for the task) either would or have returned to the South in order to capture and express the Afro-American genius and soul that enabled blacks to survive slavery.

Structured on the themes of Dante's *Inferno*, *The System of Dante's Hell* is a lyrical, fragmentary, and allusive experimental narrative of the psychological and spiritual anguish of a young male persona who moves through childhood, adolescence, and early adulthood in Newark, New Jersey, a small Southern town, and New York City.

[3]This first novel is Soyinka's scathing satire of contemporary urban Nigeria by way of telling the disjointed, episodic stories of five young, intellectual men with foreign education whose lives, upon their return to solve the problems of newly independent Nigeria, "interpret" their West African society caught in the throes of upheaval as the traditional ways are uprooted in the storm of change after colonialism.

Works Cited

Achebe, Chinua. *Arrow of God*. 1967. Garden City: Anchor-Doubleday, 1969.

Barrett, Lindsey. *Song for Mumu*. 1967. Washington, D.C.: Howard UP, 1974.

_____ *The State of Black Desire*. Paris: Alençon, impr. Corbiere et Jugain, 1966.

Braithwaite, Edward K. "The African Presence in Caribbean Literature." *Daedalus* 103.2 (1974): 73-109.

_____ "Jazz and the West Indian Novel: II." *Bim* 12 (1967): 45.

Campbell, Joseph. *The Hero With a Thousand Faces*. 1949. Princeton UP, 1968.

Cima, Richard. "Fiction." Rev. of *Song For Mumu*, by Lindsay Barrett. *Library Journal*, 90 (1974), 3214.

Equiano. Olaudah. *The Interesting Narrative of the Life of Olaudah Equiano, or Gustavas Vassa, the African*. Excerpted in *Black Writers of America*. Ed. Richard Barksdale and Kenneth Kinnamon. New York: The Macmillan Company, 1972. 738.

Krishnamurti. J. *Think on These Things*. Ed. D. Rajagopal. 1964. New York: Harper, 1970.

Levin, Martin. "New and Novel." Rev. of *Song For Mumu*, by Lindsay Barrett. *New York Times Books Review*, 29 Sept. 1974, Section VII: 40.

Royster, Philip M. "The Narrative Line of Lindsay Barrett's *Song for Mumu*." *Obsidian* 8.2&3 (1982): 57-70.

Soyinka, Wole *The Interpreters*. 1965. New York: Macmillan, 1970.

Nella Larsen's Use of the Near-White Female in *Quicksand* and *Passing*

Vashti Crutcher Lewis

Nella Larsen wrote two novels, *Quicksand* and *Passing*—both during the height of the Harlem Renaissance. *Quicksand* was published in 1928 and *Passing* in 1929. Unlike major 19th century Black women novelists—Harriet Wilson, Frances Ellen Harper, Pauline Hopkins and also unlike Jesse Redmond Fauset, a 1920s Renaissance novelist, Larsen does not idealize her female mulatto characters. Moreover, unlike earlier Black women novelists—except Harriet Wilson, she does not create a world in which they ultimately find refuge from a hostile environment. In this respect, Larsen moves away from the popular and traditional genteel image of the near-white female. Although she does not romanticize the Black poor as Addison Gayle suggests,[1] her depictions of mulatto females indicate that she viewed upper class Black gentility as peculiarly stifling and confining—a world view that foreshadows the highly individualized characterization of the mulatto heroine, Janie Mae Crawford, in Zora Neale Hurston's 1937 novel *Their Eyes Were Watching God*.[2]

Mulatto heroines and major female characters in Larsen's novels suffer emotionally and intellectually with popular images that American culture prescribes for them. To most Black Americans in her novels, they are repositories of gentility; yet to whites they are exotic primitives. In both *Quicksand* and *Passing*, Larsen not only questions but "intensifies the pathos of the mulatto image,"[3] that in most earlier novels by Black women is inextricably wed to an upper-middle class lifestyle and the best of all possible worlds. Like earlier Black women novelists, however, Larsen uses near-white female characters as vehicles to expose readers to Black intellectual thought and cultural activities during the period in which the novels are set.

Much of the complexity in Larsen's characterizations, which is lacking in those of mulatto females in the fiction of Black women who preceded Larsen—including Fauset—, is due to the small degree of sexuality that she allows her heroines. For example, in *Quicksand* the mulatto heroine's life is replete with contradictions as she struggles to repress feelings of sexuality that she accepts as both primitive and exclusively Black. In *Passing*, a major mulatto female character causes the death of another near-white female with whom she suspects her husband is sexually involved.

Quicksand, Larsen's first novel, is considered by most critics to be her more provocative work.[4] It is set during the 1920s in vastly different communities, albeit ones the author knew well—a small southern rural college campus much like Tuskegee Institute, Chicago, Harlem, and Copenhagen, Denmark.

Basically, *Quicksand* is a character study of Helga Crane, a biological mulatto not light enough to pass for white but "too dark to mingle socially...among fashionable and artistic circles of Copenhagen."[5] The biological heritage of Helga is significantly different from the traditional near-white female archetype used by nineteenth and early twentieth century Black women, since her father is Black and her mother is white and they are legally married. This reversal of the popular image of a mulatto heroine may not have held any particular literary significance for the author since her own racial background was the same as Helga's. It is true, however, that interracial marriages between Black men and white women had increased significantly by the 1920s despite the fact that they were illegal in all southern states and many northern ones.[6]

After her father deserts his family, Helga's mother who is destitute marries a man who, like herself, is Danish. Her white stepfather and white half-brothers are abusive to Helga, and she begins to distance herself from both Blacks and whites. When she is fifteen, a rich white uncle finances her education at an all Black private school where for the first time she experiences a sense of community and discovers that Black people are not "necessarily loathsome," (page 52). However, this sense of community does not compensate for her lack of strong family ties. After graduation she accepts a teaching assignment at an all Black southern college. There she is sorely unhappy and a misfit. Like Jesse Redmond Fauset, Larsen rejects the accommodationist philosophy of Booker T. Washington and preference for industrial training for Black youth over higher education in the arts and sciences. Helga is offended by the conciliatory attitude of her colleagues who are essentially snobs and who intimidate their Black students when they do not measure-up to genteel images that Caucasians are purported to have. She chafes when one Black teacher admonishes her students: "And please at least try to act like ladies and not like savages from the backwoods" (page 26).

When Helga resigns from Naxos, her reason seems clearly to be her inability to adjust to the conservative ideology of the school. However, Larsen's protagonist is also motivated in that decision by her repressed sexuality. At this point in the novel the author begins a subtle examination of Helga as a sexual being—an examination that will lead to Larsen's conclusion that Black women, particularly near-white mulattoes, often live in fear of actually being either aloof genteel snobs or exotic sexual beings that American popular culture suggests they are. In questioning her restlessness at Naxos, Helga strains for answers:

The uneasy sense of being engaged with some formidable antagonist, nameless and un-understood, startled her. It wasn't she was suddenly aware, merely the school and its ways and its decorous stupid people that oppressed her. There was something else, some other more ruthless force, a quality within herself, which was frustrating her, kept her from getting the things she had wanted. Still wanted (page 23).

Entering the Black principal's office to hand in her resignation, she confronts Dr. Anderson, a new administrator to whom she is obviously attracted. The affectionate feelings she has for him terrify her:

...at his "Miss Crane?" Her lips formed for speech, but no sound came. She was aware of inward confusion. For her the situation seemed charged, unaccountably with strangeness and something very like hysteria. An almost overpowering desire to laugh seized her. Then, miraculously a complete ease, such as she had never known in Naxos, possessed her (page 41).

The principal sympathizes with Helga and understands her stated reasons for resigning and he pleads with her to remain. She partially relents, but when he refers to her as a "lady" with "dignity and breeding" (page 46), she bristles against this popular stereotype of the genteel mulatto and leaves the school immediately. Rebelling against a genteel image that near-white Black women in earlier novels by Black women accept without question causes Helga to repress her own feelings of sexuality, thereby compounding her sense of marginality and isolation.

She returns to Chicago, and after repeated rejections at employment agencies, where only domestic-servant jobs are available to Black women, Helga finds work as a secretary to a Black woman who is a prominent civic and social leader in the city and who is spokeswoman for the Negro Women's League of Clubs. Accepting the popular notion that only the miscegenated talented tenth are qualified leaders for Black people, Larsen presents a schizoid treatment of Helga's relationship to her employer, Mrs. Hayes-Royre. A woman without a college education who seasoned her speeches with a "peppery dash of Duboises" (page 83), Mrs. Hayes-Royre is touted as a race leader because of her affiliation with the Black women's club which is a carefully drawn fictional counterpart of the National Association of Colored Women founded in 1896.[7] Although Helga finds despicable the idea that a woman of Mrs. Hayes-Royre's background is influential in matters of race, she never-the-less trusts Mrs. Royre as a confidante to whom she reveals her marginal background and terrifying loneliness. In fact, she is the person closest to Helga in the novel, and Helga moves with her to Harlem where Mrs. Royre introduces her to socially prominent Black-Americans.

In Harlem, Larsen depicts her heroine amidst the cultural activity of the Renaissance. Paradoxically, much like her elitist colleagues at Naxos whom she despises for their snobbery towards the illiterate Black masses, Helga sneers at Harlem night life and finds being in large groups of Black people unsettling. She is comforted by the fact that many of her acquaintances hold W.E.B. Dubois in high esteem and view small industrial arts colleges, such as Naxos, with scorn. At the same time, she questions attitudes of upper-middle class Blacks who were

> ...obsessed by the race problem...frequented all the meetings of protest, subscribed to all the complaining magazines, and read all the lurid newspapers spewed out by the Negro yellow press...talked, wept, and ground...teeth dramatically about the wrongs and shames of race. But...aped their clothes, their manner, and their gracious ways of living [white]. While proclaiming loudly the undiluted good of all things Negro,...yet disliked the songs, the dances, and the softly blurred speech of the race. Toward these things...showed only a disdainful contempt, tinged sometimes with faint amusement (pages 106-7).

Recognizing the contradictions of race pride of the Black intelligentsia, but unable to find solace with the masses of uneducated Blacks, coupled with her distaste for white Manhattan and its restrictions on Black people, Helga seeks exile in Denmark with her mother's relatives. Underscoring and intensifying her stated reasons for leaving the United States, however, is the return of her sexual feelings for Dr. Anderson, the Black man to whom she had tendered her resignation from the Black school in Mississippi. When she encounters him at a party in Harlem, "A peculiar, not wholly disagreeable, quiver ran down her spine. She felt an odd little faintness. The blood rushed to her face. She tried to jeer at herself for being so moved by the encounter" (page 109). Again, he is impressed with Helga, but not trusting her feelings of sexuality she refuses his attentions. Her feelings of total isolation return when she discovers Dr. Anderson has turned his attention toward another woman.

In Denmark, where Helga lives for three years as an expatriate, she finds that she must constantly conform to or struggle against the prescribed image that Danish people have about racially mixed persons. Immediately upon her arrival, her relatives insist that she turn what they see as an exotic appearance to her advantage by wearing large hooped earrings, large buckles on her shoes, vari-colored bracelets, and clothes of vivid colors. They are pleased with the attention that she receives, but "Helga herself felt like nothing so much as some new and strange species of pet dog being proudly exhibited" (page 153).

Like most mulattoes of antebellum fiction, Helga renounces a white suitor. In her case, it is a Danish artist whom Helga's relatives and all of Copenhagen society consider a good prospect for marriage. In earlier novels by Black women, when mulatto women reject the proposals of Caucasians, it is because the men request that they renounce their African heritage and live as white women. The reason that Larsen attributes to Helga's refusal to marry a white person indicates a view that is essentially different from that of the earlier Black women novelists—a world view that suggests there is something uniquely different between Blacks and whites, a difference that cannot be bridged through marriage. Rejecting the artist Helga explains:

"You see I couldn't marry a white man. I simply couldn't. It isn't just you, not just personal, you understand. It's deeper, broader than that. It's racial" (page 196).

Although Helga does not seem to experience sexual frustration in Europe, she decides, after three years, to leave Copenhagen. Upon her return to Harlem, she discovers that a very close friend of hers has married Dr. Anderson. At a party where many are under the influence of alcohol, Anderson embraces Helga. She mistakes the impulsive gesture for genuine affection and suggests that they meet cladestinely. At their meeting, Anderson apologizes for his impulsive, intoxicated behavior. His apology causes Helga to become consumed with guilt and remorse.

In an analysis of Helga's self flagellation in response to Dr. Anderson's rejection of her, Larsen depicts the emotional and psychological damage that can result in the lives of mulatto women who totally or partially internalize culturally prescribed images of themselves as either genteel or exotic primitives.

Desire had burned in her flesh with uncontrollable violence. The wish to give herself had been so intense that Dr. Andersons's surprising, trivial apology loomed as a direct refusal of the offering. Whatever outcome she had expected, it had been something else than this, this mortification, this feeling of ridicule and self-loathing....(page 244).

Through the characterization of Helga, Larsen also suggests the possibility that Black women who are sexually frustrated because of their failure to see themselves as individuals rather than culturally prescribed images may become so distraught that their emotional needs can be met only through religious experiences. This is a view not suggested by women novelist preceding Larsen. Guilt-ridden and remorseful, Helga seeks solace in a store-front church although she had never been a religious person. She even accepts the congregation's labeling of her as a "scarlet woman" and a "Jezebel" who has at last "come to Jesus" (251), although no one there knows her. She marries the uneducated minister of the church, accompanies him to a small, rural southern Alabama town where she lives in quiet desperation attending to him and their four children born in five years. Through Larsen's final comment on her protagonist, Helga Crane has become a human representation of the culturally prescribed popular image of sexually primitive Black women: "And hardly had she left her bed and become able to walk again without pain, hardly had the children returned from the homes of the neighbors, when she began to have her fifth child" (301).

Set in Chicago and Harlem in 1927, Larsen's second novel, *Passing* is the story of Irene Redfield and Clare Kendry, near-white mulattoes who can and do pass for white, but for different reasons. They are childhood friends who have lost contact with each other until a chance meeting in an exclusive all-white Chicago restaurant. When they meet, Irene is assuming a white identity merely for convenience, but Clare has permanently passed for white for twelve years. Irene is a socially prominent member of Chicago's and Harlem's Black upper-class and is happily married to a Black physician. Clare is married to a wealthy white industrialist but is lonely without the company of Black people. Using their childhood friendship as an excuse, Clare imposes upon Irene's hospitality in order to mingle socially with Black people, albeit as a white woman. Jealous over her husband's attention to Clare, Irene causes Clare's death at the end of the novel.

Through the characterization of Irene Redfield, Larsen seems to suggest that some near-white mulatto women who show no trace of their African ancestry, who were reared in upper-middle class homes in the 1920s, and who accept the culturally prescribed popular genteel image of themselves are not only sexually repressed, but will also destroy anything or anyone who threatens their way of life. The author also suggests that women such as Clare Kendry, who were reared in poverty and choose to permanently pass for white to better their lives, find that no amount of money can substitute for the sense of community a Black woman feels with her own race; moreover, in their attempts to return to the Black community, they can become ruthless and desperate, and bring heartache and pain not only to themselves, but to everyone whose lives touch theirs.

Irene Redfield resembles the nineteenth-century popular archtype of the mulatto in physical appearance, parentage, and lifestyle. Although she is not a biological mulatto, she looks like a white woman and has been reared in more than comfortable circumstances. Her father is a physician in Chicago, a city which was the "focal point of the Great Migration" between 1915 and 1920 and which by 1920 boasted 195 Black physicians for a Black population of 109,458.[8] Her mother is a socialite in the Black community, and servants perform the household chores in their home. After graduation from college, Irene marries a prominent physician and moves with him to New York, where they, too are financially able to employ servants and where Irene enjoys her life as one of Harlem's most active socialites. When the novel opens, Irene's social-correctness and restraint are clearly evident in her uneasiness and suffering on a crowded downtown street in Chicago—suffering that results from a situation far removed from the auction block experience of both William Wells Brown's 19th century depiction of genteel Clotel and Frances Ellen Harper's Iola Leroy.[9] Accustomed to the serenity of her own elaborately furnished home, Irene cannot cope with the vicissitudes of the crowed urban street.

It was while she was on her way to a sixth place that right before her smarting eyes a man toppled over and became an inert crumpled heap on the scorching cement. About the lifeless figure a little crowd gathered. Was the man dead or only faint? Someone asked her. But Irene didn't know and didn't try to discover. She edged her way out of the increasing crowd, feeling disagreeably damp and sticky and soiled from contact with so many sweating bodies.

For a moment she stood fanning herself and dabbing at her moist face...Suddenly she was aware that the whole street had a wobbly look and realized that she was about to faint...she lifted a wavering hand in the direction of a cab...the driver jumped out and guided her to his car. He helped, almost lifted her in...[10]

Clare Kendry's first appearance in the novel is in direct contrast to Irene's. Clare is presented in a downtown Chicago restaurant as a sensual woman who seems unperturbed by life: "A sweetly scented woman in a flattering dress of green chiffon..." (p.14) who is smiling, talkative, and accompanied by a man whose presence she enjoys. Since the story is told from Irene's genteel point of view, the reader is led to believe that Clare is easy and flirtatious. Irene does not recognize Clare at first but makes the observation that the woman's friendly conversation with the waiter is "just a shade too provocative" (p. 16). Even after the two women recognize each other, Irene continues to label Clare as a woman of questionable morals as she recalls that her friend always got what she wanted—"always had a having way" (p. 27).

Through flashbacks in Irene's conversation with Clare, the reader learns that Irene's background is far different from Clare's. Just as Larsen broke with the genteel mulatto tradition in *Quicksand* in her depiction of Helga Crane, whose father is Black and poor, she also presents Clare as the daughter of a poor Black man. Clare's drunken father dies on a barroom floor, and she is reared by two spinster white aunts who never allow her to forget that, as a descendent of Ham, she needs to prove her worth through hard work. At sixteen, she runs away and marries a white youth who becomes rich through speculation in oil. Although she lives luxuriously as an adult, Clare is the first major female mulatto character in novels by Black women who spends all of her childhood in poverty—although Larsen's Helga Crane spent the first four years of her life in a Chicago slum, her mother's remarriage elevated her from poverty.

In *Passing*, as in *Quicksand*, Larsen suggests that distinctions exist between Black and white people due to their different racial experiences. Larsen first gives evidence of this assumption in *Passing* when Clare states her reasons for wanting to return to the Black community. Unlike Jesse Redmond Fauset's Angela Murray in *Plum Bun*, who returns to the Black race because she is disillusioned when she discovers the extent to which whites hold Black people in contempt, Clare wants to return simply "to be with them [Blacks] again, to talk to them again, to hear them laugh." (p. 129). Although she is a wealthy matron, who lives on two continents, Clare finds that material possessions are not a substitute for the warm feeling of community that she experiences with Black people. Indeed, given her rigidity and coldness, Larsen uses Irene primarily as a vehicle through which Clare can recapture fond memories of times spent on the south-side of Chicago with Black people, before the death of her father.

Although Larsen portrays Irene as genteel and aristocratic, she allows Irene, as well as Clare, to recognize differences between Blacks and whites. For example, Irene informs a white artist, modeled after Carl Van Vechten,[11] a patron of the arts movement of the Harlem Renaissance, that it would be impossible for a white person to assume a Black identity despite the fact that Black people regularly pass for white. Irene suggests that a white person's inability to pass for Black does not result from anything they say or do, "anything in appearance. Just—something. A thing that couldn't be registered" (p. 141). It is not difficult to assume that something is racial and therefore cultural.

What Larsen fails to have her antagonist explain to the artist is that Black people have been exposed to the white majority culture as well as their own. They have cooked for whites, cared for and nursed their children, gone to their schools and studied their art, music and languages—they have internalized white culture. Very few white have done more than visit in a Black home or work with a Black person.

When the artist shows concern over the attention white women pay to Black men at integrated dances, Irene's response suggests Larsen's attempt to identify a cultural difference between Black and whites. "You got to admit," Irene explains, "the colored man is a better dancer than the average white man..." (p. 138).

Ironically, despite her proclamation of differences between Blacks and whites, it is Irene, rather than Clare, who internalizes a value system that denies the problem of race in America. She insists that her sons should have no exposure to racial subjects and resents her husband's openness with them about American intolerance. When they question their father about lynching, Irene interrupts to say: " 'I do wish you wouldn't talk about lynching before Ted and Junior' " (p. 191). She becomes indignant at her husband's pragmatic answer that "they've got to live in this damned country, they'd better find out what sort of thing they're up against as soon as possible. The earlier they learn it, the better prepared they'll be" (pp. 191-193).

Although there is no evidence in the novel that Clare is concerned with intellectual or political concepts of race, she seems not to recognize class distinctions in the manner of Irene. For example, she is as gracious towards Irene's servants as she is with Irene's upper-class friends. In addition, she is not uncomfortable with people who have little sophistication, and she is more at ease with Irene's sons and husband than Irene. Irene's restraint with her family, as well as her friends, is a telling indication that she has lost an essential human quality of warmth in the preservation of assumed gentility.

Perhaps the most devastating comment that Larsen makes about mulatto women who see themselves as inheritors of a popular genteel tradition is the tendency on their part to equate sexuality with class—women who seem disinterested in themselves as sexual beings are assumed to be aristocratic and genteel and any display in dress or gesture of sexuality is viewed as primitive and low-class. Because of this assumption every act of kindness and friendliness by Clare towards men has sexual connotations for Irene—especially given Clare's childhood of poverty in the house with a drunken father.

When students at the public school that her son attends begin to inquire about sex, Irene suggests that he transfer to a private school. In his rejection of this suggestion, Irene's husband indicates that he does not approve of her Puritanical values:

"...And you're trying to make a mollycoddle out of him. Well, just let me tell you, I won't have it. And you needn't think I'm going to let you change him to some nice kindergarten kind of school because he's getting a little necessary education...He'll stay right where he is. The sooner and the more he learns about sex, the better for him..." (p. 105).

Irene does not see sexuality as a desirable human quality, and she is paranoid about the attention her husband shows Clare. Before a party in Harlem to which Clare's white husband follows her and where, in the confusion Irene pushes Clare out of sixth-story window to her death, Irene had considered several options for keeping them apart.

One of the options is to inform Clare's white husband that Clare spent most of her time in Harlem when he was out of the city. In panic and desperation, Irene chooses to murder Clare. She also shows concern over whether or not she has really succeeded in killing her, and asks herself: " 'What if Clare was not dead?' " (p. 213).

Although Larsen's characterizations of Clare Kendry and Irene Redfield, as well as that of Helga Crane in *Quicksand*, strongly emphasize their physical appearance, their depictions also indicate changing cultural attitudes, during the late 1920s of Black people, towards the concept of color as it relates to gentility and class in the Black community. Larsen's presentations reject the concept in earlier novels by Black women that gentility is inextricably connected with color, and they also reveal the pathos that results in the lives of Black women who accept culturally prescribed, popular images of themselves. More importantly, Larsen questions the idea of an homogeneous American culture and suggests that there are basic cultural differences between Black and white people. For each of these reasons, Larsen breaks new ground for the emergence of new paradigms in the cultural and literary image of the Black woman.

Notes

[1] Addison Gayle, *The Way of the New World* (Garden City, New York: Doubleday, 1975), p. 110.

[2] Zora Neal Hurston, *Their Eyes Were Watching God* (1937; reprint, Urbana, Illinois: University of Illinois Press, 1978). For an analysis of Hurston's treatment of Janie Mae Crawford see: Vashti Crutcher Lewis, *The Mulatto Female as Major*

Character in Novels by Black Women Writers, 1892-1934 (Ph.D. dissertation, University of Iowa, Iowa City, Iowa, 1981), Ch. IV.

[3]Barbara Christian, *Black Women Writers* (Westport, Connecticut: Greenwood Press, 1980), p. 43.

[4]For a short summary of the critical acclaim which *Quicksand* received see: Amritjit Singh, *The Novels of the Harlem Renaissance*, (University Park, Pennsylvania: The Pennsylvania State University Press), p. 100.

[5]Nella Larsen, *Quicksand* (New York: Alfred A. Knopf, 1928), p. 50. All further references to this work are from this edition, and references appear within the body of the text.

[6]Ernest Porterfield, *Black and White Mixed Marriages* (Chicago: Nelson Hall, 1970), Tables 2-1, "Summary of Earlier Studies of the Number of Black-White Intermarriages: 1874-1937," p. 26.

[7]Allen H. Spear, *Black Chicago, The Making of A Negro Ghetto* (Chicago: University of Chicago Press, 1967) p. 101.

[8]Spear, pp. 129-153.

[9]See Vashti Crutcher Lewis, *The Mulatto Females as Major Character in the Novels of Black Women Writers* (Ph.D. dissertation, University of Iowa, Iowa City, Iowa, 1982) pp.

[10]Nella Larsen, *Passing* (1929 reprint, New York: Arno Press, 1969), pp. 11-12. All further references to this work appear within the body of the text.

[11]For an interesting interpretation of Van Vechten's role in the lives of Black artists of the Harlem Renaissance, see Langston Hughes, *The Big Sea* (1940; reprint, New York: Hill and Wang, 1963), pp. 252-253.

Afro-American Core Culture Social Dance: An Examination of Four Aspects of Meaning

Katrina Hazzard-Gordon

Most scholarly work on Afro-American social dance has been concerned with its structural aspects, primarily the question of African retentions. The work of Melville Herskovits, Joann Kealiinohomoku, Linda Wharton and Jack L. Daniel, Chadwick Hansen, Robert Farris Thompson, John Q. Anderson, Gertrude P. Kurath, Jan Hertzberg, Lydia Parrish, and others has touched on this issue.[1]

Though this approach to the study of Afro-American vernacular dance is far from exhausted, it ignores certain significant aspects of black dance culture. Once it is established that the structural aspects of Afro-American dance are in fact African-derived, the researcher is free to raise questions concerning the function, meanings, and uses of the dance.

The anthropologist-dancer Katherine Dunham has stated that dance has greater tenacity than any other cultural form and that it is the most permanent cultural link with the past.[2] Certainly the dance of Afro-Americans is identifiable on the basis of its continuity with both traditional and contemporary African movement. Until recently, Afro-Americans conducted their lives in relative isolation from most whites. Isolation rather than inherent tenacity may explain the similarity between their dance forms and those of contemporary Africans. Except for encounters in the workplace and marginal socialization among the middle class, blacks still maintain a high degree of autonomy, particularly in their social lives. Blacks still prefer their own forms of entertainment and leisure activity, though they have struggled to strike down statutes and customs that have barred them from access to white-controlled public facilities. Both of these phenomena have been particularly true of dance arenas. In the century (117 years) since emancipation, Afro-Americans have established seven institutions for secular dancing and socializing. Four of these are exclusively Afro-American: the classical jook and its derivatives—the honky tonk, after hours joint, and rent party. These arenas comprise the jook continuum and exist in both northern and southern black communities. The jook was the first dance institution to arise among blacks after emancipation; it served a rural constituency. According to Zora Neal Hurston:

Reprinted from CORD *Dance Research Journal*, 15:2, Spring 1983.

Jook is the word for Negro pleasure houses. It may mean a bawdy house. It may mean the house set apart on public works where men and women dance, drink and gamble. Often it is a combination of all these.[3]

In addition, blacks in the urban environment have adopted three dance arenas that also appear in white communities—dance halls, membership clubs, and cabaret night clubs. These seven settings have provided the institutional context for the development of Afro-American social dance. I have outlined the rise and development of these institutions in another work and will not discuss them here.[4]

The purpose of this article is to examine four unexplored theoretical areas of Afro-American vernacular or social dance. Among working-class blacks four aspects of meaning appear: identity, cultural integrity, ingroup-outgroup, and political resistance. Knowledge of these aspects is important for an understanding of Afro-American social dance. So that their scope is clear, I have assigned definitions to each:

I. *Identity:* This aspect of meaning appears on the psychological level. Identity is the defining aspect if the individual feels that he or she should be able to dance.

II. *Cultural Integrity:* This aspect appears on the level of black cultural participation. It is the primary aspect if being able to dance proves one to be "blacker."

III. *Ingroup-Outgroup:* This aspect appears on the social-psychological level. It is the functioning aspect of meaning if dancing is seen as a quality necessary to enhance one's membership in a voluntary association such as a gang or peer group.

IV. *Political Resistance:* This aspect functions on the political level. This is the aspect of meaning engaged if one views black dance in contradistinction to white dance; for example, if blacks see themselves as better dancers, if blacks ridicule whites who attempt to "dance black," or if they make distinctions that imply resentment, superiority, and a distaste for whites who may be attempting to emulate general aspects of black culture.

These aspects of meaning which inform Afro-American dance may also function in other groups in American society such as white working-class youths or an ethnic-minority such as Italians. What may be different in Afro-American culture is the degree of intergenerational permeation of both the dances and the four levels of meaning.

Contemporary Afro-American dances are frequently a recycled version of dances performed in previous generations, some dating back to pre-emancipation and few traceable to Africa. Both "the itch," a dance involving rhythmic movement imitative of scratching, involving pulling and tugging clothing, and the "snake hips," a dance involving stiff-legged manipulation of the hips, are good example of this recycling. Both dances appeared prior to 1900. The most recent appearance of the itch was in the 1950s. The snake hips appeared in the 1950s and early 1960s, renamed "poppin' the hips," and again in the late 1970s and early 1980s as the "pop." Such dances are frequently learned from parents, older teenagers, or adults in the context of a community dance arena such as a jook or house party.[5]

Unlike Afro-American dance, the popular dances of white youth are often adopted directly from black culture and are rarely passed on inter-generationally. Examples of this include the twist and the pony, popular dances of the 1960s, as well as the black bottom and the Charleston, popular dances of the 1920s and 1930s.

The identity component focuses judgements about dancing ability in the psychological makeup of the individual. This aspect functions of the individual feels that dancing ability will somehow enhance his or her personal self-esteem.[6] When this component is at work, the individual feels that he or she should be able to dance in a particular context.

The feelings of Malcolm X clearly illustrate the identity aspect at work:

> Like hundreds of thousands of country-bred Negroes who had come to the Northern black ghetto before me, and have come since, I'd also acquired all the other fashionable ghetto adornments—the zoot suits and conk that I have described, liquor, cigarettes, then reefers—all to erase my embarrassing background. But I still harbored one secret humiliation: I could not dance.[7]

Lack of dancing ability was seen by Malcolm X as a great personal deficiency, a "secret humiliation." Do white youths see deficiency in dancing ability as a "secret humiliation?" I would say not. This aspect can be strong when coupled with situational expectations such as those present at a teenage party. Gradually, as Malcolm learned to dance, his self-esteem increased.

The second aspect, cultural integrity, is a widespread phenomenon among blacks. Unlike the identity component, this one is not age-specific. It occasionally operates across both age and socioeconomic lines within the black community. The cultural integrity component implies the assertion of blackness. It helps define one as a participant in Afro-American culture. Dance becomes a litmus test for cultural identity. Proper Afro-American dance demands the demonstration of certain postures and gestures held in esteem in black culture; through the dance, one proves that one is a member of the cultural body, that one is truly in touch with the cultural material.

Malcolm X provides an excellent illustration of how the cultural integrity component works:

> Whites are correct in thinking that black people are natural dancers. Even little kids are—except for those Negroes today who are so "integrated" as I had been, that their instincts are inhibited.[8]

This aspect informs those conceptions of dance as an Afro-American phenomenon. It enables challenges to cultural participation to be made, and it also enables one to dispel those challenges. Malcolm X viewed integration as an undesirable phenomenon. His statement quoted above makes it clear that "integration" leads to the rejection of characteristics in one's own cultural background, in this case dancing ability. Here dancing ability is viewed as a valid indicator of whether one is "integrated." Inability to dance indicates that one's cultural base is not black, that one has taken on another cultural identity. The concept of "integration" as used here by Malcolm X has subtle overtones, implying notions about assimilation: the denial of that which is "natural" to the Afro-American. The "integrated Negro" is no longer a member of the cultural group in the full sense of the word; he lives a denial of that which is "instinctual."

Malcolm articulates what many black Americans experience in their everyday encounters within black culture. One such experience ("for those what are not too integrated") is learning to manipulate dance and other parameters of movement which are held in esteem in Afro-American culture. These dance behaviors included improvisational ability such as that described by Maya Angelou:

He spoke to the other players, counted down four and the music began. I started dancing, rushing into movement, making up steps and changing direction. There was no story, no plan; I simply put every dance I had ever seen or known into my body and onto the stage. A little rhumba, tango, jitterbug, Suzy-Q, trucking, snake hips, conga, Charleston and cha-cha-cha. When the music finished I had exhausted my repertoire and myself.[9]

Other approved dance behaviors include isolation and movement of the pelvis, individual manipulation of other body parts such as torso, head, arms, phrasing ability, flat-footed movement style, flexed leg position, and percussive use of rhythm.[10] Many black children learn dance behaviors that elicit approval from parents, peers, and significant others such as community elders or close family friends. They develop certain neuromuscular patterns that attest to the cultural participation of the performer, verifying in motion the cultural identity and integrity of the dancer.

In an interview, Ralph Ellison gives another example of the cultural integrity aspect at work in Afro-American culture. The discussion centers on the role of black writers in black culture. The interviewer has mentioned charges that black intellectuals such as Ellison have deserted the culture. Ellison responds:

Part of my pride in being what I am is that as a dancer, as a physical man...I bet you I can outdance, outriff most of those intellectuals who're supposed to have come back.[11]

This statement provides an example of the informative scope of the cultural integrity aspect. Ellison offers his dancing ability as proof that he is as much a participant in black culture as any other Afro-American. The fact that he can dance is pointed to as indicative of his cultural integrity; therefore, the charge is repudiated. Symbolic reference to the black experience is provided through the dance.

The cultural integrity aspect does not manifest itself in the same degree across age groups or socioeconomic strata. In periods of intensified racial conflict or awareness in the black community, as in the 1960s, however, the cultural integrity aspect permeates layers of black culture that otherwise could not experience it or would experience it on a diminished level. A previously unaffected group such as the black elite, seeking to express solidarity with core culture blacks,[12] begins to experience this aspect at work. Many members of the black elite previously rejecting black dance as undesirable experienced in the 1960s a change of perspective and used opportunities to perform the latest black popular dance. Nathan Hare provides an example:

At exclusive gatherings of top society folk, you can now sit back and watch some 20 couples lined up on a patio busily executing the Wobble and the Watusi. They are unaware that a good many such dance crazes were imported from the Southern backwoods, as well as Miami and Baltimore. Whereas it once was a mark of status to be "the smoothest dance couple on the floor," this acclaim now goes to the "best twisters" at Virginia Beach, or some other integrated locale. But since they are generally latecomers to the Twist,...their styles are a burlesque of the pioneer Negro twisters.[13]

The dances carry with them an implied context of sociocultural experience. They help to define one as a black person, but especially as a black person who has not been removed from one's people and cultural roots.

Another example of the cultural integrity aspect is found in the dialogue between two of Alice Walker's characters in the novel *Meridian*. The following example clearly illustrates two levels of meaning—the cultural and the political. The scene involves a heated argument between Truman, a black man, and his estranged white wife, Lynne. She is blaming him, or at least her marriage to him, for her failure in life. She states:

Look at me...you think you can step over me and just keep on going...ruin my life.

Truman responds:

Don't bring up your lousy dancing career...if you people could dance you wouldn't have to copy us all the time.

Lynne, searching for a defense, snarls:

You asshole, you're a fine one to talk. You're the only nigger in the free world who can't dance a lick.[14]

Lynne's final words are an attempt to challenge Truman's cultural integrity. The author of *Meridian* is black and uses her characters to reveal at least one component of the cultural integrity aspect. Had Lynne made such a statement to a white man, it would have had almost no meaning.

The third aspect, ingroup-outgroup, appears to be highly age-specific and functions most prominently among youth. In certain age groups, dance functions as an approval-soliciting mechanism among peers and significant others. Although this aspect frequently overlaps with the two previously discussed aspects, it is distinctive in that dance is seen as necessary to enhance one's inclusion in a specific group, usually a voluntary social group. As one youth put it:

If you can't dance, you just ain't hip, you don't get invited to nothin'.[15]

This aspect involves other components that relate to the total concept "soul." Youth music and dance contain highly observable and frequently demonstrated aspects of black culture. Once again Malcolm X's autobiography is illustrative. Throughout the chapter entitled "Laura," he recalls the ingroup-outgroup aspect at work in the social atmosphere of his peer group:

All I remember is that during some party around this time, when nearly everyone but me was dancing some girl grabbed me—they often would take the initiative and grab a partner for no girl at those parties ever would dream that anyone present couldn't dance...[16]

If one could not dance, why would one attend the party? Dancing was the most observable activity, and ability to dance was necessary for successful inclusion in such a social situation. It would not occur to participants that anyone would attend who could not dance.

As Malcolm's social life led him from small house parties to large public dances at the Roseland ballroom, he discovered that to be considered a "favorite," to win peer approval, and to become a veteran of "showtime" one had to be an outstanding dancer. Malcolm writes:

Now Count Basie turned on the showtime blast and the other dancers moved off the floor, shifting for good watching positions, and began their hollering for their favorites...The Count's band was wailing. I grabbed Mamie and we started to work...I remember the very night that she became known as one of the showtime favorites there at the Roseland...she got barefoot and shouted and shook herself as if she were in some African jungle frenzy, and then she let loose with some dancing, shouting with every step...The crowd loved any wayout lindying style that made a colorful show like that. It was how Mamie had become known.[17]

Her dancing ability earned for Mamie, and later for Malcolm and Laura, inclusion among the showtime favorites. Mamie could have attended every dance and never have become known, but her style of dancing earned her the title of "favorite," a high-status position in the context of the weekly Roseland dances.

The ingroup-outgroup aspect, as well as the other three, posits an implied level of dance competence. This competence includes subtle postures that fall outside the realm of acrobatic virtuosity and may be as subtle as a tilt of the heard, a facial expression, or position of the arms. These subtle postures derive from an African cultural base, and in conjunction with other variables such as personal demeanor, presentation of self, or personal style help to define who has access to status. They are necessary but not sufficient to accrue status in certain situations.

R. Lincoln Keiser, in his study of the Vice Lords, a Chicago street gang, provides a further example of the ingroup-outgroup aspect at work:

Vice Lords value soul. To tell someone he has soul is a compliment, while to say he has a "hole in his soul" is a definite criticism. There are certain social situations in which judgements are made in terms of soul. These are contexts involving music. Music is an extremely important part of Vice Lord life. Vice Lords closely follow the music form Chicago's black radio stations, and are constantly singing songs that are broadcasted there. Dancing is even more important in Vice Lord life. Almost all Vice Lords take intense pride in their dancing ability, and lose few opportunities to demonstrate it.

Vice Lords judge one another's singing and dancing in terms of soul ideology...Singing and dancing are important activities in two Vice Lord scenes. These are called by Vice Lords sets and hanging on the corner. A set can be translated as a party. Vice Lords usually display their dancing ability in this scene, and it is here that judgements are made in terms of soul.[18]

In the case of the Vice Lords, dancing ability is a necessary prerequisite for complete ingroup status. Without it, a Vice Lord would be incomplete, and the status of the entire group would be diminished.

The final aspect for discussion here is the fourth variable, political resistance. this aspect boldly presented itself in the dialogue quoted earlier from the novel *Meridian*. Lynne says:

Loot at me...you think you can step over me and just keep on going...ruin my life.

Truman responds:

Don't bring up your lousy dancing career...if you people could dance you wouldn't have to copy us all the time.[19]

Truman's statement about whites copying blacks is heavy with resentment. He is voicing a feeling shared by millions of black Americans. In a strict interpretation, Truman's statement is a reference to the political realities of race. He is alluding to the deep-seated bitterness that Afro-Americans feel as they directly witness the violation of attributes they recognize as culturally theirs.

In both sides of the exchange, Walker uses dance as the focal point to reveal black's feelings, for she recognizes the fundamental nature of nonverbal behavior expressed as dance. Truman's reply is particularly exact. He is not only stating the feelings of many Afro-Americans but is also answering the question of who is capable of "stealing" from whom. He is sensitive to the fact that as a cultural and political group, blacks have limited power to appropriate and export culture, even their own. Obviously, Truman disapproves of whites copying the way blacks dance. But he must be pushed to feel anger and hostility before he will reveal the extent of his resentment.

The inference of dual standards of judgement is another important component in Truman's statement. Who gets measured by which standards is largely a function of where one finds oneself cultural and racially. Black Americans have long maintained at least two standards with which to judge dance, as Malcolm X reveals:

She didn't dance well, at least not by Negro standards. But who cared? I could feel the string eyes of other couples around us.[20]

In this passage, Malcolm is referring to a white girl with whom he danced at a large, predominantly black, public dance. The standard that blacks apply to their own dancing is charged with political and other meanings. Therefore, they silently (if not overtly) ridicule white persons attempting to dance in the presence of blacks, particularly if that dancing involves the emulation of Africanisms.

Afro-Americans, unaware of and unable to articulate the implied political meanings carried in the dance, merely voice the bitterness with which such activity is received. Their remarks range from pity, hatred, and ridicule to unaffected acceptance. In *Soul on Ice*, Eldridge Cleaver gives an account of the political resistance at work. He is candid in his description of whites performing dances of black origin:

The stiff Mechanical Omnipotent Administrator and Ultra-feminines presented a startling spectacle as they entered in droves onto the dance floors to learn how to Twist...They were swinging and gyrating and shaking their dead little asses like petrified zombies trying to regain the warmth of life, rekindle the dead limbs, the cold ass, the stone heart, the stiff mechanical, disused joints with the spark of life.

Cleaver continues:

This spectacle truly startled many Negroes, because they perceived it as an intrusion by the Mind into the province of the Body, and this intimated chaos because the Negroes knew, from the survival experience of their daily lives, that the system within which they were imprisoned was based upon the racial Maginot Line and that the cardinal sin, crossing the line—which was, in their experience, usually initiated from the black side—was being committed, en masse, by the whites.[21]

Many Afro-Americans perceive the activity to which Cleaver is referring as much more than crossing "racial lines"; they perceive it as an invasion, a profaning of sacred ground. it is viewed as proof of the white man's ultimate inabilities. In spite of his political reign over Afro-Americans, his ultimate cultural and physical paleness and lack of vigor are revealed in the dance and the degree to which white Americans attempt to imitate Africanisms and assimilate them into their social dancing styles.

Dance is the arena in which black confronts white and wins. It is the province over which black rule has prevailed relatively unchallenged. When whites attempt to "dance black," they pose what is perceived in the black mind as a challenge to that rule. To the black observer they usually appear ridiculous or obnoxious or both.

Cleaver gives an account of black response to whites performing the "twist":

Man what done got into them ofays? one asked. They trying to get back, said another. Shit if you ask me I think it must be the end of the world. Ooo-wee! said a Negro musician who had been playing at a dance and was now standing back checking the dancers. Baby, I don't dig this action at all! Look here baby, pull my coat to what's going down! I mean, have I missed it somewhere? Where I been baby? I been blowing all my life and I ain't never dug no happiness like this. You know what man, I'm gon' cut that fucking weed a loose. Ooo-wee! Check that little bitch right there! What the fuck she trying to do? Is she trying to shake it or break it? Ooo-wee.[22]

A Negro girl said, "Take me home I'm sick"; another said, "No let's stay! This too much." And a bearded black man who was not interested in learning how to twist but felt that if he was interested in doing it, he could get up from the table right now and start twisting, said, "It ain't nothing. They just try to get back, that's all."

Each of these comments is in pejorative terminology. This response is a group sensitivity that reflects the almost territorial guardianship with which most blacks, even those incapable of dancing, view the dance.

Cleaver continues:

And the dancers, they were caught up in a whirl of ecstasy, swinging like pendulums, mechanical like metronomes or puppets on invisible strings being manipulated by a master with a sick sense of humor. They look like Chinese doing communal exercise, said a Negro. That's all they're doing calisthenics! Yea said his companion, They're trying to get in shape.

In the eye of the black spectator, the white dancers do not meet the mark. One needs more than pelvic manipulations as standardized popular social dances[23] to pierce the political barrier of racism. What the white dancer perceives as the total reality, the movement itself, is merely a contingent component of a wider reality. To the untrained white observer, African movement appears independent of interlocking relationships that permeate its presence. This view can only elicit reactions of derision form most black observers.

For the Afro-American dancer, social dancing is a central and fundamental carrier of meaning. The dance is more than personal entertainment, fun, and good exercise. The dance is imbued with individual, socio-psychological, cultural, and political meaning.

The four meaning aspects—identity, cultural integrity, ingroup-outgroup, and political resistance—can be roughly correlated with changes across the life cycle. The identity aspect often appears in the early home environment in which parents and other encourage youngsters to dance or "cut a step"[24] almost as soon as they can walk. It is not uncommon in black homes and community affairs such as block parties or rent shouts[25] to find neighbors, adults, and older siblings giving or withholding approval on the basis of how well a three-to-six-year-old child imitates the current dances. The identity aspect is more prominent than the other three until preadolescence, age ten or eleven, and occasionally will extend beyond this point.

At age eleven or so, during the preteen and early teen years, the ingroup-outgroup aspect begins to show itself. During the early adolescent years the dance is a significant socialization mechanism, particularly for black urban youth. During this period the dance party becomes important enough in the lives of some urban youth to assume the stature of a "rite of passage." Attendance at dance parties demarcates the onset of a new phase in the life cycle: moving away form childhood and the home-centered phase of life.

If the dance party is viewed as a ceremony that enables individuals in transition to move from one status to another, then the significance of the dance in the life of black urban preadolescent youth can be more clearly understood.[26] Dance is absolutely necessary because it is the primary although not the only activity at these functions. According to R. Milton Clark:

In certain dances definite encouragement, group identification, and unity is seen developing among the participants. Males and females in close proximity slap hands and smile at each other. The words "we" and "us" are used. If the music stops, someone may start a chant of "We don't need no music" which is taken up by the crowd. The effect is one of a unit, an entity. One name given to this dance is "the soul train line." As individual males and females "come down the line" one hears shouts of "go ahead on girl," "right on," "Do your thing." Both males and females are actively involved in this process. Even though the participants may not know each other there is tacit approval of each other because no one feels threatened. There is a spirit of "soul" solidarity and togetherness at this point.[27]

The approval of dancing ability which the child first encounters in the home soon finds it locus in the preadolescent peer group. Here it is highly functional as a key ingredient in the definition and process of ingroup relations. At these parties, dance is pivotal in facilitating the emulation of numerous adult behaviors. Open contact with the opposite sex, practice in the adult social graces, and facilitation of a new individual identity through ingroup processes are only three specific ways in which dance is used in this situation.

The cultural integrity and political resistance aspects may appear any time after early adolescence. They usually do not appear before that time because of the limited exposure of the black child to the racism of the wider society and also the child's limited political understanding and sophistication. These two aspects surface earlier in working and lower-class blacks than in their middle-class counterparts. The black elite generally encounters fewer negative experiences with the dominant cultural milieu and has more cultural options such as elite balls and dinner parties at its disposal.[28] As a result, the aspects that relate most heavily to race and power relations generally appear later in the life cycle and tend to emerge more strongly in an institutional context.

The ideas discussed here demonstrate the vast unexplored territory with respect to the role, function, and meaning of dance in Afro-American culture. However, they are predicated on the existence of blacks as a separate socio-cultural entity in America. As more Afro-Americans find their way into mainstream American society these aspects of meaning could become relics of the past.

Notes

[1]Melville Herskovits, *The Myth of the Negro Past* (Boston: Beacon Press, 1941); Melville Herskovits, "What Africa Has Given America," *The New Republic*, September 4, 1935; Joann Kealiinohomoku, "A Comparative Study of Dance as a Constellation of Motor Behavior among African and United States Negroes," CORD *Dance Research Annual, VII* (1975); Linda F. Wharton and Jack L. Daniel, "Black Dance: Its African Origins and Continuity," *Minority Voices 1*, no. 1 (Fall 1977); Chadwick Hansen, "Jenny's Toe: Shaking Dances in America," *American Quarterly* 19, no. 3 (1967); Robert Farris Thompson, "Dance and Culture, an Aesthetic of the Cool: West African Dance," *African Forum* 2, no. 2 (Fall 1966); John Q. Anderson, "The New Orleans Voodoo Ritual Dance and Its Twentieth-Century Survivals," *Southern Folklore Quarterly* 24, no. 2 (June 1960); Gertrude P. Kurath, "African Influences on American Dance," *Focus on Dance* 3 (1965); Jan Hertzberg, "African Religious Survivals in the U.S." (1977, typewritten); Lydia Parrish, *Slave Songs of the Georgia Sea Islands* (New York: Creative Age Press, 1942).

[2]Edith J. R. Isaacs, *The Negro in American Theatre* (New York: Theatre Arts, Inc., 1947), pp. 72-73.

[3]Zora Neal Hurston, "Characters of Negro Expression," in Nancy Cunard, ed., *Negro Anthology* (New York: Negro Universities Press, 1969), pp. 39-46.

[4]Katrina Hazzard-Gordon, "Atibas a Comin': The Rise of Social Dance Formations in Afro-American Culture" (Ph.D. dissertation, Cornell University, 1983).

[5]For a more detailed description of these dances see Marshall and Jean Stearns, *Jazz Dance* (New York: The Macmillan Co., 1968), pp. 24, 27, 31, 99, 154, 235-37, 242; see also Georgia Writers' Project, WPA, *Drums and Shadows* (Athens: University of Georgia Press, 1940), p. 115.

[6]Alfred B. Pasteur and Ivory L. Toldson suggest that psychomotor or movement aspects of the personality are necessary for a healthy personality and that blacks demonstrate a predisposition to bodily movement *Roots of Soul* [Garden City, N.Y.: Anchor Press/Doubleday, 1982], pp. 237-45.

[7]Malcolm X with Alex Haley, *The Autobiography of Malcolm X* (New York: Grove Press, 1966), p. 56.

[8]Ibid., p. 57.

[9]Maya Angelou, *Singin' and Swingin' and Gettin' Merry Like Christmas* (New York: Random House, 1976), p. 56.

[10]Kealiinohomoku, pp. 122-28; Wharton and Daniel, pp. 73-80.

[11]Ralph Ellison and James McPherson, "Indivisible Man," *The Atlantic,* December 1970, p. 50.

[12]The concept "core black culture" refers to working-class black traditions and includes such cultural products as soul music, dance, soul food, black English, and street corner fellowship. See Richard W. Thomas, "Working-Class and Lower-Class Origins of Black Culture: Class Formation and the Division of Black Cultural Labor," *Minority Voices* 1, no. 1 (Fall 1977): 81-103.

[13]Nathan Hare, *The Black Anglo-Saxons* (London: Collier-Macmillan Ltd., 1965), p. 87.

[14]Alice Walker, *Meridian* (New York: Pocket Books, 1977), p. 148.

[15]From conversation with black youths in Cleveland, Ohio, June 1980.

[16]Malcolm X, p. 56.

[17]Ibid., p. 64.

[18]R. Lincoln Keiser, *The Vice Lords* (New York: Holt, Rinehart and Winston, 1969), p. 52.

[19]Walker, p. 148.

[20]Malcolm X, p. 57.

[21]Eldridge Cleaver, *Soul on Ice* (New York: Dell Publishing, 1968), p. 181.

[22]All quotations in this section are from Cleaver.

[23]For an account of such dancing, see Sharon Leigh Clark, "Rock Dance in the United States, 1960-1970: Its Origins, Forms and Patterns" (Ph.D. dissertation, New York University, 1973).

[24]The concept "cutting" is both familiar and traditional in core black culture to both musicians and dancers. For musicians it has meant unstructured competitive playing. It has a similar meaning for dancers engaged in spontaneous competitive dancing. For an account of "cutting" used by dancers see Hazzard-Gordon, chapter entitled "Block Parties."

[25]For an explanatory account of both block parties and rent shouts, see Hazzard-Gordon.

[26]R. Milton Clark, "the Dance Party as a Socialization Mechanism for Black Urban Pre-Adolescents and Adolescents," *Sociology and Sociological Research* 58, no. 2 (1974): 146.

[27]Ibid., p. 150.

[28]For accounts of black elite lifestyle, see E. Franklin Frazier, *Black Bourgeoisie* (New York: Free Press of Collier-Macmillan, 1957); see also Nathan Hare, *Black Anglo-Saxons*; Gerri Majors, *Black Society* (Chicago: Johnson Publishing Company, 1976); Stephen Birmingham, *Certain People: America's Black Elite* (Boston: Little, Brown and Company, 1977).

Vacant Places:
Setting In The Novels of Toni Morrison

Audrey Lawson Vinson

A cosmic structure with its basis in the familiar American puritan ethic can be identified in settings in the novels of Toni Morrison. This ethic with its Heaven and Hell is often the panoply against which Morrison's characters improvise their lives—improvise because the traditional law of existence, the Christian ethic itself, for her characters often increases frustration and thereby intensifies their dilemmas. Its requirements of hard work, plenitude, and moral discipline are foiled by the society (Cleanth Brooks and others, *American Literature: The Makers and the Making*, pp. 7-8). Like participants in an ancient, inchoate dance, Morrison's characters create, according to their individual emotions, responses to their milieu, and the resulting rules of expediency are shown against the foil of setting.

The immediate setting of the first three novels is a small midwestern town, the central focus of character and action. Radiating from this center in varying geometric forms are remote ancestral homes, the memories of which are draped in a mixture of the ideal, insecurity, longing and often terror; ideal refuges which are longed for as release from the harshness of life; and temporary havens which blend the real and ideal, but offer no finite resolution to frustrations. In her fourth novel, Morrison chose a Caribbean island as the setting. It contains, however, many of the same elements of the works with American settings, the island lending a concentration of fantasy and magic to the plot.

In *The Bluest Eye* Cholly seems to have emerged from the jaws of Hell to become the hope of Pauline whose background was by comparison idyllic. Pauline is lame, and Morrison utilizes her lameness to symbolize an unconscious susceptibility to evil. She capitulates, in each segment of her environment, to forces both good and evil which erode the lives of her children and herself. Once she is transported to the midwestern town from rural Kentucky, she immerses herself in the imaginary setting of the silver screen, becoming the avatar of her daughter Pecola in yearning to be white and wanting to enjoy the good environment associated with being white. The void of her own world—the bleak storefront home, her deteriorating relationship with Cholly, money problems, and her perception of ugliness in her child—created an environment so frustrating that she could only reflect hatred for her family and herself. Consequently she wrapped herself in a blanket of virtue that was "easy to maintain," and she maintained it to the exclusion of her family. Her gratification took the form of her total absorption in the setting of the white family's home. There she found order. Her other retreat, religion, reinforced the first by providing a rationale or justification for her zealous attention to the needs of the white family and her willful neglect of her own family. The American puritan ethic of hard work and loyalty to one's responsibility was followed assiduously at the house fronting the lake. Pauline's diligence on behalf of the white family was her obedience to God. She saw her own family as an obstruction to her order, including her Christian rectitude. Hence, she was quick to pound into them their sinfulness and unworthiness with the result that her son ran away and her daughter retreated into a pathetic self-hatred that ended in her complete loss of contact with reality.

The emptiness of the setting—its being a "vacant" place—is seen through the device of contrast with the imaginary perfection of family life and place as found in the first grade reader whose characters, Dick and Jane, live in attractive, secure surroundings. Morrison's repetitive superimposition of passages from this book emphasizes the starkness of the lives of Pecola and her friends. Two headnotes which open the novel suggest first the fertile abundance in an imaginary textbook setting and secondly the reminder that Marigolds in the real setting of the novel did not grow in the town that year. Vacancy, sterility and futility are conveyed by this description of setting.

In *Sula* Morrison recognizes the rich folk culture in the isolated environment of blacks in the community, but she is keenly aware of the suffocating vacuum which keeps them separated, poor and discouraged. The mound of dirt which stood as a reminder that a bridge was to have been constructed with labor from the Bottom symbolizes the unfulfilled dreams of economic relief.

The theme of vacancy in setting is treated with an irony reflected in the creation of the Bottom where blacks resided. Years before Sula's birth, white townspeople had moved the black population to the Bottom, actually a mountaintop which provided the proper separation the whites desired. As in nearly all such isolated areas, a rich folk culture thrived amid the poverty, violence and often sterile life. The descent from the Bottom was difficult and uncertain; hence, few left except for the strong and defiant ones such as Sula who spent some years in a large city before returning to the Bottom. As in *The Bluest Eye* the juxtaposition of traditional values and immediate needs creates the irony which highlights the actions of the characters. The setting itself is unyielding in the absence of jobs and money. Upon Sula's return to the Bottom, the setting becomes starker as if her presence, with its lack of a morality, places a curse on the area thereby causing wildlife to die and human beings to shrink in fear of her.

The cosmology of *Sula* consists of the Bottom with its footbridge connecting it to the white section of Medallion, the bridge site, and the remote forest with its river where Shadrack the crazed veteran resides. In addition, the large, mysterious cities, such as those seen by Sula, lie far away beckoning the daring.

Nearly every conceivable sin is committed in the Bottom—gambling, whoring, murder, theft, drug addiction and a multitude of other violent acts. They are committed against the background of joblessness and poverty so severe that at one time the only things standing between Eva Peace's family and starvation are two beets. The ambivalence with which the reader is forced to regard Eva's alleged action to get money for her family by letting a train sever one leg is the kind of duality which Morrison elicits from much of the violence which erupts from settings that seethe with such potential. One feels revulsion and sympathy simultaneously. Is Eva peace a madwoman or a heroine? Morrison creates in this setting a Euripidean fury which springs from the combination of milieu and character.

In her third novel, *Song of Solomon*, Morrison has refined her craft to create a complex setting and cosmogonic system on both the psychological and physical levels. The psychological "climate" exists not only in terms of the burden of racism, but racism as its effects are felt in an isolated environment. This setting in itself spawns much of the action. Yet the longing of Milkman Dead for his real identity establishes the crucial psychological climate of the novel. On the physical level Morrison skillfully weaves a cosmic pattern which encompasses Heaven and Hell and reflects her craftsmanship in its poetry and wholeness.

It is not difficult to identify the Paradise-Hades pattern in Morrison's treatment of physical setting. The images which describe the midwestern town, the Edenic Pennsylvania farm, and the remote cavernous Virginia country are highly suggestive as archetypal symbols. *Song of Solomon* is set in places which correspond to the ideal fecundity and dark caverns of the previous novels. Yet it seems to present deeper association within the reader as the combination of imagery and plot conducts one through the complete cosmogonic cycle. The idea of the cosmogonic cycle is adapted from Joseph Campbell's *Hero with a Thousand Faces*.

Setting in the novels is also enriched by imagery. Maud Bodkin in *Archetypal Patterns* has demonstrated the significance of certain images including mountain-garden, cavern, and river as they reflect the Heaven-Hell pattern. These images are prominent in *Song of Solomon* where the microcosm of a Michigan town lies within the macrocosm of the Michigan-Pennsylvania-Virginia universe. For Milkman Dead, his own home, nearby streets and office represent the limited boundaries of his life, and he longs to extend himself beyond them. This "earthbound" environment is complemented by the excursions to their Honore Island beach house with its idyllic setting. In his microcosm, Macon Dead, Milkman's father, regards Honore as heaven and for him it is the ultimate status symbol next to his business, his home and car. Diametrically opposed to his "heaven" is the dark depths of Pilate's winehouse which completes the Heaven-Hell pattern of Milkman's microcosm.

Encircling this smaller universe is the macrocosm consisting of Michigan, Shalimar, Virginia and Montour County, Pennsylvania where Lincoln's Heaven once caressed the first Macon Dead. This heaven has a direct reference back to Solomon's Leap from which old Solomon flew back to his original home. The river which Milkman crossed to reach Solomon's Leap was his last stage of progression from the forested underworld in Virginia to the promontory of heaven.

The emptiness of the microcosm is illustrated in Magadalene's pointing out that the maple tree which she planted in the yard had died. Like the little girls, Frieda and Claudia in *The Bluest Eye*, she places her hope in life on the dependable fertility of nature. When that fails, hope itself fails, for without nature the universe is indeed empty. Yet the emptiness itself might yield something. Pilate's rock collection—each rock taken from one of the places where she was rejected—though worthless, attracts Milkman and Guitar and the collection becomes a talisman which leads Milkman towards his destiny. Even vacant places yield something as long as human beings keep their hopes for the future alive. Morrison places Pilate in her permanent setting, the winehouse, which exudes hope and fecundity.

The emptiness is shown, furthermore, by a rhetorical technique in which negatives are juxtaposed with positive values. In *Song of Solomon* blacks called the street on which their one well-to-do physician lived with his family, Doctor Street. When the post office refused to deliver mail to this unofficially named street, and after it served notice that it was not Doctor Street, blacks quickly accepted Not Doctor Street as the name. The negation correlates with the denials in general made by the predominant society against the residents of the town who are black. Similarly, Mercy Hospital, because it would not admit blacks up to the time of Milkman's birth, is called No Mercy Hospital. Hence, life is filled with negation for the black residents of the town, and these negative elements represent the absence of meaning in the language used by the dominant society.

Significant also in Morrison's treatment of setting in her novels is what Maud Bodkin calls the "magic of place-names." A portion of Bodkin's review of observations on place names made by writers of psychological insight follows:

Marcel Proust has described vividly the effect of certain place-names upon the mind of an imaginative child. An unknown place becomes, he says, individual by having, like a person, a name for itself alone. Some character in the sound of the name, together with fragments of description assimilated in connection with it, would give rise, Proust tells us, in his childish fancy, to a vision unique, and as personal as love for a human being. An accumulated store of dreams was "magnetized" by the name, so that the place behind the name seemed "a thing for which my soul was athirst." ...Within the name was enclosed the magic of "the life not yet lived," of "Life intact and pure." It is such an illusion of the very life of life awaiting one at some point within the unknown that has lured travellers forth to distant lands; and the same readiness of our dreams to be magnetized by place-names has given to these a distinctive value and power in poetry. (102)

The second Macon Dead remembered his idyllic early life at Lincoln's Heaven. The Pennsylvania farm, acquired after his father attained his freedom, was the longed for Eden which provided a secure and prosperous family life. As Eden, it was earthbound, for it collapsed with the murder of the first Macon Dead. Yet its memory, transmitted to his grandchildren, caused Milkman Dead to yearn for it and the purity of life that the mere name elicited. Its magic widened his aspirations to seek the longed for Edenic flight at Solomon's Leap, a place-name which carries the highest human longing of not only the descendants of Solomon, but of all the blacks in Milkman Dead's milieu. Shalimar, in Virginia, is itself the affectionately corrupt version of Solomon, the name which was so "magnetized" that it drew to it a song and children's game which contained those fragments needed by Milkman to possess a vision of his origin, the place to which he was compelled to go for his ultimate personal fulfillment.

In *Sula*, the significance of names is evident in the ancestral home of Nel on Elysian Fields Street in New Orleans. This home remained a memory of the enchanting smell of gardenias for Nel who was too young, upon returning there for her great grandmother's funeral, to know that her own mother was the daughter of a Creole whore who worked at Sundown House with its red shutters. The mother's refuge was the House on Elysian Fields where high morality was practiced and which was guarded by "the dolesome eyes of a multicolored Virgin Mary, counseling her to be constantly on guard for any sign of her mother's wild blood" (17). From the house on Elysian Fields Nel's mother went to Medallion to live a conservative life against the moral dangers that might beset her daughter. The names Elysian Fields and Sundown House suggest the moral spectrum of Paradise-Hades.

In addition, Medallion as a name suggests something memorialized, and it is obviously intended to tie in with the attraction for the incidents related to National Suicide Day and the veteran Shadrack. Furthermore, memories, both gentle and terrible, become a large part of the plot which takes place in Medallion. The naming of the Bottom was a promise of good land in the valley from a slave owner.

...The slave blinked and said he thought valley land was bottom land. The master said, "Oh, no! See those hills? That's bottom land, rich and fertile." "But it's high up in the hills," said the slave. "High up from us," said the master, "but when God looks down, it's the bottom, That's why we call it so. it's the bottom of heaven— best land there is. (5)

This "nigger joke" is the favorite version of how the Bottom got its name, and when told among themselves increased the fondness with which Medallion's blacks regarded their part of the village. It is another example of names giving meaning to setting in Morrison's novels.

Isle des Chevaliers in *Tar Baby*, the island of the wild horses, suggests utter freedom and untamed nature on the isle where the rules of society are set aside. It is the kind of place which Shakespeare scholars call the Green World where life is license and freedom. "...what was unthinkable in Philadelphia was not so on that island" (195).

Nearly all of the elements of setting found in Morrison's earlier novels exist in *Tar Baby*. The central character has a quasi-birth or rebirth (similar in some respects to Byron's Don Juan) out of warm waters which push him gently into the setting of Isle des Chevaliers. Unlike Don Juan, who met Haidee, a naive island girl, Son meets Jadine, a sophisticated black American. The island is a place for the two young blacks to be free of the realities of Paris, Eloe, Florida and New York. But freedom itself, like the dance of Gautier's Giselle, propels one to the blind fury of one's inner desires. In *Tar Baby* the down-to-earth, uneducated, sexually attractive black man is loved by, but cannot be a permanent refuge for the sophisticated Paris model, a Sorbonne graduate. After they try life in the milieu in which she feels comfortable, and in Eloe where he is comfortable, her rational rules send her back to Paris despite the magnetism of her black roots, and his unbridled passion sends him to the darkest side of the isle where wild, blind, black horsemen rip past trees and lush growth, feared even by the islanders who by American and European norms are themselves free. Jadine chooses a "vacant" place, Paris, where she can pose, recreate herself, over the tenacious, passionate island swamp which symbolizes the deep roots of life which she found in Eloe and which rips off everything which she has become and makes her feel inferior as a woman. She first feels her mask ripped off in Paris in her encounter with the African woman. She feels it again in Eloe where the black women envelop Son and make her feel rootless and outside. This conflicts, of course, with her genuine relationship with Son who brings out the real, unmasked Jadine. Morrison suggests a kind of Ur-Blackness which magnetically pulls Jadine wherever she encounters it. On the surface she rejects it, but inwardly she yearns for it. The place of the desire lies within her true identity as a black. The masks of the worlds of Paris and New York are, at best, temporary refuges from the complexities and contradictions of being black. Except for the Paris education and stylish career, she might blend well with the women of Eloe. She does not, however, and her experience in the Parisian setting provides her with an alternative to which she responds rationally. Her instinct is to remain with Son, but logic dictates that she return to the materially secure, but emotionally vacant, setting of Paris. She understands its form and elects it as her method of surviving in the universe. This, she feels, is better than the frustration of trying to convince Son that he should go to college and "move up" to her level of experience. In *Tar Baby* Morrison has added to her "vacant places" the empty, deluding whirl of Paris and New York.

By contrast, the verdant island reduces everything to unmasked reality which includes the Streets seeing themselves without the trappings of their Philadelphia manners, Jadine finding emotional security in Son, and her aunt and uncle seeing their true relationship to the Streets. The island with its enchantment is concomitantly disturbing and evokes the dark areas of the psyche which reveals some truths, long masked, that are not pleasant to encounter. They include memories, dreams, magic and ritual. All of these elements deserve more specific treatment of the important ways in which they are utilized in the development of the novel. In brief, they are each combined with images of nature—landscape and animal images—to reflect the unlimited richness and fertility of a prelapsarian paradise.

Setting in Toni Morrison's novels can be described against the foil of the American puritan ethic with its inherent discipline and against the "norm" of the white society. which is constantly visible as an economic and social backdrop to the problems confronted by her characters. The milieu of whites often serves to emphasize the emptiness of setting in these works. Yet Morrison's characters emerge as persons in a realistic world which is often reconstructed to form that which can be utilized for living. The alternative to such re-creating is death of the spirit. Survival in spirit, a goal which underlies all her novels, is the heroic result of creating in a vacuum. Setting, therefore, is an antagonist, a character itself, which possesses countless means of stifling the ideals and yearnings of other characters.

Early Criticism of Jean Toomer's Cane: 1923-1932

Ronald Dorris

In *The Development of American Literary Criticism*, John H. Raleigh contends in his article, "Revolt and Revaluation in Criticism: 1900-1930," that in the closing years of the nineteenth century and in the early years of the twentieth, "The subject matter and interests of criticism were enormously enlarged in various ways; there was first a horizontal extension, particularly into psychology, sociology, philosophical esthetics, and the other arts, and a further extension culturally by the taking into account of foreign critical theory."[1] Despite such trends applicable to the development of literary criticism, examination of the 1923-32 criticism of Jean Toomer's *Cane* highlights the failure or refusal of critics to do an indepth analysis of the novel's content, revealing instead personalized accounts of *Cane* based on an assessment of the book's title or of Toomer himself.

Initially, *Cane* was published in 1923. One of the first reviews to focus on Toomer's book came from Paul Rosenfeld in *Men Seen*, published in 1925.

Toomer received a six and one-half page review in *Men Seen*. Although Rosenfeld's appraisal is heartwarming, he is subtle in his approach. He does not credit Toomer with the clarity of vision which evolved from the author's philosophical development. Instead, he presents Toomer as a writer who could respond to the clearness of two of his contemporaries.[2]

Both Sherwood Anderson and Waldo Frank have helped to rouse the impulse of Toomer. Yet it was the imagists with their perfect precision of feeling that fevered him most for work. Some clarity in himself must have responded to the clearness of these poets. That his definiteness remains as yet less intense than theirs is plain. Perhaps because his gift is warmer and more turbulent, it is also less white and clear...Large as is the heralding which comes through him, Toomer remains as yet much of the artist trying out his colors, the writer experimenting with a style. And still, these movements of prose are genuine and new. Again a creative power has arrived for American literature: for fiction, perhaps for criticism; in any case, for prose. Other writers have tried, with less happiness, to handle the material of the South. They have had axes to grind, sadisms for whites; masochisms to release in waking resentment for blacks. But Toomer came to unlimber a soul, and give of its dance and music.[3]

From firsthand experience, Waldo Frank was one man who understood that Toomer had come "to unlimber a soul, and give of its dance and meaning." By the time Frank wrote the introduction to *Cane*, he had written a number of unpublished manuscripts, published four works, visited Wyoming and Montana, lived in Paris, worked as a reporter on the city staff of New York *Evening Post*, served as an associate editor of *Seven Arts*, traveled to the South twice, first with Jean Toomer to live among blacks while passing as a Negro, and registered for the draft as a pacificist. For a brief period in their lives, the relationship between Toomer and Frank was fruitful. They encouraged each other and from the experiences of their Southern tour, Toomer published *Cane*, and Frank published *Holiday*, both in 1923. Each was interested in the essence of man, Frank having a concern that meaning and values not be limited to striving after things on earth in isolation from the rest of the cosmos. He disagreed with a realism which assumes that the individual is real and immortal, portrayed analytically in back and forth motion. For him man was an unreal individual transformed in truth instantaneously, in circular motion, only as the timeless and spaceless Presence speaks in him. Sharing a spiritual view similar to that of Toomer, Frank appraised *Cane* as a harbinger of literary maturity.

It seems to me, therefore, that this is a first book in more ways than one. It is a harbinger of the South's Literary maturity: of its emergence from the obsession put upon its minds by the unending racial crises—an obsession from which writers have made their indirect escape through sentimentalism, exoticism, polemic, "problem" fiction, and moral melodrama. It marks the dawn of direct and unafraid creation. And, as the initial work of a man of twenty-seven, it is the harbinger of a literary force whose incalculable future I believe no reader of this book will be in doubt.[4]

Matthew Josephson was the associate editor of *Broom*, a transatlantic magazine edited by Harold Loeb from 1921-24. The magazine focused on creating a bridge between the continents of Europe and America by presenting significant solutions of the art and literature of the two continents. Josephson was very appreciative of the various allies and helpmates who gathered to give support to the American edition of Broom when the European office was closed in 1923. He recognized Toomer as a gifted Negro novelist "whose studies of Negro life in America were essentially naturalistic,"[5] and wrote a review of *Cane* in the books review section of *Broom* (October, 1923). Josephson did not review *Cane* as a work of philosophy that came from a spiritualist, despite the fact that he was in favor of a "Humanistic revival that would perhaps appear again, as in a cycle, attended by a romantic search for the 'soul of man'...of man at his finest development..."[6] Josephson spoke of Toomer as a Negro naturalist who evoked praises to the soil that the black man in America has tilled.

Toomer is close to his soil, his book is dripping of the Negro South, and beyond this, he writes with a prodigious intensity of sight and hearing. Hitherto this unconsciously gifted race has expressed itself in America through a superb folk-music and folk-poetry. *Cane* is unique in that it is the expression of an artist working deliberately in the literary medium, young, headstrong, unreserved, but ultimately faithful.[7]

Another review of *Cane* is linked with the message of art from an America of the 1920s. Literature, as one component of art, gave focus to the New Negro on one side of the color line, and the Lost Generation on the other side, to name two literary movements among others. In terms of the former, Alain Locke, considered the dean of the movement, strove to place the New Negro in congruence with American democracy, alongside "a mass movement toward the larger and more democratic chance..."[8]

The Negro today is inevitably moving forward under the control largely of his own objectives. What are these objectives? Those of his outer life are happily already well and finally formulated, for they are none other than the ideals of American institutions and democracy. Those of his inner life are yet in process of formation, for the new psychology at present is more of a concensus of feeling than of opinion, of attitude rather than of program. Still some points seem to have crystallized.[9]

The philosophy presented by Toomer was different from the preachings of Locke. Toomer believed that no outer life was happily and finally formulated under democracy or any other type of government as an end unto itself. For a prosperous life, he counseled man to turn to the inward institution of developing and appreciating individual essence. Toomer further believed that inner life was already formed; it need only be enhanced by self-acceptance in order to be extended.

With Alain Locke attempting to place the New Negro securely within the framework of American democracy, and Jean Toomer attempting to release him from it, the difference in their point of view is sharpened when Locke states, "...Toomer gives a musical folk-lilt and a glamorous sensuous ecstasy to the style of the American prose modernists."[10] W. E. B. DuBois, another chief supporter of the New Negro movement, reinforces Locke's point of view, and admits confusion in a collaborative article with Locke on the "Younger Literary Movement."

Toomer does not impress me as one who knows human beings; and from the background which he has seen slightly and heard of all his life through the lips of others, he paints things that are true, not with Dutch exactness, but rather with an impressionist's sweep of color. He is an artist with words but a conscious artist who offends often by his undue striving for effect...His emotion is for the most part entirely objective. One does not feel that he feels much and yet the fervor of his descriptions show that he has felt or knows what feeling is. His art carries much that is difficult or even impossible to understand...Toomer strikes me as one who has written a powerful book but who is still watching for the fullness of his strength and for that calm certainty of his art which will undoubtedly come with years.[11]

A number of Toomer's contemporaries focused attention on characters caught in a world squeezed between the Spanish American War and the First World War. Their breeding ground was the American city, an urban vacuum stuffed with pre-war and post-war conditioning. Some of the writers of this era saw the city as a herculean effort that produced a split between social energy and social intelligence in an arena that seemed to leave no fields unexploited. For Toomer to give "glamorous sensuous ecstasy" to the style of American prose modernist would have been wasted effort to his own sense of philosophy. Instead of showing that the American cultural spirit struggled with the changes of breathtaking physical transformation, Toomer showed that the permanent character of an individual—one's essence, far surpassed any physical transformation that could take place. In this sense, only William Stanley Braithwaite emerged in *The New Negro* publication with a clearer picture of what Toomer had attempted to achieve.

Finally in Jean Toomer, the author of *Cane*, we come upon the very first artist of the race, who with all an artist's passion and sympathy for life, its hurts, its sympathies, its desires, its joys, its defeats, and strange yearnings, can write about the Negro without surrender or compromise of the artist's vision. So objective it is, that we feel that it is a mere accident that birth or association has thrown him into contact with the life that he has written about. He would write just as well, just as poignantly, just as transmutingly, about the peasants of Russia, or the peasants of Ireland, had experience brought him in touch with their existence. *Cane* is a book of gold and bronze, of dusk and flame, of ecstasy and pain, and Jean Toomer is a bright morning star of a new day of the race in literature.[12]

In 1932, personnel of *Opportunity* magazine commissioned Eugene Holmes, a young student of literature, to do a critical estimate of Toomer as a writer. As with critics before him, Holmes' assessment did not go beyond the title of the book or an attempt to explain the "significance" of its author. Calling Toomer an "Apostle of Beauty," Holmes wrote of him as a poet who surpassed race to emerge as an artist, filling his work with a message that went beyond rebellion and propaganda. Holmes saw Toomer as not wanting to commune with God and nature in isolation, but with God and nature in each man's understanding of self. Yet, Holmes did not draw this out in relation to the text of *Cane* itself. Despite the words of Eugene Holmes that Toomer "woke up to the spiritual realities, and to the ethical side of our existence,"[13] his hope that other writers might assess *Cane* as the philosophical work of a man with mystical interests was in vain. By now *Cane* had been out of print for a number of years and Jean Toomer had re-located to the American desert of the Southwest.

The chance of a work of art to stand the test of initial reception or of time depends on a number of factors. If public acceptance of *Cane* depended on an indepth analysis of content, examination of criticism about the book issued from 1923-32 can help us to understand why, after two brief publications totalling five hundred copies, *Cane* faded into obscurity until the 1960s. On December 12, 1922, Toomer forwarded a letter to Waldo Frank to explain what he had attempted to achieve: "The book is done, From three angles, *Cane's* design is a circle. Aesthetically, from simple forms to complex one, and back to simple forms."[14] None of the early criticism examines this design.

In keeping with his mystical interests and his own understanding of life, Toomer accepted that the hidden meaning of all things to be realized and felt would come about in an environment which gives birth to the impulse to keep the painful details and episodes of an experience alive in one's consciousness. *Cane* highlights the South as an environment that could keep alive a particular experience in the life of a people. Toomer explained: "One should, I think, view an environment in terms of what it actually is, and not in terms of its possibilities,—keeping in mind the essential fact that not the place itself but your ability to function in it is the important thing. Having done this there are three main factors to be considered: first, the physical factor, the obvious physical geography of the place; second, the human factor, the people themselves, the obvious living conditions, the subtle human atmosphere; and, third, the supernatural factor, the extraphysical, the extra-human the soul of the place."[15] None of the early criticism examines Toomer's interest in environment.

To write of the essential character of a people—the potential of beings to realize and actualize themselves in a world of chaos—was to Toomer the creation of a message. None of the early criticisms of *Cane* incorporates an indepth analysis of the creation of this message.

It is often stated that Toomer and *Cane* failed because the author stood apart from his contemporaries. Perhaps Jean Toomer did not stand apart from his contemporaries as much as the early critics stood apart from a wholesome assessment of *Cane*.

Notes

[1]Floyd Stovall, editor, *The Development of American Literary* Criticism, (Chapel Hill: Univ. of North Carolina Press, 1955), pp. 194-95.

[2]Paul Rosenfeld, *Men Seen* (New York: Dail Press, 1925), v-vi.

[3]Rosenfeld, pp. 232-33.

[4]Jean Toomer, *Cane*, with an Introduction by Waldo Frank (New York: Boni & Liveright, 1923), ix.

[5]Matthew Josephson, *Life Among the Surrealists* (New York: Harcourt, Brace & Company, 1930), p. 260.

[6]Matthew Josephson, *Portrait of the Artist as American* (New York: Harcourt, Brace & Company, 1930), p. 305.

[7]Matthew Josephson, review of *Cane*, *Broom*, Volume V, Number 3 (New York: October, 1923), p. 179.

[8]Alain Locke, "The New Negro," *The New Negro* (New York: Albert & Charles Boni, 1925), p. 6.

[9]Locke, "New," p. 10.

[10]Alain Locke, "Negro Youth Speaks," *The New Negro* (New York: Albert & Charles Boni, 1925), p. 51.

70   Perspectives of Black Popular Culture

[11]W. E. B. DuBois and Alain Locke, "The Younger Literary Movement," *Crisis*, Volume XXVII (New York: 1924), 162.

[12]William Stanley Braithwaite, "The New Negro Literature," *The New Negro* (New York: Albert & Charles Boni, 1925), p. 44.

[13]Eugene Holmes, "Jean Toomer—Apostle of Beauty," *Opportunity*, Volume X, Number 8 (New York: August, 1932), p. 260.

[14]The Jean Toomer Papers are presently housed at the Beinecke Rare Book and Manuscript Library, Yale University.

[15]Jean Toomer, A drama of the Southwest (Unpublished MS), Box 49, Folder 14, Jean Toomer Papers, Fisk University Library, Nashville.

Cultural Challenge, Heroic Response:
Gwendolyn Brooks and the New Black Poetry

D. H. Melhem

A new poetry, strong and true, has been developing in this country. Born of the constant quest in the Black community for emancipation and leadership, it expresses the democratic intentions of American civilization.[1] Antithetical to the art of alienation, Angst, solipsistic confession, it vigorously challenges negative aspects of the majority culture by responding with cohesion, spirituality, and heroic power. This literature, often described by the poets themselves as "revolutionary" or calling for "revolution," may be viewed as a politicized spiritual energy.[2]

We observe a great range in the new Black poetry, from historical affirmation, as in Robert Hayden's "Runagate, Runagate" and "The Ballad of Nat Turner"[3] and the consciousness-raising prevalent in nearly all black poets, to the activist voices of poets like those discussed here. The variations, a matter of degree more than of kind, share a common concern with racial identity that sparks and spurs the work, whether it be personal, social, or both. The perspective taken here is that of a new heroic genre of contemporary American literature.

Certain features set the poetry apart from its predecessors. The focus of so much Black life, the search for leadership, now includes the poet's own assumption of a leadership role. We see Gwendolyn Brooks traveling across the country and to Africa and Europe, giving readings and stimulating Black creativity and unity, having turned her publishing to the black press [more recently to her own company]; Dudley Randall pioneering with Broadside Press; Haki Madhubuti founding and guiding Third World Press and the Institute of Positive Education; Amiri Baraka promoting a political stance, formerly with Spirit House and now with an organized group and with the Advanced Workers, a musical/political/educational ensemble; Sonia Sanchez combining her role as poet and teacher, formerly in the service of the Nation of Islam. Pedagogical energies directed by these and other black poets emerge from total commitment that shapes a poetry of social concerns. These artists point out, moreover, that a poetry which eschews politics is itself making a political choice.[4]

There is no gender distinction for the heroic role. Audiences confirm this. A lively interaction obtains between poet and listeners, one analogous to that between preacher and congregation (as with "call and response") in many Black churches. The eight poets selected below usually encourage such responses. Their differences, nevertheless, give some idea of the rich diversity within the genre. The inquiry begins with the poetry of Gwendolyn Brooks.[5]

There are three salient reasons for starting here. First, her poetry reveals and responds to social change, as George E. Kent points out.[6] Significant historical events and their cultural modifications clearly imprint Brooks's work from *A Street in Bronzeville* (1945) onward. Second, it is prototypically heroic in both style and content. This structural distinction enhances its formal vigor, notably in the "brief epic" *In the Mecca* (I imply the meanings Barbara Lewalski establishes for Milton's *Paradise Regained*).[7] Although Brooks's poetry has always been humanistic, infused with political and spiritual life, she has developed toward a more urgent and sermonic mode. This is a process of prophecy, of perfecting the poetic voice as an instrument of communication. Third, Brooks has influenced contemporary Black poetry by the impact of her personality as much as by her work per se. She has achieved this through her support and championing of poets and by propagation of the new consciousness, which dramatically confronted her at the Second Fisk University Writers' Conference in 1967. The tribute anthology by black poets, *To Gwen With Love*, her most cherished award, edited by Patricia L. Brown, Don L. Lee (Haki R. Madhubuti), and Francis Ward (1971), attests to this significance. [See also *Say That the River Turns: The Impact of Gwendolyn Brooks*, edited by Haki R. Madhubuti (1987).] While some poets have been contending lately with personal statement, Brooks has been steadfast in maintaining the goals of cultural identity and cohesion, by looking past the navel of solitude toward the lives of others.

Stylistics of the leading black poets variously retain the elements of Black music and speech identified by Stephen Henderson.[8] What distinguishes Brooks, however, and what places her in the heroic/epic tradition of literature in English is a unique configuring of the incantatory Black sermonic with the Anglo-Saxon alliterative and metonymic mode. In her later work one may discern, to borrow a modifier from Matthew Arnold, a "grand heroic" and a "plain heroic" style; the first more formal and public, audible in her "Sermon(s) on the Warpland" where she urges her people:

> Build now your Church, my brothers, sisters. Build
> never with brick nor Corten nor with granite.
> Build with lithe love. With love like lion-eyes.

and enjoins them, "Nevertheless, live./Conduct your blooming in the noise and whip of the whirlwind." The second mode is more conversational and personal, as in poems like "Walter Bradford" and "Speech to the Young." In the latter poem, lines like

> Taking Today (to jerk it out of joint)
> the hardheroic maim the

leechlike-as-usual who use,
adhere to, carp, and harm.

carry great phonic weight, with the vigor of consonants that make *Beowulf*, the great Anglo-Saxon epic, so powerful to the ear. The kenning, an Old English figure of speech, is suggested in Brooks's frequent compounding in phrases like "tall-walker" for proud Black youth, "sun-slappers" and "harmony-hushers" for negative people, and in other metonymic figures such as the magnificent description of the Wall of Respect in Chicago, decorated with a mural of Black heroes, including Brooks, and since torn down: "This Wall this serious Appointment/ this still Wing/ this Scald this Flute this heavy Light this Hinge." Her new work, particularly since publication of *Riot* with Broadside in 1969, and subsequently of *Family Pictures* (1970), *Aloneness* (1971), and *Beckonings* (1975), is honed to directness and musicality. She describes it as "clarifying rather than simple." Her increased usage of the ballad form is important in this respect. Yet the subtlety and complexity of her later poems is borne not by allusiveness or symbolism found in earlier works but by their structural, semantic, and phonic elements. Brooks's art, beyond its Judeo-Christian grounding and its skepticism, is a social act, an act of prophecy and maternal extension.

Like Brooks, Sonia Sanchez offers a poetry of leadership.[9] She is a strong poet who creatively uses Black English,[10] phonetic spelling, and the rhythms of Black music. [Formerly] committed to the Muslim faith, her work, with its nearly stern moral cast, is a heroic stance and call to black people. This morality, the hallmark of Black writing as a whole, is hurled against the hostile and decadent culture as both armor and weapon. In her first book, *Home Coming* (1969), appear the stylistic traits and themes that will be developed in succeeding volumes. Writing as a Black woman in touch with her own feelings and the everyday problems of Black life, its cultural existence within a menacing society, her work is an affirmation of pride and solidarity. The lowercasing of the first person singular, together with phonetic spelling, suggests the influence of e. e. cummings and allies her with Haki Madhubuti, who introduces the volume and shares her condemnation of white capitalist American society. Sanchez writes poems against taking drugs and consuming alcohol, against economic and social inequality, in a straightforward idiom designed to reach masses of people.

A poem like "summer/time T.V./ (is witer than ever)" in her second book, *We A BaddDDD People* (1970), attacks the commercial values of American life, along with both whites and blacks who perpetuate its pretensions to democracy. The very title of the book, in which "bad" means "the very best" in Black English, indicates, according to Clarence Major's definition, "a simple reversal of the white standard."[11] It is useful here to bear in mind his comment regarding what he calls "Afro-American slang," that "beneath the novelty or so-called charm of this speech a whole sense of violent unhappiness is in operation" (Introduction, p. 9). *We A BaddDDD People* is dedicated to black women, "the only queens of this universe."

It directly addresses itself to Black life in America by means of a spare, conversational style and a Black musically influenced rhetoric, heavily syncopated, compelling in the poet's oral delivery. The title poem is dedicated to Gwendolyn Brooks and begins

```
    i mean.
                we bees real
    bad.
                we gots bad songs
        sung on every station
        we gots some bad        N A T U R A L S
        on our heads
                and brothers gots
        some bad loud ( fo real )
                dashiki threads
                    on them.
```

Sanchez's images are concrete, everyday, indigenous. There is no attempt at any point to modify or translate the speech into polite and/or standard white diction. The repetition of "bad" insists upon the legitimacy of the Black English usage. There are no compromising apostrophes, which usually bracket poetry as "dialect," as in some poems by Paul Laurence Dunbar and Sterling A. Brown. Lowercasing, moreover, serves to convey a reflective, subjective mode, one that is democratic, equalizing rather than distinguishing people by capital letters. Capitalization that does occur, as in the fully capped "N A T U R A L S" here, for example, is consequently emphasized and conceptualized.

It's A New Day (1971), a book dedicated to "young brothas and sistuhs," inspires her sons, Morani and Mungu, with a confidence that they as "black princes" "will be the doers" whose deeds "will run red with ancient songs." Both the Muslim religion, with its Spartan abstinence and ideals of self-discipline and the African heritage, itself partly joined with Mohammedan culture, feed Sanchez's work. Exemplary figures in Black life, men and women like Elijah Muhammad, Martin Luther King, and Gwendolyn Brooks are invoked in the title poem. The sermonic and pedagogic role of the poet is especially appealing in "don't wanna be," where the urban villains and victims—the pimps, numbers runners, and junkies—are identified as negative phenomena to be shunned.

A Blues Books for Blue Black Magical Women (1974) is dedicated to her father and to Elijah Muhammad "who has labored forty-two years to deliver us up from this western Babylon." The book carries an epigraph from the Qur'an, a significant emblem for its sermonic impulse and its style. The Qur'an itself, along with African, especially Swahili poetry, should be examined for its influence on the later work of Sanchez and of Madhubuti. The anaphoric repetitions, which bear relation to the chanted sermon,[12] as well as to the blues, also appear in the work of Audre Lorde, and they figure prominently in the later poetry of Brooks. *A Blues Book* constitutes an important shift to the lyrical and to the assumption of a full prophetic voice, both reflections of Scriptural antecedence. Moving from the Introduction, a rhetorical, discursive exhortation to Black women to help build the Nation of Islam, the poet offers an autobiographical summary of past, present, and rebirth, and a vision of the future. As the sequence becomes more lyrical and elevated in tone, the poetry grows luxuriant and vivid, with suggestions of Blakean, Whitmanic, and Scriptural incantation and imagery. The closing poem, "in the beginning," which opens with

> in the beginning
> there was no end
> in the beginning
> there was no end
> (to be sung) in the beginning
> there was no end
>
> all continued
> nothing stopped

calls for a renewal of the "circle of Blackness" which is made of "you and me," the ideal of Black solidarity. This is a humanism rather than the theism of "In the beginning was the Word" (John 1:1), and it contrasts with T. S. Eliot's "In my beginning is my end," which introduces the "East Coker" section of *Four Quartets*. Sanchez's view of continuity and recurrence is social; Eliot's, while similarly spiritual in tone, is ultimately personal.

The combination of maternalism and leadership, found in the work of Brooks and Sanchez and characterizing the poetry of many black women, is evident in the work of Audre Lorde.[13] Although, at times, rhetorical demands overtake her, she is movingly effective in combining maternal and social perceptions. In *From A Land Where Other People Live* (1973) the vision is outward, mother to child, daughter to mother, with a periplum of understanding toward past, present, and future. There is great tenderness in her work, a lyricism both incantatory and reflective that utilizes concrete imagery and, occasionally, African myth. She is a heroic mother, encouraging her children to see the ferocious reality of their environment, to struggle against it and, if necessary, to rebel even against her. The last poem, "Prologue," is aptly placed and titled, for its aim is to understand her own past as a step toward action in the future. "The time of lamentation and curses," she says, "is passing." She is turning away from Jeremiad lamentations toward possibilities of constructive living.

New York Head Shop and Museum (1974) moves from the didactic and sometimes aphoristic mode of Lorde's previous book to an angry confrontation with New York realities. In the first poem, "New York City 1970," she states, "I have come to believe in death and renewal by fire." The fire image invokes Biblical reference (2 Peter 3:10) and recurs throughout prophetic literature as emblem of destruction and revival. Along with other literary associations, including James Baldwin's *The Fire Next Time*, it recalls Brooks's *In the Mecca* where, suggesting Shadrach, Meshach, and Abednego, "Don Lee" "stands out in the auspices of fire/ and rock and jungle-flail." "To My Daughter The Junkie on A Train" compassionately appraises the unknown, afflicted child, from whom

> women avert their eyes
> as the other mothers who became useless
> cursed their children who became junk.

The poet's urgency sometimes directs her toward the discursive, as in "The American Cancer Society or There Is More Than One Way To Skin A Coon." Lorde employs a scattering of rhyme, in "The Ballad From Childhood," for example, with its deadly irony of the need to kill illusion. "Sacrifice," the penultimate poem, calls for a resolute stoicism:

> Learning all
> we can use
> only what is vital
> The only sacrifice of worth
> is the sacrifice of desire.

The last poem, "Black Studies," ends on a somewhat elegiac and self-questioning note. The poet, a teacher, speaks as both teacher and mother, proffering her student/children the certainty of questions and of her love. *Coal* (1976) includes reprints of some earlier, unavailable pieces. Her latest book, *Between Our Selves* (1976), is the most personal of her volumes. It seems to mark a temporary retrenching into an introspective passage, where her motivations, beliefs, and origins are deeply probed.

Another poet of remarkable power and intensity, one who shapes her copious imagery into working-class perspectives, is Jayne Cortez.[14] Her first book, *Pissstained Stairs And The Monkey Man's Wares* (1969), only hints at the strength she develops in subsequent work, although it lays out the terrain of engaged sensibility she later explores. Born in Arizona, the poet grew up in the Watts community of Los Angeles and adapted her rugged purviews to the New York scene. In both *Festivals and Funerals* (1971) and *Scarifications* (1973), the raw language expresses an unequivocal indictment of capitalist America. Through erotic and sensuous imagery, she transforms her woman's body into an emblem of the depredations upon and triumph of Blackness. In so doing, she calls attention to the power of the individual—and therefore of the group—in confronting a hostile society. Poems like "I Am New York City," "Lexington/96 Street Stop," and "Herald Square" present a hard, urban scene without sentimentality; "Do You Think," which asks, "Do you think this is a sad day, or sad night/ full of tequila/ full of el dorado/ full of banana solitudes" and ends, "Do you really think time speaks English in the mens room?" describes the cultural ghettoizing of minorities. Like the other poems in *Scarifications*, including the eulogy, "Song for Kwame," the late President Nkrumah of Ghana, it suggests the scars of ghetto life which can yet be made into emblems of warrior courage and beauty.

With *Festivals and Funerals*, Cortez's many visits to West Africa since 1967 emerge in a synthesis of African, Afro-American, and Hispanic elements. The book title refers to the fact that some of the festivals involved funerals, like that for the Asantehene, King of the Ashanti people in Ghana, and implicates the poet's own philosophical insight. In "African Night Suite" she describes herself as an African woman:

> my neck of four lines
> my nose of gold studs
> my lip ring flashing signals
> to the moon against mount kenya
> greeting myself
> > welcome
> > perdido of the mambo sun
> > afro star
> > afro light
> > afro suite of crickets in
> > the african blues tribe

and combines musical elements, the mambo, blues, syncopated rhythms, associating them with their African origins, and identifying herself simultaneously with popular culture and oppressed people. This ethnic dynamo of her work, impelled by commitment, propels its urgency.

Like the other poets discussed here, Dudley Randall calls for revolution in earlier works, but his poetry is more reflective and interpretive than incendiary.[15] *After the Killing* (1973) probes the meaning of rhetoric and facile slogans in poems like "Words Words Words" and "Tell It Like It Is." In the poem "Courage," he names "mercy" as the apex of three degrees of courage, the others being courage to die and to kill. He speaks out against the perpetuation of vengeance in "After the Killing," where his use of compounding in the word "blood-thirster" is reminiscent of Brooks's important stylistic trait.

Randall's first individual volume (after *Poem Counterpoem*, with Margaret Danner) was the chapbook *Cities Burning* (1968). It indicates, in poems like "Primitives," "The Rite," and "Hail, Dionysos," the range of the poet's varied cultural and literary interests, and suggests both his social engagement and critical temperament. In the first poem, "Roses and Revolutions," with its Whitmanic eloquence and spiritual breadth, the natural rose becomes "the terrible and splendid bloom/ the blood-red flower of revolution." The poet writes with bitter humor in "Black Poet, White Critic," of the attempt to reduce the subject-matter of poetry to "a white unicorn." He is technically at ease with conventional forms as well as free verse and utilizes the communicative potential of the ballad in poems like "The Ballad of Birmingham" and "Dressed All In Pink."

Sanely paternal in approach, Randall cuts through false rhetoric in a poem like "An Answer to Lerone Bennett's Questionnaire On A Name for Black Americans" in *More to Remember* (1971). There he points out that the social positions of blacks and whites would be the same if the names were reversed. "The spirit informs the name," he writes, "Not the name the spirit." "Ancestors" in the same volume, a poem which, like Brooks's sonnet from *Annie Allen* appears at the end of Herbert G. Gutman's *The Black Family in Slavery and Freedom, 1750-1925* (New York: Pantheon, 1976), features the serious humor, democratic and working-class orientation of his poetry. He asks:

> Why are our ancestors
> always kings or princes
> and never the common people?
>
> Was the Old Country a democracy
> where every man was a king?
> Or did the slavecatcher
> steal only the aristocrats

and wonders ironically whether the ordinary working people, "fieldhands/ laborers/ streetcleaners/ garbage collectors/ dishwashers/ cooks/ and maids" were left behind.

Randall's poetry is complemented by that of Etheridge Knight,[16] whose perspective is also humanistic and working-class. Knight's personal history, his courage in contending with drugs and despair, has inspired others and become a significant act of leadership. "I died in Korea from a shrapnel wound and narcotics resurrected me," he writes in *Poems form Prison* 1968). "I died in 1960 from a prison sentence and poetry brought me back to life." His first book, written while an inmate of Indiana State Prison, is introduced by Gwendolyn Brooks as "a major announcement." It presents keenly rendered portraits of prisoners like "Hard Rock" and of prison life, various reflections on life and on heroic figures like Malcolm X and Gwendolyn Brooks, the latter whom he addresses as "Effulgent lover of the Sun!" In a lyrical prose poem, "The Idea of Ancestry," he muses upon the forty-seven family pictures taped to the wall of his cell. Drawing strength from their presence he observes, "I am all of them, they are all of me;/ they are farmers, I am a thief, I am me, they are thee."

Belly Song (1973) extends the range of the poet's first book in subject-matter and style, combining his sense of family and Mississippi roots with an awareness of African heritage. In the tour-de-force, "Ilu, the Talking Drum," the instrument unites the "15 Nigerians and 1 Mississippi Nigger." The repetitions, phonic and rhythmic structuring precisely achieve a poetic synthesis. Knight skillfully employs the haiku; in "Dark Prophesy: I Sing of Shine" he adapts the ballad form, subordinating the anti-white sentiment to Shine's working-class confrontation with the millionaire banker, his daughter, and the preacher. A Black folk-hero, the ship's stoker escapes the

sinking Titanic and refuses to help any of the passengers who call to him
in turn, "Shine Shine save poor me" and offer him treasures or, in the
case of the preacher, a heavenly command, "save me nigger Shine in the
name of the Lord." Shine's most violent reaction is in defending himself
lethally against the drowning clergyman's assault and the hypocritical racism
he represents. The stoker is last seen dancing in Harlem when news of the
sinking reaches shore. Knight's impressive gifts, particularly the lyrical and
satiric, vividly deploy the images and personae of the poem.

His work rarely and then subtly employs the sermonic mode. He is
most direct in a poem like "For Black Poets Who Think of Suicide," keenly
moving as he calls for the poets to become instruments of their people.
He concludes:

> For Black Poets belong to Black People. Are
> The Flutes of Black Lovers. Are
> The Organs of Black Sorrows. Are
> The Trumpets of Black Warriors.
> Let All Black Poets die as trumpets,
> And be buried in the dust of marching feet.

The fine simplicity and seriousness, the capitalizations and metonymy, and
the heavily alliterated first line invoke Brooks's grand heroic style. The
passage may be compared with lines from "The Wall," quoted above. But
the statement and impulse are very much Knight's own. One may well reflect
that through poetry and personal response the ultimate outcast of the social
structure, the prisoner and former drug addict, may yet become a cultural
hero of opposition and affirmation.

The most dramatic expression of the poet as teacher and leader animates
the work of Haki R. Madhubuti (don l. lee)[17] and Amiri Baraka (LeRoi
Jones).[18] Their name changes in themselves are noteworthy in rejecting
Anglo-Saxon, dominant cultural referents for names that combine Arabic,
Muslim, African (Swahili, in particular), and Eastern associations. The
rejection for both poets includes a disaffection toward organized Christianity,
viewing it as passive and supportive of exploitation. The work of Madhubuti,
seriously poetical as well as polemical, has become, like that of Baraka,
almost completely didactic. The titles of his books, *Think Black* (1965-67),
Black Pride (1967-68), *Don't Cry, Scream* (1968-69), *We Walk the Way of
the New World* (1969-70), *Book of Life* (1973), indicate the tone and vision
with which he addresses his people. While there are culture heroes in these
works, like Malcolm X, John Coltrane, and Gwendolyn Brooks, and African
leaders like Kwame Nkrumah and Amilcar Cabral, Madhubuti's own voice
becomes increasingly directive and prescriptive. His remarkable ability to
use rhythms and onomatopoeic effects, as in "Don't Cry, Scream," his tribute
to John Coltrane, and his typographical sensitivity, like that of Sonia Sanchez,
enliven his earlier work. In the Coltrane poem, the poet's voice is employed
as a musical instrument, eulogizing the tenor saxophonist's art in terms
of a modulated scream of rage, grief, and pride.

> we ain't blue, we are black.
> We ain't blue, we are black.

he insists, identifying with "soultrane," the "man-maker," and asks, finally,

> can you scream—brother?   very
> can you scream—brother?   soft
> i hear you.
> i hear you.

> and the Gods will too.

Madhubuti's poetry also features usage of Black English, Brooks-type word coinage and compounding like "worldman" and "show-upper" in "Knocking Donkey Fleas off a Poet from the Southside of Chi," a poem dedicated to the poet Ted Joans who now makes his home in Timbuctu.

A recent work, *Book of Life*, expresses aphoristically the poet's role of teacher/prophet. In "Spirit Flight into the Coming," dedicated to Amilcar Cabral, the revolutionary leader of Guinea and Angola; Amiri Baraka, and the Congress of Afrikan People, he defines contemporary black slavery as powerlessness reinforced by adoption of white competitive values. Madhubuti calls for development of identity, purpose, direction, cooperation, and asks for guidance from the Congress of Afrikan People and from Baraka. He excoriates blacks who move away from separatism and pan-Afrikanism, who view the issues as human and economic class confrontation. The title poem, "Book of Life," is of especial interest for its structure as ninety-two didactic stanzas of varying length, quiet in tone, yet in the assured mode of revealed wisdom. The poet extols belief in oneself as a step toward belief in one's people. Significance of names is discussed in stanza 91 and may be applied to Madhubuti himself:

> your name
> tells us who you are,
> where you come from,
> where you are going,
> how you may get there
> and who is going with you.
> your name
> is legitimization of the past
> confirmation of the present
> and direction for the future.

He speaks from African and Afro-American cultural roots, family- and nation-oriented, in quest of the "self-definition" which he cites as "the first step toward/ self control."

The didactic/prophetic mode of Madhubuti's *Book of Life* is carried to a rhetorical apotheosis in Baraka's *Hard Facts* (1973-75). Some of the pieces, in fact, are undisguised speeches, like "A New Reality Is Better Than A New Movie!" which begins:

How will it go, crumbling earthquake, towering inferno, juggernaut, volcano, smashup, in reality, other than the feverish nearreal fantasy of the capitalist flunky film hacks tho they sense its reality breathing a quake inferno scar on their throat even snorts of 100% pure cocaine can't cancel the cold cut of impending death to this society.

The piece ends with incantatory references to the coming revolution and the dictatorship of the proletariat. Other poems carry titles like "Stop Killer Cops," "Horatio Alger Uses Scag," "Watergate." In "It Can Be Understood" he writes:

> Evolution is what turns the cycle
>
> Revolution is what
> completes
> it.

The anguished rage of his "When We'll Worship Jesus" insists on an activist philosophy:

> We'll worship Jesus
> When jesus do
> Somethin...
>
> we worship revolution

"Literary Statement On Struggle!" presents his poetic creed:

> A poem is
> the naked advice
> of the heart—...
> shd try to make people progress
> our life here go forward

Baraka's work reflects significant transitions, not only in his own thinking, as with the earlier, self-absorbed and amorphous fury of *Preface to a Twenty Volume Suicide Note* (1960) and *The Dead Lecturer* (1964), but also in the social channeling of that rage toward group cohesion and action. Having turned away form both religion and capitalism, he adheres to a Maoist communism which combines revolutionary goals with individual self-discipline. The most influential male poet among blacks, he has dedicated himself to political causes in Newark, most assiduously after the riots of 1968.

Baraka's earlier poetry, carefully crafted and disciplined, shows connections with the Beats and the Projectivists, both in personal association and, to some extent, tone and style.[19] It manifests the incursions of Western and popular culture; radio, music, and the movies, for example, are referents in his work. The presences of T. S. Eliot and Ezra Pound haunt the imagery, along with the "hard, dry images" demanded by T. E. Hulme, and the acedia of Eliot's earlier mood. The "Crow Jane" poems of *The Dead Lecturer*, inspired by the "Crow Jane" of Mississippi Joe Williams, recall W. B. Yeats's wryly philosophical series on "Crazy Jane."[20] Baraka's novel, *The System of Dante's Hell* (1965), which utilizes the *Divina Commedia* as a structural and symbolic referent, suggests the connections between prose and poetry made in a later book, *Hard Facts*. What may be viewed as a middle work, *Black Magic* (1969), comprises three books, *Sabotage*, *Target Study*, and *Black Art*. In form and content they demonstrate the progression from LeRoi Jones to Amiri Baraka, the movement toward rhetoric and a more relaxed, prosaic line that expresses increased political militancy.

Baraka's politics have acquired a new, practical dimension with the Advanced Workers, a jazz/rock group, which takes it s name from Leninist theory and for whom he writes political lyrics with titles such as "Better Red," "3rd World Blues," "America," "New Days," "Party of A New Type," and "You Was Dancing, You Shd've Been Marching." The insistent refrain of one song is "Revolution is the leading trend in the world today." The simple lyrics are repeated to the heavy beat of amplified sound which, when diminished, serves as background for the reading of Baraka's poems. In conversation with me recently, the poet distinguished his earlier work with jazz in the sixties as ad hoc and issue-oriented, while the current productions express a comprehensive ideological position. Of the poets mentioned above, Baraka embraces most flexibly the media of popular culture to further his political beliefs.

In conclusion, we observe that the new heroic genre of contemporary Black poetry combines interpretive, pedagogic, exemplary, parental, and prescriptive roles into the poets' assumption of leadership. Their art organically functions as total commitment to racial and communal welfare. Their perspective, based on moral, religious, and political structures, has validity not only for blacks but for whites, as well. It re-positions the artist within a social context and extends poetic breath to the breadth of humanity. Such an art, responsible and responsive, merits particular attention in times of social disintegration like our own.

Notes

Editor's Note
Bracketed interpolations update the text presented in April 1977. For other work by the author on many of these poets, see *Heroism in the New Black Poetry: Introductions and Interviews* (1990) and *Gwendolyn Brooks: Poetry and the Heroic Voice* (1987), both from the University Press of Kentucky. Grateful acknowledgment

for quoted material is made to Amiri Baraka, Gwendolyn Brooks, Jayne Cortez, Etheridge Knight, Audre Lorde, Haki R. Madhubuti, Dudley Randall, Sonia Sanchez, and to their publishers.

[1]See Lerone Bennett, Jr., *The Challenge of Blackness* (Chicago: Johnson, 1972), Introduction.

[2]Woodie King, in his Introduction to the anthology *Black Spirits* (New York: Random House/Vintage, 1972), generally places the new work into the last of Frantz Fanon's three categories for the literature of colonized peoples: assimilationist, precombat, and the fighting phase where the writers become awakeners of the people and produce, thereby, a revolutionary, national literature (p. xxvii).

[3]Robert Hayden, from *A Ballad of Remembrance*, rpt. in *Angle of Ascent* (New York: Liveright, 1975), pp. 128, 125.

[4]While the limits of this paper extend to Black poetry alone, and it seems the salient grouping in development of the genre, the category is not exclusive. It may include other ethnic distinctions and individuals of any racial origin or environment.

[5]Gwendolyn Brooks's cited works appear in the omnibus volume, *The World of Gwendolyn Brooks* (New York: Harper & Row, 1971), and in the following: *Riot* (1969); *Family Pictures* (1970); *Aloneness* (1971); *Beckonings* (1975); all published with Broadside Press, Detroit. [See also the omnibus *Blacks* (Chicago: The David Company, 1987].

[6]George E. Kent, "The Poetry of Gwendolyn Brooks," Part I, *Black World*, September 1971, rpt. in *Blackness and the Adventure of Western Culture* (Chicago: Third World Press, 1972), p. 104.

[7]Barbara Kiefer Lewalski, *Milton's Brief Epic: The Genre, Meaning and Art of Paradise Regained* (Providence, R.I.: Brown Univ. Press, 1966).

[8]Stephen Henderson, *Understanding the New Black Poetry: Black Speech and Black Music as Poetic Referents* (New York: William Morrow, 1973). See especially "Structure," pp. 28-61.

[9]Sonia Sanchez's works cited appear in the following: *Home Coming* (1969); *We A BaddDDD People* (1970); *It's A New Day* (1971); *A Blues Book for Blue Black Magical Women* (1974); all published by Broadside Press.

[10]I have used the term "Black English" generically throughout to embrace both the designation by J. L. Dillard in *Black English* (New York: Random House/Vintage, 1973) and by William Labov, who prefers the term "black English vernacular" in *Language in the Inner City: Studies in the Black English Vernacular* (Philadelphia: Univ. of Pennsylvania Press, 1972).

[11]Clarence Major, *Dictionary of Afro-American Slang* (New York: International Publishers, 1970), s.v. "bad." Further citations in the text.

[12]See the important discussion of the chanted sermon as an art form in Bruce A. Rosenberg, *The Art of the American Folk Preacher* (New York: Oxford Univ. Press, 1970).

[13]Audre Lorde's works cited appear in the following: *From A Land Where Other People Live* (1973); *New York Head Shop and Museum* (1974); both published by Broadside Press, Detroit; *Coal* (New York: Norton, 1976); *Between Our Selves* (Point Reyes, Calif.: Eidolon Editions, 1976).

[14]Jayne Cortez's work cited appears in *Pissstained Stairs and The Monkey Man's Wares* (New York: Phrase Text, 1969); *Festivals and Funerals* (published by the author in New York, 1973); and *Scarifications* (New York: Bola Press, 1973).

[15]Dudley Randall's work cited appears in *Cities Burning* (1969); *More to Remember* (1971); *After the Killing* (1973); all published by Broadside Press, Detroit.

[16]Etheridge Knight's work cited appears in *Poems from Prison* (1968) and *Belly Song* (1973), both published by Broadside Press, Detroit.

[17]Haki R. Madhubuti's (don l. lee's) work cited appears in *Think Black* (1965-67), *Black Pride* (1967-68), *Don't Cry, Scream* (1968-69), *We Walk the Way of the New World* (1969-70), rpt. in *Directionscore: Selected and New Poems* (Detroit: Broadside, 1971); *Book of Life* (Detroit: Broadside, 1973).

[18]Amiri Baraka's (LeRoi Jones's) work cited appears in *Preface to a Twenty Volume Suicide Note* (New York: Totem/Corinth, 1961); *Sabotage* (1961-63), *Target Study* (1964-65), *Black Art* (1966-67), rpt. in *Black Magic: Collected Poetry, 1961-67* (Indianapolis: Bobbs-Merrill, 1969); *The Dead Lecturer* (1964), *The System of Dante's Hell* (1965), rpt. in *Three Books by Imamu Amiri Baraka (LeRoi Jones)*, (New York: Grove Press, 1975); *Hard Facts* (1973-75), (Newark, N.J.: Revolutionary Communist League, 1975).

[19]See the clarifying distinction between the two made by Donald Phelps in his essay "Depressed Art 2: Tone," *For Now*, No. 8, pp. 84-96, n.d.

[20]The comparison is also made by Karl Malkoff in *Crowell's Handbook of Contemporary American Poetry* (New York: Crowell, 1973), p. 54.

Positive Negatives and Negative Positives: Confronting Black Stereotypes Through Visual Artistic Expressions

Floyd Coleman

Since the aggressive Black liberation movement of the 1960s, scholars of various ideological persuasions have attempted to examine manifestations of Black culture more closely. Yet, an aspect of the Afro-American cultural experience that has not been explored to the extent of literature and song is the visual arts—the images of Blacks that are presented to us on the pages of popular magazines, in books, and on cereal boxes and more recently in the paintings and prints of Black American artists.[1] Perhaps the dearth of scholarly explorations of plastic and graphic expressions dealing with Black life can be attributed, at least in part, to a general lack of understanding of the messages conveyed by visual imagery, and a reluctance to accept the full implications of any visual arts statement as an expression of a particular cultural perspective.[2]

Moreover, we might add that formalist art criticism has had a profound influence on the art of the 20th century. Formalist criticism, simplistically stated, places little emphasis on the context from which the work arises, but upon the uniqueness of the aesthetic object;[3] hence, supporting the notion of a work of art as a singular expression, not a culmination of many aesthetic and extra-aesthetic concerns. And, too, the Western regard for individualism—individual genius—has helped to further inhibit the recognition of the fact that a work of art is more than the expression of a single artist. Andre Malraux,[4] among others, has expressed the view that the creative work of an individual artist is not due to his efforts alone, but is built upon the work of other artists, those who have shaped his vision.

In this paper we will be guided by the assumption that works of art, whether popular or elite, are hypotheses about the nature of the society from which they spring. It should be added that in interpreting a work of art it may be quite obvious that the artist has dealt with more than one hypothesis, yet there is one—the controlling idea—that has influenced the artist's hand throughout the creative enterprise and is, indeed, the most salient.

Specifically, the aims of this paper are twofold: 1) to show that the Euro-American ideology of race and white supremacy is almost universally reflected in the portrayal of Blacks, from the obviously stereotypic images of Uncle Tom and Aunt Jemima to seemingly positive images of Black superheroes; and 2) to show that the Black Art Movement of the 1960s was an outgrowth of earlier effort on the part of artists of African ancestry to confront racist and white supremacist views by re-employing racist stereotypes in their work in order to promulgate the idea of Black unity and liberation.

Ever since their initial contact with peoples of African ancestry on a large scale, Westerners have shown their preoccupation with Blacks in very deliberate ways. In the 1830s, minstrel entertainment was one such way. That genre of entertainment which involved blackening of the face developed at a time when the idea of racial inferiority of Blacks had long been "proven" by supposedly irrefutable scientific evidence.[5] It seems curious, though, that negative stereotypes were being so universally espoused long after slavery had become a way of life, after millions had been brought from Africa to the Americas, after African civilizations had been systematically destroyed through slaving and by outright conquest. Some interpreters of Black history and culture suggest that the stereotypes were developed to justify the then current atrocities and beliefs of white supremacy. Whereas it was more perhaps an attempt to wash away the guilt of the past, for from the middle of the late Nineteenth Century, white military power had eclipsed most of the indigenous development on the part of Black people in Africa or elsewhere.[6]

White entertainers blackening their faces were acting out what white people felt about Blacks, as if their scripts were drawn directly from the pages of Carl von Linneas' *Systema Naturae* (1735), where he describes *Homo Afer* as black, cunning, lazy, lustful, careless, and governed by caprice.[7] White entertainers made the minstrel show one of the most popular forms of entertainment in the United States, and as one author suggests, "a national institution."[8] During this time racist and white supremacist ideas, having been "verified" earlier by science, were given sanction and popularized by art.

Just as the "godfather" films have influenced recent thinking about Italians and Italian-Americans, the minstrels shaped the views that whites had about Blacks in the Nineteenth Century. Those not so complimentary images and ideas about Blacks have persisted until the present day in American literature and theatre. In the area of film, D. W. Griffith's motion pictures of the 1920s developed the stereotypes that were to remain in that genre throughout the decades. The scared darkie—Mantan Moreland, Birmingham Brown, and Stepin Fetchit—was drawn from this early mold.[9] Griffith's white actor in black face became the universal image of Blacks in the cinema. To be sure, the literary images had their impact too. Perhaps the role played by Hattie McDaniels in *Gone With the Wind* would not have possessed the degree of character definition if it had not been for the Black literary images of Mark Twain, William Faulkner, and the articulation and development of Black images by Black intellectuals and writers such as W.E.B. DuBois.

One might question my reference to literature and film since this paper is concerned primarily with the plastic and graphic arts. Obviously, however, the reason is that all involve visual thinking.[10] To be sure, Twain had to have a clear visual image of Nigger Jim to make him come alive in *Huckleberry Finn*, the same could be said of many of the characters in Faulkner's novels. With the latter, Black images were as clearly defined as Faulkner wished them to be—in one instance, a rude outline, another, a fully developed portrait.[11] Thus, when the various modes of expression, such as painting, film, and theatre are examined, they all exhibit many of the concerns for form and follow many of the same artistic conventions. In no form do these modes merge so much as in the so-called "comic strip."

That the early ideas about Blacks have persisted with only superficial changes until recent times, becomes quite evident when we examine a few comic strip characters.

The Captain America comic strip presents a typical positive negative character in the Falcon. The Captain America strip reached its greatest popularity in the late 1960s and early 1970s, it featured a very potent duo, Captain America and his loyal companion, the Falcon. In more than one frame, the Falcon, a strong Black figure, along with his avian companion, is shown socking it to white men. Alas, a Black superhero! But a white artist depicting a Black man beating up white folks? There must be a catch. And there often is. Frequently the costumes of the white men provide a clue. If they are wearing capes and monocles and carrying whips—symbols that are not associated with the white ideal of fair play—they are evil white men. Then, of course, it is all right for a good black character to beat up scoundrels, even if they are white.

But the true heroic status of the Falcon can be determined by studying the figurative relationships that exist between the principal figures as the story unfolds in the frames of the comic strip. While the image of the Falcon is frequently larger than those of the bad characters, it is not uncommon for the entire body of the Falcon to not approach the size of even the head of Captain America. One compelling image shows a close-up of the head of the white superhero, staring straight forward, engaging the viewer, and seemingly visualizing the action that is taking place in the foreground. The Falcon, Sam Wilson of Harlem, could only become a superhero after being taught by the superhero of superheroes, Captain America. This point is confirmed when elsewhere in this issue of Marvel Comics the Falcon says:

You...the one who's been helping me...training me...who *made me* the Falcon...YOU ARE CAPTAIN AMERICA![12]

This statement is quite revealing, indeed. It reflects the idea that whatever the Black man has produced or thought has been due to his sustained contact with whites. It was, and still is, believed that Blacks are incapable of producing by themselves anything of value. So, despite his apparent strength and intellect, his superhuman gifts, the Falcon is, in fact, nothing more than a rude pastiche of Captain America, symbol par excellence of white supremacy.

When we continue to examine the frames of this serial we see what Black soldiers, from World War I to Vietnam, have come to know. In the face of the enemy the Black man and the white man are partners; they are brothers who share the same values, the same concern for "freedom." Similarly, the differences that separate the Falcon from Captain America are overshadowed by the immediate threat of the evil characters. And predictably they join forces to destroy them.

It is in this light that the Falcon does not escape the role we have seen for decades: Harriet Beecher Stowe's Uncle Tom, Daniel Defoe's Friday, and in the comics, Tonto of the Lone Ranger, and, of course, the Spirit's Lil'Ebony. Faithful companions of superheroes, they are incapable of thinking or acting for themselves. The idea that "the Negro" is but a child among the races of men is given a modern day continuation in supporting roles that range from the inglorious to the glamorous.

Lt. Flap of the Beatle Bailey comic strip, like the Falcon, creates at first the illusion of Black status and increased progress in white America. It takes no unusual insight to see that Lt. Flap is entirely predictable. You know what he is going to say before the last frame is read; the character is a placebo. His creation is an attempt to satisfy the Black community's demand for more "positive" Black images. Robert Chrisman writes about the movie and television industries' response to similar demands:

The result from the movie studios and television networks was a character that satisfied the most basic appetites and lusts of blacks for power and beauty and success, but which at the same time sustained the white American value systems and absorbed blacks into them.[13]

Within our discussion, the Falcon and Lt. Flap are positive negative images. That is, their positive characteristics cannot withstand close analysis. Undoubtedly, they were created for commercial reasons rather than from any outgrowth of a substantive change in the way white Americans deal with the question of race.

In an area where there is the appearance of equality and respect for Black talent—collegiate and professional sports—we find the same thing: racism and white supremacy. This is apparent when we observe the Black quarterback situation in professional football. On this issue, Chrisman, writing in 1976, is again quite insightful: "to concede Harris (James Harris formerly of the Los Angeles Rams) the right to quarterback would be to relinquish a basic tenet of white supremacy: that talented blacks need white leadership to get the job done."[14] One would think that the belief that the quarterback position on a professional team in the National Football League was the last bastion of white male supremacy had died a slow, but sure, death by 1988. It has not. When Doug Williams replaced Jay Schroeder as the starting quarterback for the Play-Off bound Washington Redskins, it nearly eclipsed the Reagan-Gorbachev summit that was taking place during this same time in the nation's capitol. In the Super-Bowl showdown against the Denver Bronchos, Williams "out-guned" the highly touted quarterback John Elway and won the contest. It would be surprising if next year Williams and all of the other Black quarterbacks were not labeled "chokers"..."they just can't win the big ones."

Above we have looked briefly at a few images of Blacks that were created by white artists. Now we want to see how Blacks have viewed themselves.

From the time of Scipio Morehead of the late 18th Century to the evolution of the Black professional artist as exemplified by Edmonia Lewis (1845-1890), Edward Bannister (1828-1901), Robert Duncanson (1821-1872) and others, artists of African ancestry have created images of their fellows that were in every respect positive.[15] It must be acknowledged, however, that the forementioned artists did not paint or sculpt a superabundance of images of Blacks. They were struggling with some of the same problems that contemporary Black artists are currently facing, that is, a lack of a substantial audience. The people who buy art—the educated Black middle class—was, and still is, relatively small.

Of the early Black professional artists, one of the most prolific and widely acclaimed was Henry Ossawa Tanner. While Tanner did not paint images of Blacks for any great length of time in his career, nevertheless, he did produce images that were more than simple caricatures. His *Banjo Lesson* and *Grateful Poor* are two strong 19th Century images that fly in the face of the stereotypes that seemed to always issue forth from the hands of white artists.

While Edmonia Lewis' *Forever Free* and Tanner's *Banjo Lesson* were outstanding works that portrayed Blacks positively, it took artists of a much later period to create visual statements that reflected a self-conscious racial self-portraiture. *Forever Free* by Sargent Johnson symbolizes the growing self assertion of the Black community of the 1920s and 1930s. This sculpture expresses in visual terms what Langston Hughes said in his essay, "The Negro Artist and the Racial Mountain" (1926), that Blacks are not ashamed of their color and that they are beautiful and proud.[16] Certainly the Harlem Renaissance of the 1920s anticipated the Black Art Movement of the 1960s, in that many of the artists of this earlier period directed their art toward the Black community. Theirs was not an art of appeasement, but often one of confrontation as well as one of celebration-*joie de vivre*.

The much celebrated artists Jacob Lawrence and Romare Bearden were not old enough to be a part of the Harlem Renaissance proper, but they were its heirs. Lawrence's *Migration, Harriet Tubman, Frederick Douglas, and John Brown Series* were serialized works that dealt with the Black experience in the United States from a historical perspective. Even in later works, such as *Tombstones*, he continued to paint that which he knew best, the Harlem scene—the Black community. Likewise, Bearden drew very heavily upon his knowledge of Black music for ideas for paintings such as *The Prevelance of Ritual: Tidings* (1964) and *Three Folk Musicians* (1967).

In these and in later works, Bearden comes about as close as any artist ever has to making visual statements that approach the Blues-Jazz idiom.[17]

Still the paintings of Lawrence and Bearden were not strident, not emphatically accusing. It took artists of the 1960's to interject a stronger measure of confrontation and a decidedly political element in the visual and plastic expressions of Blacks. Artists such as Reginald Gammon and David Bradford, among others, dealt with heroic figures such as Malcolm, Stokley, Rap, and Martin. For the first time in the history of Afro-American art we see heroic figures—proud Black figures—portrayed with a degree of assuredness theretofore unseen.

Black artists not only confronted the numerous racist and white supremacist ideologies, but in their attack on the former, they confronted themselves. The problems of drugs within the Black community has been most serious. A number of artists, such as Dana Chandler, dealt with this theme; they directed their work to the Black youth. The message was essentially this: revolutionary activity is not synonymous with a syringe and pills, and that drugs destroy!

The Black artist of the 1960s was politically aggressive; he did not let the stereotypic images, such as Uncle Tom, Aunt Jemima, and others, go unchallenged. Paintings of Uncle Tom, like this one, entitled *New Money*, reflects the Black artist's concern for humor as well as the absurd. The three dollar bill with an image of Uncle Tom is a reflection of this artist's view of America: bankrupt—a forecast of an end to America's imperial rule. Humor is expressed here as somewhat concealed malice.

While more than one artist painted images of Uncle Tom, one of the most frequently encountered negative positives from the hands of Black artists is that of Aunt Jemima. Bettye Saar, Jon Lockard, and others, made highly effective statements on the transformation of Aunt Jemima. Works by such artists which deal with the Aunt Jemima theme are perhaps visual symbols of the idea that was frequently uttered during the height of the Black movement in the 1960s, that is, in every "Negro" there is a Black man, a potentially positive force for Black liberation.

One of the earliest treatments of the Aunt Jemima theme is this work done by Murry DePillars, entitled *For Ron Smith and John Carlos*. Before this time, Aunt Jemima smiled contentedly from the sides of pancake and syrup containers, just like Uncle Ben, Elsie the Cow, and the nameless but loveable pooch that is always used to sell dog food. However, in this work by DePillars, Aunt Jemima is assuming a role that is completely different from her historic one. This Aunt Jemima, with its full-length figure and stern facial expression, indicates the emergence of an image of heroic proportions. Here Aunt Jemima joins Sojourner Truth and Harriet Tubman in the struggle for Black liberation.

In retrospect, the work of Black artists of the 1960's reflected the mood of the Black community. It was an art of confrontation. the ideological posture was not veiled in the artifice of formalist expression. That it sprang from the Black folk, not just from the intelligentsia, is reason for its aesthetic toughness, an achievement not frequently seen in the works of earlier artists. And it is clear that the Black artist could not make such statements until they were thought and expressed in the actions of a significant portion of the Black community. Hence, there is nothing strange about the character of Black American art, for it, like that from any other distinct cultural milieu, reflects the values and world view of its cultural constituents.

In the 1970s and 1980s it is not too uncommon to hear from the mouths of Blacks and whites alike that the Black liberation struggle has been defeated. But the Black community's apparent withdrawal from direct action and confrontation of street marches is like the narrator in Ralph Ellison's *Invisible Man*. It is mere postponement, not defeat. It "is a covert preparation for a more overt action."[18] And we can be sure that the persistent images of the Uncle Toms and Aunt Jemimas will be confronted, appropriated and used by Black artists as the struggle for self-definition and Black liberation continues.

Notes

This is a revision of a paper that was presented at the Eight Annual National Convention of the Popular Culture Association, April 21, 1978. For their helpful suggestions in preparing the original paper and this revised version, I wish to thank Professors Harry Shaw, John Adkins Richardson, and William Colvin.

[1]Notable exceptions are Alain Leroy Locke, *The Negro in Art; A Pictorial Record of the Negro in Art* (New York: Hacker Art Books, 1968); Ellwood Parry, *The Image of the Indian and the Black Man in American Art, 1590-1900* (New York: G. Braziller, 1974). For an overall treatment of Black popular culture in the 1970s see the penetrating essay by Robert Chrisman, "Blacks, Racism, and Bourgeoise Culture," *Black Scholar* Vol. 7, No. 5 (Jan.-Feb., 1976), pp. 2-10.

[2]In highly literate cultures visual imagery is not frequently recognized for its documentary significance; in essence, there is a general distrust of visual data. See Rudolf Arnheim, *Visual Thinking* (Berkeley: University of California Press, 1972), pp. 2-6, for a discussion of sensory perception.

[3]For a discussion of formalist art criticism, see John Adkins Richardson, *Modern Art and Scientific Thought* (Urbana: University of Illinois Press, 1971), pp. 116-117.

[4]See Andre Malraux, *Psychology of Art: The Creative Act* (New York: Pantheon Books, 1949-50), p. 121.

[5]Carlos Moore, *Were Marx and Engels White Racists?* (Chicago: Institute of Positive Education, 1972), p. 11ff.

[6]Moore, pp. 11-12.

[7]John S. Haller, Jr., *Outcasts from Evolution: Scientific Attitudes of Racial Inferiority, 1859-1900* (Urbana: University of Illinois Press, 1971), p. 4.

[8]Robert C. Toll, *Blacking Up: The Minstrel Show in Nineteenth Century America* (New York: Oxford University Press, 1974), p. 8.

[9]For a most perceptive analysis of the visual portrayal of Blacks, see Darwin T. Turner, "Images of Blacks in Visual-Auditory Media," a paper presented at the

Eight National Popular Culture Association meeting, Cincinnati, Ohio, April 20-22, 1978.

[10]Arnheim, p. v.

[11]See Faulkner's treatment of Lucas in *Intruder in the Dust*. For a most insightful analysis of the portrayal of Blacks in Faulkner's novels, see Charles H. Nilon, *Faulkner and the Negro* (New York: The Citadel Press, 1965).

[12]*Captain America*, Marvel Comics, October, 1969, p. 11.

[13]Chrisman, p. 7.

[14]Chrisman, p. 8.

[15]James A. Porter, *Modern Negro Art* (New York: Arno Press, 1968).

[16]Langston Hughes, "Negro Artist and the Racial Mountain," *Nation*, CXXII (June 23, 1926), pp. 692-694.

[17]See Ralph Ellison, "Romare Bearden: Paintings and Projections," *The Crisis* (March, 1970), pp. 81-88, for reference to "poetry of the blues" in a discussion of Bearden's works.

[18]Ralph Ellison, *Invisible Man* (New York: The New American Library, 1964), p. 16.

Self Definition and Redefinition in
Paule Marshall's *Praisesong for the Widow*

Joyce Pettis

Is the Black female character created in recent fiction by Black women writers defining herself differently or is she only her "old self" in new times? If Paule Marshall's protagonist Avatara Johnson in *Praisesong for the Widow* is any indication, the former is correct. Distinctive changes are evident in women characters in recent fiction by Black women writers. Women characters in the fiction of the 1920s, for example, seem linear in contrast to the roundness, complexity, and diversity of women in fiction since the 1970s.

In fiction preceding the 70s, with few exceptions, women defined themselves in relationship to perceptions of middle-class standards or in reference to biological roles. Both Jessie Fauset and Nella Larsen, significant novelists of the 1920s, depicted class conscious female protagonists reactive to the allure and sterility of materialism and White middle-class ideals of beauty. The women of Fauset's *The Chinaberry Tree*, for example, emphasize beauty (fair skin, straight black hair), style, poise, and marriage to a socially acceptable man. For Laurentine Strange, Fauset's protagonist, self definition is inextricably bound to class consciousness, economic position, and sex role.

Similarly, in Nella Larsen's *Quicksand*, attention focuses on Helga Crane's appearance—"skin like yellow satin...curly blue-black hair" (159). Helga's ancestry, however (White immigrant mother and Black gambler father who abandons the mother), limits the social acceptability that would be assured through her physical looks and contributes to her ongoing crisis of identity. Hence, Helga's vacillation between the different cultures of her parents and problems with identity account for the complexity of her character in comparison to Laurentine. Nonetheless, through physical appearance, education, taste, and sophistication, her orientation is middle-class. In Ann Petry's *The Street* (1945), and Dorothy West's *The Living is Easy* (1948), Lutie Johnson and Cleo Judson are propelled by materialism and the demands of motherhood. Although Cleo's husband is an anomaly, a successful Black businessman in the early 1900s, she contributes to his financial ruin through imitation of the upper middle-classes in Boston.

Redefining the self as theme is rarely, if ever, the focus of Black women in fiction before 1970. More recently, however, redefinition of self, rejection of middle-class values, and self autonomy have become characteristic of Black of narrowly conceived ideas and images. Guided in reformation of self by their unique culture, by a community of nurturing women, by feminine intuitiveness, myth, or by combinations of these, they are satisfyingly individualistic when redefinition is completed. Highly visible among such redefined women are Toni Morrison's Pilate in *Song of Solomon* (1977) and Alice Walker's Shug Avery and Celie in *The Color Purple* (1982).

Avatara Johnson (Avey), protagonist in Paule Marshall's *Praisesong for the Widow* (1982), illustrates the difference between depictions of earlier women such as Laurentine Strange and Helga Crane and contemporary portrayals of Black women, although she embodies characteristics from both periods. Significantly, the emphasis on physical beauty is not replicated by Avey's physical description, for she is tall and dark with an underlip marked by a "spillover of raw pink across the top...." During the middle years of her life, however, Avey endorses the values and practices of a materialistic society, but confrontation with her distorted values compels her both to reexamine and to redefine herself. Moreover, she questions the process responsible for her present status. Marshall's protagonist is one of the earliest to make such a positive journey backward to her cultural mooring. Initially, middle-class economic status is not her goal either, for both Avey and husband Jerome are working class and live in a fifth-floor walkup apartment on Halsey street.

Halsey Street is a metaphor for hundreds of similar streets in hundreds of cities, where economic deprivation dominates, where underfed, ill clothed children, and hopeless and defeated men and women eke out an existence. It is synonymous with 116th Street in Ann Petry's *The Street*, Brewster Place in Gloria Naylor's *The Women of Brewster Place*, or Fulton street in Marshall's *Brown Girl, Brownstones*. The disease of Halsey Street stalks and infects Avey and Jerome during her successive pregnancies, when income is reduced to Jerome's paycheck. In his battle against the ruin and defeat endemic to Halsey Street, Jay symbolizes the efforts of innumerable Black men threatened with defeat by a racist society. Although Jay is not defeated, he and Avey are transformed during the twenty years before they acquire resources to leave Halsey Street. Avey's transformation situates her with Helga Crane and Laurentine Strange—regal, cultured, and sophisticated, solidly middle class oriented—although she is less comfortable with it all than her husband.

Escaping the economic poverty embodied by Halsey Street and embracing the middle-class status symbolized by the future house in North White Plains produces an unanticipated problem that Avey has to recognize prior to her redefinition. What Jerome and Avey have lost on their climb to social position and economic prosperity is an essential consideration in the novel. When they were poor, they were anchored by Black cultural traditions, but as they shed poverty, inadvertently they shed certain levels of their cultural identity until Avey imagines another face superimposed over Jay's familiar features and sometimes fails to recognize herself in the mirror or recall her name. Thus the house in North White Plains, the symbol of financial stability, is also a symbol of cultural vacuity. Realization of the cultural loss is too late for Jerome who has died, but Avey's recognition and redefinition reclaim her.

Journeys crisscross this text, anchor it, and underscore Avey's metaphorical and literal travel. Other elements of the novel—dreams, symbolism, and myth—are intertwined with real, psychic, and metaphorical journeys, establishing the motifs of circularity, progress, and completion. The ocean cruise with which the text begins is an empty trip, merely indicative of middle-class leisure and money. Ironically, this trip precipitates the crucial journey to Carriacou, a small Caribbean island, where Avey's ritual redefinition occurs. Her metaphorical journey to redefinition begins onboard the ocean liner with a vivid dream of her deceased Southern relative, Aunt Cuney, one of the "old people" revered and respected in the Black community. Thus it is unimaginable, even in the depths of dream, that Avey would physically resist the old woman by striking her arm.

The disturbing dream onboard the oceanliner acts as catalyst for Avey's recalling a childhood journey. Aunt Cuney, who summarily demanded Avey's relocation from Harlem for vacation on Tatem Island on the South Carolina Tideland, begs her to return. During these vacations Avey and Aunt Cuney walked twice weekly to Ibo Landing, where the Aunt narrated an account of another journey, of Ibos brought enslaved to the island and their rejection of the place. Aunt Cuney's "gran" had passed the story on to her.

And the minute those Ibos was brought on shore they just stopped, my 'gran' said...And they seen things that day you and me don't have the power to see. 'Cause those pure-born Africans was peoples my 'gran' said could see in more ways than one...they turned, my 'gran' said, and looked at the white folks what brought 'em here. [Then] they turned...and walked on back down to the edge of the river here...They just kept walking right on out over the river here...my 'gran' declared she just picked herself up and took off after 'em. In her mind. Her body she always usta say might be in Tatem but her mind, her mind was long gone with the Ibos. (37-39)

The twice weekly journeys to Ibo Landing are rituals to which Avey is being introduced. Keith Sandiford has noted the careful preparation in which Aunt Cuney always engaged, wearing the same clothes and following the same routine in putting on the pieces, including two belts and high-topped brogans. Her goal was to initiate Avey "properly into the mystery of the past and into the truth of her own particular racial reality" (376).

In the manner of her Aunt, Avey *had* narrated this story to her friends and had taken Jay to the Landing for vacation in the early years of their marriage (He believed it.), but she has forgotten its meaning. She is as distanced now from the memory of those activities as the Caribbean Islands are from South Carolina. Moreover, she is distanced from those Black culturally anchoring activities shared with Jerome in the early years—listening to the jazz of Coleman Hawkins or Billy Holiday, reading the poetry of James Weldon Johnson, or dancing. The dream about Aunt Cuney poetry of James Weldon Johnson, or dancing. The dream about Aunt Cuney and Avey's resistance, coupled with indigestion and hallucination, compel her to leave the cruise and spend one night in a Grenadian hotel before flying home to New York.

The psychic journey that Avey takes sitting on the hotel balcony of her room transports her backward through the years of her marriage. Symbolically, she must travel backward before forward motion is possible; she understands whom she has become before redefinition can occur, although at this point, Avey has little understanding of where these strange events will lead. Using memory and dream, Marshall forces the protagonist's painful remembering of the years that have led to Avey's present self definition as a middle-class matron living the leisurely life. Dominating her reverie is Halsey Street and the poverty, pregnancies, jealousy, despair, and fear that had transformed her into a raving, unrecognizable drudge. Seeing that his family was not immune to the destructiveness of that street, Jay committed himself to defeat it the only way a Black man legally could—through education. Their schedules placed them both in such rigid routines that time for the small pleasures they had previously enjoyed was eliminated. After college (He enrolled at age 32.) when the companies downtown still refused to hire a Black accountant, Jay built his own firm, acquiring accounts from Black businesses.

The crucial part of Avey's balcony reverie is the unanswerable question: Wasn't it possible "to have wrested, as they had done over all those years, the means needed to rescue them from Halsey Street and to see the children through, while preserving, safeguarding, treasuring those things that had come down to them over the generations, which had defined them in a particular way. The most vivid, the most valuable part of themselves!" (139) This unanswered question is nonetheless important as well as indicative of their tremendous losses, which she now perceives. The aptly titled second book of the novel, "Sleeper's Wake," thus ends with Avey's new perceptions, her rage, at how pursuing economic stability has robbed them of their essential "selves." Recognition of their immense and irretrievable losses devastates and disorients her.

While the first half of the novel, then, has revealed Avey's awakening to their displaced identities, in the second half she experiences the rituals that will restore her. Being recalled to her roots through Aunt Cuney's intercession necessitates preparation similar to a rite of passage, "where formal and usually very severe, exercises of severance, whereby the mind is radically cut away from the attitudes, attachments, and life patterns of the stage being left behind" occurs (Campbell 10). Marshall thus repositions the mythic dimension that has functioned as a subtext in the novel, interweaving it with Avey's literal activity. In other words, forces beyond human explanation now direct the process of Avey's redefinition. The first stage in preparation for the symbolic spiritual rebirth is a return to innocence. The night of sleep in the Grenadian hotel following her painful remembering empties her mind of the past thirty years, leaving her "slow and clumsy as a two-year-old," with a mind "wiped clean, a *tabula rasa* upon which a whole new history could be written" (151). When she walks away from the hotel the next morning, she is physically only a remnant of her former well groomed, matronly identity, having haphazardly thrown on wrinkled clothing pulled from the suitcase.

Like a child who thoughtlessly ambers away from familiar surroundings until it is lost, Avey wanders aimlessly down the deserted beach until "she felt the caul over her mind lifting." This walk begins the series of short trips that will transport her through the ritualistic stages of confusion and revelation preparatory to redefinition and full spiritual rebirth. The motifs of journey, circularity, and completion are equally reinforced.

Distanced from the tourist hotels Avey enters the deserted rum shop of Lebert Joseph, a primary director in the continuance of Avey's literal and spiritual journeys. While Joseph's role is real, his mythic dimensions place him in a surreal sphere. His age and physical appearance appear to vacillate, for example. And like Aunt Cuney, he exhibits androgynous qualities. In the words of Barbara Christian, "[Aunt] Cuney strides the field like a warrior in her husband's brogans and Lebert dances the Juba in an imaginary skirt" (*Callaloo* 6:79). He is the ancestral counterpart to Aunt Cuney, who seems to have reached from the grave to grab Avey, pull her back, and reground her in African-American and African culture. Like Aunt Cuney he embodies wisdom, myth, and continuity with the vision of the Ibos—his penetrating look marking him "as someone who possessed ways of seeing that went beyond mere sight and ways of knowing that outstripped ordinary intelligence (*Li gain connaissance*) and thus had no need for words" (172). Continuing Aunt Cuney's role, Joseph stresses *knowing the place and people of one's origins* and the necessity of reverence for the "Old Parents." Initially mistaking Avey for an islander, he discovers that, unlike him, she does not know her origins or "nation," can not recognize the remnants of names—Arada, Cromanti, or Yarraba—or the old time dances, except Juba, remembered from her vacation summers in the South with Aunt Cuney. Heritage and ritual, vital components of memory, are given literal expression through Joseph's participation in the annual Carriacou Excursion.

Avey's uncharacteristic decision to accompany Joseph on the Excursion continues the journey motif as well as places her in the revelatory stage of the progressions that lead to redefinition. Avey's definition of self through economic status has erected physical as well as emotional barriers between her and other social classes, the tenants of Halsey Street of thirty years ago, for example, as well as the present Islanders assembled at the wharf in Grenada. During revelation, however, she recalls occasions when she felt connected to other people. When her family took its annual boat ride up the Hudson River to Bear Mountain along with hundreds of other passengers, "slender threads stream[ed] out from her navel and from the place where her heart was to enter those around her" (190). The disjuncture Avey has experienced during her middle-class status, therefore, is alien to her natural predisposition.

Aboard the schooner enroute to Carriacou, Avey is lulled into the sphere of memory by the rocking of the vessel, and recalls a Sunday from childhood and an Easter Sunday sermon. The subjects—the power of God's love, salvation, deliverance, and the Resurrection—parallel the process in which Avey is unknowingly engaged. Reliving the preacher's vocal rocking of the church and her childish futility at controlling the corresponding rocking of an overfilled stomach, she regurgitated then as she does now on the schooner, steadied over the rails by two elderly women who recall church mothers from her childhood in their ministering to her. When nothing more remains on her stomach, nevertheless, the contractions continue, pushing down to her lower intestines and forcing expulsion there. The old women lead her into the darkened deckhouse where she lies down. Alone there, Avey feels the presence of other bodies crowded with her. "A multitude it felt like lay packed around her in the filth and stench of themselves, just as she was. . . Their suffering—the depth of it, the weight of it in the cramped space—made hers of no consequence" (209). Significantly, many of the journeys involving Avey—the Ibos's walk, the Hudson River Voyage, the trip to Carriacou—entail passage across bodies of water. These passages reflect African-American history and serve to reinforce Avey's separation from its meaning. Mythic memory controls her sensation in the deckhouse, however.

Through the process of redefinition, Avey has been returning to the forgotten realization of her shared origins: different tribes, sexes, and ages bound in commonality in the belly of a slaveship. Hence this experience reestablishes her severed union to her African ancestors and reestablishes her inseparableness from the inarticulate pain of that act. The regurgitation and defacation of the bloated mass clogging her stomach symbolize ridding the internal body of the remaining dregs of middle-class excess.

The cleansing continues on Carriacou in the house of Lebert Joseph's daughter, except that now, it is the washing and massaging of Avey's external body by Joseph's daughter. The ritualistic washing and massaging, performed in spite of Avey's gentle objections, restore and regenerate moribund flesh. These are essential stages for a woman who has retreated from confraternity with other human beings to "helpless aversion to being touched." Moreover, the external washing and massaging, the last rites in the preparation of Avey's physical body, are performed with the solemnity that the occasion requires, with Joseph's daughter performing the steps. That the restoration and regeneration are executed through a woman's hand significantly engenders the relationship between women as nurturers and healers and confirms Avey's suspicion that Lebert Joseph's daughter has inherited his supernatural ability to know and to see without being told.

The ritualistic restoration of Avey's physical body is consistent with the rituals practiced to honor and remember the Old Parents, the justification for the Carriacou Excursion. As Lebert Joseph's questions about Avey's "people" and the old dances indicate, the Islanders have retained African cultural connectedness. Establishing and maintaining contact between the living and the departed are common to every African society, according to

Mbiti. Certain rituals indicate that the dead have not been forgotten and act to appease them if offense has been given (267).

The second night after her arrival in Carriacou, Avey climbs a hill with Lebert Joseph. It is the climatic last journey in the stages of redefinition where she witnesses ritual and ceremony through song and movement that is non-dance, performed in remembrance of the old people and of their origins.

It was the essence of something rather than the thing itself she was witnessing. Those present—the old ones—understood this. All that was left were a few names of what they called nations which they could no longer pronounce properly, the fragments of a dozen or so songs, the shadowy forms of long-ago dances and rum kegs for drums. The bare bones. The burnt-out ends. And they clung to them with a tenacity she suddenly loved in them and longed for in herself. (240)

Avey moves from observer to participant as the circle of dancers widens and she is taken into it by "what [seems] an arm made up of many arms [reaching] out from the circle to draw her in." Gradually, unconsciously, she performs the flat-footed glide and stamp as if it were native to her and feels again the threads of sisterhood and brotherhood between herself and the dancers. Moreover, she recalls childhood summers in the South, standing in the dark with Aunt Cuney observing execution of the Ring Shout inside the church from which her aunt was excluded. Avey's participation in the circle of dance (the Carriacou Tramp) is the final symbol of reunion with her people and her culture. The completion of redefinition, however, initiated by Lebert Joseph and followed by all, is paying homage to Avey through "a profound, a solemn bow that was like a genuflection" (250). Asked by one aged dancer, "And who you is?", Avatara Johnson is privileged to speak her full name: "Avey, short for Avatara," the name sent by Aunt Cuney before her birth. Avatara. One regarded as the incarnation or embodiment of some known model or category.

Thus Avey returns redefined to a role mythically predetermined, a role from which she has been detracted by materialism and economics. Certain individuals, regardless of gender, are apparently predestined to possess or are gifted with special powers of knowing, such as Aunt Cuney, Lebert Joseph, Joseph's daughter Rosalie, Avey, and Avey's daughter Marion, who has already travelled to Africa and knows its culture. They are to function as griots or cultural preservationalists, to prevent their common culture and its origins from being obscured, displaced, distorted or forgotten. Avey will be like Coleridge's ancient mariner, seizing the young "as they [rush] blindly in and out of the glacier buildings, unaware, unprotected, lacking memory and a necessary distance of mind (no mojo working for them)" (255). She will use Aunt Cuney's coda to the Ibos story: "Her body might...might be in Tatem but her mind, her mind was long gone with the Ibos" (39). The story is a paradigm for Avey's and others' lives; a dualistic separation between the mind and body is essential in hostile environments that do not respect all individual differences equally. A balance is possible only when one's sense of connectedness with the human family and unique culture is established as well as maintained. Avey's redefinition is not selfserving, therefore, but beneficial to her community.

The settings of this novel as well as the journeys and motifs of circularity, progression, and completion reinforce this connectedness. African-Americans in the Caribbean Islands, the South, the Northeast, Canada or wherever located are historically and culturally linked. The customs, rituals, or practices may have become altered over time, but nonetheless are identifiable, as the Ring Shout and Carriacou Tramp are essentially similar, or as the ritual of bathing administered by Rosalie recalls the childhood bathing of Avey by Aunt Cuney. Similarly, the journeys lend shape to the motifs; Avey's primary trips, literal and metaphorical, transport her through confusion and revelation to self knowledge and cultural stability.

The character of Avatara Johnson represents a new woman for a different time. Her rejection of distorted materialistic values and their replacement through cultural anchoring and connectedness, rituals and ceremonies, earn the widow a praisesong. Although Avey embodies characteristics from Laurentine Strange and Helga Crane, her development transcends the superficiality and limitation of beauty and social class. Transcendence through redefinition earns Avatara Johnson a distinct presence among Black women in recent fiction, securely placing her among complex, diverse, autonomous, and culturally conscious sisters.

Works Cited

Campbell, Joseph. *The Hero With a Thousand Faces*. Princeton: Princeton University Press, 1968.

Christian, Barbara. "Ritualistic Process and the Structure of Paule Marshall's *Praisesong for the Widow*." *Callaloo* 6 (1983): 74-84.

Fauset, Jessie. *The Chinaberry Tree* (1931; reprinted New York: Negro Universities Press, 1969).

Larsen, Nella. *Quicksand* (1928: reprinted New York: Negro Universities Press, 1969).

Marshall, Paule. *Praisesong for the Widow*. New York: G. P. Putnam's Sons, 1983.

Mbiti, John. *Concepts of God in Africa*. New York: Praeger Publishers, 1970.

Sandiford, Keith. "Marshall's *Praisesong for the Widow*. *Black American Literature Forum* 20:4 (1986): 371-392.

The Early Development and Growth of America's Oldest Black Resort— Idlewild, Michigan, 1912-1930

Ben C. Wilson

Racism affected every phase of the day-to-day existence of Black Michiganians between years 1912 and 1930. Cognizant of the realities of Jim Crowism in the state, certain non-Black Michiganian entrepreneurs with keen foresight, realized a profit could be made by servicing desperate middle class Blacks hungry for fun. Realizing that Blacks were denied at the most renowned resort areas and desperate for an escape from the burdens on ghetto life, some non-Black businessmen became aware that they were "ripe for the picking." They created Black vacation spots in Michigan, the Water Wonderland.

The enterprising few decided to buy land, from either lumber firms, farmers, or realtors, and then decided to develop their resorts on spring-fed inland lakes. The most popular started and began to blossom, between the years 1912 and 1930, in Lake County. It was called Idlewild.[1] One of the publicity brochures produced by the promoters described the resort in the following manner:

...It is renowned for its beautiful lakes of pure spring water, among which beautiful Lake Idlewild stands out like a diamond among the gems of the earth. It is renowned for its sparkling streams of crystal waters, two of which practically border on Beautiful Idlewild. It is renowned for its profusion of wild flowers and berries, all of which abound in Beautiful Idlewild. It is renowned for its myriads of game fish, with which its lakes and steams are fairly teeming, and for the game of all kinds which roam through the woods. Idlewild the Beautiful is truly named for its Beautiful Idlewildness.[2]

The Idlewild experience was started in 1912 by Erastus Branch, Albert Branch, Wilbur Lemon, Mamye Lemon, Alvin E. Wright and Madolin Wright. All were non-Black. Their corporation—the Idlewild Resort Company (hereafter referred to as I.R.C.)—purchased nearly 2,700 acres of cut-over timberland, including Lake Idlewild,[4] for their purposes. There is a mystery concerning who sold the real estate, especially Idlewild Island,

Reprinted with permission from the *Journal of Regional Cultures* Volume 2:1 Spring/ Summer 1982.

to the company. One source indicates that Mr. Branch played the role of a squatter on the Island and acquired the and eventually.[5] As realtors the Branch Brothers were certainly in ideal occupations to become knowledgeable of certain land sales in advance.

Once the land was acquired, the first objective of these astute businessmen, especially the Branch Brothers—the realtors from White Cloud, Michigan—was to sell the I.R.C. and its purpose to the black communities of Midwestern America, notably Chicago, Detroit, Cleveland, Fort Wayne, Gary, et. al. The notion of a vacation playground for Blacks where beaches,[6] hotel accommodations,[7] unpolluted water, opportunities to participate and enjoy all of the outdoor leisures such as boating, swimming, possibly golf and tennis, horseback riding,[8] night-clubbing, etc., was enough bait to lure many to the "rustic retreat seventy-nine miles north of Grand Rapids." According to another I.R.C. publicity brochure "the 2700 acres of land was parceled out into some 19,000 small plots 25 x 100 feet in size with a price tag of thirty-five dollars each—six dollars down and one dollar a week."[9] Impressed by Booker T.'s nascent ideas of economic self-sufficiency but followers of W.E.B. DuBois and the newly formed N.A.A.C.P., lang hungry urban middle class Blacks[10] jumped at the opportunity to acquire property in Idlewild. Within the reach of many urban middle class Blacks via newsstands and through friends, the promotional bulletin, in a rather hyperbolic manner, stated that:

This beautiful spot, which surely must have been intended by nature as a playground for her children, beckons to you to come and rest your poor, tired body, your over-worked brain and your shattered nerves within her bosom. 'Idlewild' is not an experiment, but a reality. Idlewild is not a local enterprise, nor dominated by the people of any one locality, but is national in every respect. There are now thousands of Idlewild lot owners scattered throughout the United States and Canada, and practically every state is represented. The large and rapidly growing list of lot owners is composed of the thinking, progressive, active class of people. People who do things—and what they have done and are planning on doing in the very near future at Idlewild is what has made Beautiful Idlewild the wonder and admiration of all visitors...[11]

Advertisements in the Saturday editions of the *Chicago Defender* of the mid-twenties also described an Eden-like atmosphere that engulfed the rustic retreat.

To do an effective job of soliciting those victimized by Jim Crowism, the I.R.C. decided to hire Black sales persons. Their responsibilities were to inform, lure and hopefully sell property to the urban Black elites in Midwestern America. A portion of one of the company's form letter to the salesperson reads,
...Here is our proposition to you:

Undoubtedly you have friends who would be interested in securing lots.... If you get them interested enough to buy, either from you directly or our nearest agent or through this office, we will give you a lot for every customer you get, that is to say, one of the lots that we have been selling for $10 each. All you have to do is to get your friend interested then call or write our nearest agent or communicate with the Chicago office. If you can handle the sale yourself, a location will be sent to you. If it is handled through our agent, he or she has locations on hand to offer.

If you would prefer to take out an agency yourself and work on a commission basis in place of receiving a lot for each sale you help make, you will receive a cash commission of $2 for every lot you sell, together with regular agent's outfit and assignment of lots to sell. We are only making the free lot offer to lot owners who are not agents...

If either of these propositions interests you and you want to take out an agency and work on a commission basis or refer your prospects to our nearest agent and receive a lot for every sale made, whether the sale is for one, two or any number of lots let us know. In either case, we will be glad to have your cooperation, and we feel that we can help you to make money for yourself...[12]

Most of the Blacks who became salespersons for the I.R.C. all were familiar with the experiment; some visited the community with early excursion parties. A striking example was Ms. Lela Wilson. In 1912, she and her husband, Herman O. Wilson, joined an excursion from Chicago to view Idlewild, then being developed. They did not return until 1921, but "upon returning, the Wilsons bought 80 acres surrounding Lake Idlewild and Lela promptly named it Paradise."[13] Then the couple had to make money to support the dream. "Rental cottages was one answer...Selling real estate was another. They had acquired, as fast as they could, 320 acres."[14]

Since some of the Black salespersons were quite successful[15] in their task, Mr. Erastus Branch of the I.R.C., anticipating the arrival of many summertime vacationers (circa 1921), not only constructed a land bridge to the site of the Idlewild Club House which was on the Island, but he also saw to it that small bungalows were built. He began the construction of some wooden floors, ten by twelve feet, over which tents were pitched. Eventually, before too many buyers appeared on the scene, wooden bungalows were built over the floors, replacing the canvas tent tops. The little cottages, each identifiable by a letter of the alphabet, curved along the north side of the Island, the true nucleus of the resort. There was a narrow wooden sidewalk extending in front of all the bungalows or "dog houses." The front doors opened onto the boardwalk; a window at the opposite end faced Lake Idlewild. Each cottage contained two cots, a crude nightstand, a pitcher and bowl, a kerosene heater, a night pan—usually stored under small beds— a bucket for drinking water and a vintage hot plate. Meals were usually sold in the Idlewild Club House and in some of the homes of those who took advantage of the resort opportunity early. Logically, the privies were located far behind the living quarters.

Many who once upon a time sought accommodations in the "dog houses" eventually had contractors erect more desirable living quarters designed to the likeness of the new property owners. Mr. Rollo Branch built cottages for several years and in turn the following gentlemen exhibited their carpentry skills on the different bungalows and homes constructed. Some of the other contractors[16] during the formative period were John Simmons, Archie Brott, Charles Scott, Andy White, Herman Wilson, Mr. Mills and George Webb.[17] After the resorters had settled in either their own cabins or temporarily in the "dog houses," they usually met in the Club House for entertainment and the business of discussing the future growth of the resort area. The further development of Idlewild was usually discussed near the blazing fireplace.[18] The piano was always in the background.[19]

However, before becoming serious about Idlewild, many of the Talented Tenth undoubtedly were suspicious of the grandiose endeavor because of the race of the developers, even though the I.R.C. used Afro-American "front persons" as agents. The countless years of denigration left an indelible scar on the psyche of the blacks of that era. Their reasoning was rational. That early skepticism was quite often expressed in some form of paranoia and distrust for all who benefited economically, socially and politically from the effect of racism in Michigan. The idea is vividly highlighted in the thoughts of one of Black America's leading intellectual giants, W.E.B. DuBois. He candidly mentioned that:

no one will accuse me of over partiality toward my paler neighbors. I deeply regret that as I grow older a white face is to me a sign of inherent distrust and suspicion, which I have to fight in order to be just. Now white men developed Idlewild. They recognized its beauty, bought it and attracted colored people there. They have made money by the operation. That was their object. But they have not been hogs. They have not squeezed the lemon dry, and they have apparently been absolutely open, square and just. Idlewild is worth every penny...It is worth a good deal more than most people paid for it.... White men developed it because they knew how. We pay for their experience, but we pay a very low sum. Our hats are off to the Idlewild Resort Company.[20]

After closely examining the rationale of some of the developers and the commitment of the first Black wave of resorters, DuBois eventually purchased a lot or two there. He never developed the plots because of his demanding schedule and constant struggle for human equality; the warrior-educator later sold his property. Nevertheless, others, without national reputations, would continue to flow into the resort. Instead of dumping their land, many vowed to never give up their second homes in the rural retreat.[21]

Without a doubt, the biggest drawing card to Idlewild was a doctor, a pioneer heart surgeon. Fleeing form his constant antagonists and critics in the medical profession, Dr. Daniel Hale Williams bought a large portion of land in Idlewild between 1917 and 1925.[22] Appropriately, he called his acquisition the Daniel Hale Williams' subdivision. Most of his land was located on the island.[23] Much of his property he sold to his peers and fellow professionals throughout Midwestern America. A few examples were cosmetologist Madame C. J. Walker, novelist Charles Chestnutt, Lemuel L. Foster of Fisk University, Chicago politician Louis E. Anderson, et. al.

Since such giants were present frolicking in the wilderness of Michigan, the resort began to attract others who were not so famous throughout the Black communities of America. A few of those early settlers were: Mrs. Mary Ellis, Mr. and Mrs. Cecil Barrett, Mr. Edward Wright, Mrs. Sarah Hackson, Mrs. Myrtle Hamilton, Mr. Evelyn Casey, Mrs. Clanton, Mrs. Mary E. Cox, Mrs. Laura Cannon, Mrs. Cora Riley, Mrs. Florence Powell Washington, the Reverend and Mrs. Bradby, Mr. and Mrs. Robert Riffe, Mr. and Mrs. Charles Roxborough, the Reverend and Mrs. H. Franklin Bray, Mr. and Mrs. C. Gass, Mr. and Mrs. Elsner, Mrs. Buckles, et. al.[24] Perhaps the publicity brochure was not all hyperbole when it suggested that "if you buy a lot in Idlewild you will place yourself, your family and your friends in position to reap the innumerable benefits that spring from personal contact and social intercourse with the deepest thinkers, the most active, most progressive people of the times."[25] Others continue to flow into Idlewild seeking the Black Eden, regardless of the unbelievable hardships. A striking illustration of that is described in the memoirs of Harry Solomn, former Cleveland resorter and one time township supervisor of Idlewild. In part it reads:

In August of 1928 at the age of 12, my father, mother, sisters and brothers made the trip to Idlewild. I remember it took 24 hours to get there from Detroit in a model T Ford after many flat tires. I remember that Idlewild was rugged, natural and beautiful with dirt roads, trails and very few modern conveniences....I saw for the first time in my life snakes, porcupines, deer, bears, rabbis and many variety of birds in their natural habitat.

I saw my father shave by the light of the sun. We spent two very beautiful weeks in a cottage owned by a Mrs. Hattie Martin. We had many camp type meals. This was my first real experience of what a vacation was like.

They came from not only Detroit, Cleveland and Chicago but also from St. Louis, Missouri; Alberta, Canada; Thomasville, Georgia; Indianapolis, Indiana; St. Paul, Minnesota; Richmond, Virginia; Chattanooga, Tennessee; Omaha, Nebraska; Roxbury, Massachusetts; etc.

By 1921, the I.R.C. turned the resort over to the all-Black Idlewild Lot Owners Association (hereafter referred to as the I.L.O.A.). Supposedly, $20,000 was involved in this transaction. That organization, for a number of years, conducted the business of further developing America's premier Black resort. As a matter of fact, the new owners commissioned a group of motion picture photographers from the *Chicago Daily News* to produce a promotional film on the resort. Shown primarily in the colored theater houses in Midwestern America, "A Pictorical View of Idlewild" further disseminated information on the hotspot.[26]

A debate is still going on about the reasons behind the start of Idlewild by the I.R.C. and why that association sold out. The initial investors were not that much different from their neighbors who sanctioned or benefited from Jim Crowism[27] nor was Lake County (the location of Idlewild) an island of racial tolerance. During the summer months, the money of the elite Black resorters temporarily "deracialized" the ideas of many non-Blacks in Lake County. Most importantly, Idlewild struggled through the formative years thanks to hardy Black individuals called Idlewilders.

As the Depression lurked ominously on the horizon, the character of the resort did not change; it continued to grow even through that economic catastrophe. Since it was known from coast to coast, from north to south, a more representative group of Blacks began taking advantage of Idlewild. Gradually, the rustic retreat emerged as a vital spot on the "chitterling circuit" for fledgling young Black entertainers. Between the 1930s and 1950s, the resort became known as the Summer Appolo. It certainly qualified to be called that because many performers exhibited their talents in one of the five or six nightclubs located at the resort. Among the many famous performers at Idlewild were Ziggy Johnson, Fats Waller, Sam Davis, Jr., his father and uncle, Sarah Vaughn, George Kirby, the Four Tops, Jerry Butler, Brook Benton, Jackie Wilson, Dinah Washington, Betty-Be-Bop Carter, T. Bone Walker, Earl Hamilton, Bobbie Lewis, Earl Grant, Della Reese, Arthur Prysock, Barbara McNair, B.B. King, Al Hibbler, Bill Doggett, Aretha Franklin, Steppin' Fetch' it, Chilton and Thomas, Dusty Fletcher, Big Maybelle, and Jackie "Moms" Mabley. [28] The presence of such celebrities also contributed to the success of Idlewild. The resort grew and eventually encompassed nearly all of Yates Township of Lake County. To Black America it was the Fountain Bleu and the "Summer Appolo."[29]

That its relevance to the entire Black Experience of America is gradually becoming known can be attributed to the pioneer resorters. Today, thanks to their efforts, national yet informal Idlewild gatherings have been occurring in midwestern cities to reminisce about the retreat and to speculate how the resort should exist in the future.[30]

Notes

[1]The community is located in Yates Township, Lake County, Michigan. Even though present day Idlewild resembles a retirement village, its link to the total Black Experience is unbelievable. The majority of the elders who inhabit or frequent the village are largely responsible for the gradual re-emergence of the resort. The former "Black Las Vegas" is located roughly seventy-nine miles north of Grand Rapids, Michigan.

[2]*Beautiful Idlewild*, published by the Idlewild Resort Company (Chicago, Illinois: 110 Hartford Building, circa 1912), p. 1.

[3]Interview with Mr. Rollo Branch, June 1980, Chase, Michigan.

[4]Mimeographed article entitled "Founding of Idlewild," information provided by Ann Gregory Hawkins and Henry Gregory Jr. housed in Michigan Historic Unit office Vertical Files, Lansing, Michigan.

[5]Interview with Mr. Rollo Branch, June 1980, Chase, Michigan. However, no records in the government land office in Washington, D.C. stated that this island was federal property.

[6]Once Idlewild was dredged and cleaned up, its sharp drops to deep water and currents were quite treacherous. A few summer resorters, unfortunately, never made return trips to their earthly homes.

[7]As the years passed the visitor could make a choice of living accommodations. Those who did not have their own cabins built could stay at the Oakmere Hotel, at Ma Buckles or McHenry Hotel, Mrs. Herrons' Facility, Meadowlark Haven, the Hickory Inn or Promiserania. Mimeographed article, "Founding of Idlewild."

[8]Horses for riding were provided by Sargeant Johnson, a veteran of the Spanish-American War. He owned roughly twelve saddle-broken horses. The Clover Leaf Ranch was in full scale operation in the late 1920s.

[9]*Idlewild Resort Company Brochure*, 110 Hartford Building, 8 South Dearborn Street, Chicago, circa 1917-1919.

[10]Interview with Mrs. Josephine Love, March 10, 1981, Detroit, Michigan.

[11]*Beautiful Idlewild*, published by the Idlewild Resort Company, (Chicago, Illinois: 110 Hartford Building, circa 1912), p. 1.

[12]The form letter originated in the office of the Woodland Park Resort Company Limited. Woodland Park, a very quiet Black Resort, is located roughly ten to fifteen miles from Idlewild. A central figure in the Woodland Park experience was Mr. Wilbur Lemon, co-founder of Idlewild. This company's mailing address was 808 Hartford Building, 8 South Dearborn Street, Chicago, Illinois. Its mailing address was the same as the post office box for the I.R.C.

[13]Paradise Lake is roughly three to four miles from Idlewild. Ms. Wilson built a hotel, store and the famous Paradise Night Club. Her hard work truly contributed to the success of the Lake County resort. Her travels resulted in the attraction of many southerners to Idlewild.

[14]Frances Hill, "Her Middle Name is 'Spunk'—Meet Lela Wilson," *Negro Digest* (November 1963), pp. 66-67. Lela and Herman Wilson were responsible for bringing the first electric lights and paved roads to the resort area. Their influence in purchasing lots and locating choice properties decided where many summer resorters would locate their homes. Naturally, the friendship enhanced their financial success.

[15]Some resorters bought lots without inspecting the acquisitions beforehand. Consequently, many had beach lots but no access road to them. Exchanging a lot for a better one which would allow a thoroughfare to ones cottage was rather easy.

[16]In addition to the presence of contractors, many small Black businesses developed around resorts, e.g., brick-making, dry cleaning, canning, etc., establishments.

[17]Mimeographed article entitled, "Founding of Idlewild,"...; Interview with Mr. Rollo Branch,...

[18]Interview with Mr. and Mrs. Robert L. Washington and Mrs. Thelma Hackley, May 1980, Kalamazoo, Michigan.

[19]Interview with Mrs. Jospehine Love,...

[20]W. E. B. DuBois, "Hopkinsville, Chicago, and Idlewild," *Crisis Magazine* (n.d.) volume number unknown, Vertical Files State of Michigan Library, Lansing, Michigan.

[21]Interview with Mrs. Vivian Hogan, May 1980, Grand Rapids, Michigan.

[22]According to many informants and the deed, Dr. Dan's land was mostly located on or near the island.

[23]For a detailed account of what lots were purchased and the exact location of the plots, see the Records of Deeds for the I.R.C. and the deed for Dr. Williams' landholdings. Both are in the possession of Mr. Rollo Branch, a descendant of two of the original developers.

[24]See the "Early Settlers of Idlewild Michigan List," Vertical Files of the Historic Unit, Lansing, Michigan.

[25]*Idlewild Resort Company Brochure,..., passim.*

[26]"A Pictorial View of Idlewild" is a silent film roughly twenty-three minutes long. It is now copyrighted by this writer and Mr. Edward Reed.

[27]During the 1920s Blacks could not frequent Big Star Lake Resort located in Baldwin, the sister city of Idlewild in Lake County.

[28]With the passing of the 1964 Civil Rights Act, many Blacks stopped going to Idlewild. When Caesar's Palace, the Sands, The Fountain Bleu started to accept them through the front door, some of the performers who had appeared in Idlewild were frequently on stage in Las Vegas and Miami.

[29]Arthur "Daddy" Braggs and Sonny Wilson were instrumental in developing some and bringing many performers to the rustic retreat. The presence of the performers there is worthy of an article itself. In January of 1975, WTTW (PBS Channel 11 out of Chicago) aired an excellent program pertaining to the resort. it was called "Paradise Club—Summer of '58." The one hour program was a part of the "soundstage" series and concentrated on three entertainers—George Kirby, Della Reese and Jackie Wilson.

[30]During the summer holidays—The Fourth of July and Memorial day, tourists come to the resort expecting mainly entertainment. Many leave discouraged because performing artists are opting to go elsewhere. Slowly, the resort is becoming a retirement community.

The Black Disc Jockey
As a Cultural Hero

Gilbert A. Williams

The radio disc jockey wakes us in the morning, puts us to sleep at night, and in between, his time, weather and music announcements take us through the day. But the black disc jockey has been more than an announcer. He has transcended his job as a radio station employee and becomes in many cases, a cultural hero, an individual admired and respected for his work in the black community, his concern for his fellow man, and his ability to effectuate changes in society.

This study compares early black disc jockeys (1940-50) with those of a later period (1960-80) to illustrate the various roles each group has played in the community. The earlier group was characterized by the music its members played (mostly jazz, blues, and later rhythm and blues), their language patterns, and their personalities. Their styles developed from the clash of urban and rural cultures that helped define their lives. These early black disc jockeys appealed to the lower class southern migrants by speaking their language and reminding them of "down home." Today's black disc jockeys generally do not enjoy the prestige and status that the early jockeys did. What are the reasons for their diminished roles? Are black disc jockeys the cultural heroes they once were?

The development and widespread use of formats on today's radio stations has been singled out as the major reason that "personality" radio is no longer popular.[1] Consequently, black disc jockeys say their influence on thought and action in the community is weak and their role as purveyors of cultural symbols, especially regarding language styles and the black experience, is circumscribed by the strait jacket of the format. The black disc jockey's role has changed since the 1950s, but factors other than the use of formats have contributed to it. Spaulding noted that black styles, language and culture have changed. Younger blacks in the late 1960s could not relate to the language patterns and styles of the early disc jockeys; they no longer "talked the talk or walked the walk" of this earlier generation. However, they did accept jockeys who sounded "white" and maybe even were white. Spaulding observed that "pure black dialect may have lost its appeal, both to station management and to the listening audience."[2]

Reprinted with permission from *Popular Music and Society*, Volume 10:3.

Certainly, black urban communities have changed and the resultant cultures' clashes with middle America have produced a new culture. These cultural changes explain some of the reasons that black disc jockeys are no longer the cultural heroes they once were; but other factors must be considered to fully understand why black disc jockeys do not enjoy the power (at the radio station), prestige or popularity in the community as they once did.

The purpose of this study is to: 1) show how the early black disc jockey exemplified the essence of black culture; 2) compare and contrast today's black disc jockey's working environment with that of the early jockey's; 3)formulate ideas about why today's black disc jockey does not enjoy the power, popularity and status that his earlier predecessors did.

Given this background, it is possible to generate the following hypotheses: 1) Management practices at radio stations have become more refined and as a result, sales and programming functions are tightly controlled. This development can be seen in the increasing number of jobs for account executives, sales managers and program directors. 2) Today's radio management now promotes the station's call letters, dial position, or format style more so than the names of individual disc jockey personalities. These hypotheses follow from the theory that radio is a corporate enterprise that has used black music, language, and styles to survive economically, but has little regard for the cultural symbols and rituals from which they come.

The popularity of early black disc jockeys came about when black Americans began moving from rural areas to urban centers. Black migration from the South began after the Civil War but the more dramatic increases took place after World War II. The rate of increases can be seen in the rise in the numbers of blacks in American cities. For example, in 1940 blacks made up 8 percent of the population in Chicago; by 1960 that had increased to 23 percent. In Detroit blacks comprised 9 percent in 1940; by 1960 they made up nearly 29 percent of the population. Blacks in Memphis made up 41 percent of the population 1940; by 1960 the figure was 48 percent. New York in 1940 had a 6 percent black population; in 1960 it had grown to 14 percent. In 1940 blacks in Philadelphia made up 13 percent of the city's population; by 1960 that number had doubled—26percent. Los Angeles had a 4 percent black population in 1940; however, by 1960 blacks made up 12 percent of that city's population.[3] With these changes in demographics came changes in lifestyles. The newly—arrived blacks changed the cities' neighborhoods and their people. Older black residents of these cities intermixed with the new groups and together they created a new urban culture. It was in this new urban culture that early black radio disc jockeys gained popularity, power and status. Radio was an easy way to reach the black masses. Disc jockeys used music and language styles that helped the new urban residents adjust to their surroundings, and made them feel at home. These early black disc jockeys were considered role models and heroes because their audiences identified with them; they gave them a sense of identity, and expressed the joy and pain of the black experience through the music they played, the words they spoke, and the actions they took. For the new black urban resident, the black disc jockey had entered the white world but still maintained his humanity, identity, and community spirit. Moreover, the black disc jockey allowed his listening audience to "share and imitate him." From a cultural point of view, these men and women were considered entertainers—one aspect of life where black men still preserved their masculinity, identity and other cultural traditions. Keil explained the significance of "entertainment" in black culture when he discussed the development of urban blues: "This domain or sphere of interest may be broadly defined as entertainment from the White or public point of view and as ritual, drama, or dialectical catharsis from the Negro or theoretical standpoint. By this I mean that certain Negro performances, called "entertaining" by Negroes and Whites alike, have an added but usually unconscious ritual significance to Negroes. The ritualists I have in mind are singers, musicians, preachers, comedians, disc jockeys, some athletes, and perhaps a few Negro novelists as well."[4] Black disc jockeys invented and used such styles as "riding gain" and "talking through" in musical presentations in the late 1940s. The disc jockey would "ride gain" when he boosted or lowered the power on the audio board to accent various parts of a record. To "talk through" a record, the jockey would lower the volume of the music and talk over the piece as it played; this practice is quite common today but was new and unique at that time.[5] Their audiences found these language patterns flattering and attractive. The black urban dweller could identify with the disc jockeys since many spoke in a similar manner. Black disc jockeys both borrowed from the language of the street and contributed to it. Black disc jockeys' ability to "rap" and speak eloquently made them instant heroes in the community where such language skills are highly valued. The black oral culture tradition places high values on its members who can speak well and greatly admires the best orators. Keil observed, "In White America, the printed—literacy tradition—and its attendant values, are revered. In the Negro community, more power resides in the spoken word and oral tradition—good talkers abound and the best gain power and prestige..."[6] In addition, black disc jockeys mastered timing, sound, and the spoken word, all of which as Keil puts it "are defining features" of black culture.[7]

While black disc jockeys developed entertainment skills and worked in black-oriented radio stations, white radio stations were losing status, power, and money. The major networks decided to invest in the new medium—television—and left their radio affiliated stations to fend for themselves. Part of the reason that the networks pulled the plug on their affiliates was that national advertisers were not interested in buying time on radio. A look at advertising trends clearly indicates that national radio networks did not receive as much national advertising in the years after 1950 as during radio's early years of growth. For example, in 1945 national advertisers bought 134 million dollars' worth of air time from ABC, CBS, and NBC radio networks. Just ten years later (1955), national advertisers spent only $64 million with the networks.[8] Radio station owners looked desperately for some way to offset the decline in audience sizes, ratings and revenues. It was then that many station owners started to hire and promote black radio disc jockeys. Advertisers were eager to sell their products to this growing black urban market, and radio station owners were quick to recognize the marketing potential of black disc jockeys. Station managers promoted their disc jockeys as "personalities" and gave them top billing. Furthermore, many of the jockeys were built into the advertising and marketing schemes. A radio buy included not only the radio time, but often included pictures and other promotional items using the disc jockey as the dominant sales figure for certain products. For example, in Chicago, Coca-Cola bought time on Al Benson's show and also featured him prominently in their print media advertisements. Similarly, Seven-Up bought time on another popular disc jockey's show—Richard Stam's. The company also used him as a personality in many of its retail store promotional campaigns. Disc jockeys were expected to represent the company at many social and political functions. Advertisers felt that black disc jockeys gave them additional exposure in the community through these promotional appearances.[9] As advertisers recognized the growing black consumer market, radio stations all over the country scrambled for ways to reach it. MacDonald observed: "while in 1943 only 4 stations throughout the country were programming specifically for Blacks, 10 years later, 260 such stations were attracting national and local sponsors to their broadcasts. And throughout the country many stations that traditionally had been directed toward White consumers now switched their formats and became all-Black outlets. Among these stations were WMRY (New Orleans) in 1950, WEFC (Miami) in 1952, WCIN (Cincinnati) in 1953, and WNJR (Newark/New York) in 1954."[10]

Despite the desire to hire black disc jockeys, their job situation was precarious, competitive, and highly pressured. And even though disc jockeys reflected the cultural milieu of urban America, their main function at the radio station was to sell air time. As Spaulding noted: "The prime requirements for success as an early Black disc jockey was to be a good salesman."[11] Early black disc jockeys often bought time from the radio station and then found commercial sponsors. They would then sell time at a higher rate to those sponsors—that's where the jockey made money, from commission.

The Pioneers

The first black disc jockey with a commercially sustained radio show was Jack L. Cooper, a former vaudevillian and ventriloquist who started broadcasting on WCAP in Washington, DC, in 1924.[12] Cooper had complete power over his show and introduced a number of innovative programming ideas. For example, he was the first black sports announcer; he started a daily newscast featuring items of interest to the black community and national advertisers.[13] He was a hero to his listeners in the community. Cooper had the unique combination of talents that engendered deep feelings and admiration in the black community. He was able to "give public expression to deeply felt private emotions...(that) both increase feelings of solidarity (and) boost morale."[14] Cooper's broadcasting delivery emphasized the average, middle-class American's English language usage. He avoided black dialect in his speech; none of the urban "jive talk" would be heard in his announcements. Cooper's broadcasting style came closer to that of Martin Block.

Al Benson represented a different kind of black disc jockey who expressed the feelings, emotions, and cultural idioms that made him a hero to his listening audience as well. Benson spoke with a southern black accent, mixing street talk idioms from the urban north to enhance his delivery. Lower-class blacks easily identified with this kind of delivery. Benson's broadcasting style was unique and differed completely from that of white announcers. In fact, Benson and those who imitated him moved away from the announcing styles of whites and even mocked them. Benson's style came closer to that of Arthur Godfrey, on the Martin Block (smooth) and Godfrey (folksy) dimension. Benson was influential in inventing new programming concepts: moreover, his "down-home" language style and inflections made the newly-arrived rural migrants feel at home in their urban environment. Benson's power and influence extended into the community and to a new generation of black disc jockeys that he introduced to Chicago. His popularity sprang from his "southern lower-class street language" and the music he played— "an early urban blues that revolutionized Chicago's Black radio programming."[15] Benson's audience included most of the recent lower-class migrants. According to Spaulding, Benson's "huckster style of delivery, filled with idiomatic expressions" appealed to the southern migrants. In addition to his use of language and ability to entertain the masses, Benson was admired for his stand against racial discrimination. He was known to personally integrate nightclubs, where owners were fearful that Benson's popularity and influence would hurt them if they refused to allow his entry. One story has it that Benson, a native Mississippian, once hired an airplane pilot to drop leaflets on the state's capitol to protest the discriminatory practices blacks faced in the state.[16]

Throughout the 1950s and 1960s, other black disc jockeys endeared themselves to black audiences. Many in Chicago had been influenced by Al Benson's style. There were other jockeys, however, who created their own identities and styles; they, too, embodied the qualities of a cultural hero. Black disc jockeys during this time period represented something new and different, just as the music they played. Much of the music, however, would have been unavailable were it not for the independent record companies that recorded it. These record companies recorded lesser—known rhythm and blues artists. Major record companies, such as RCA and CBS, upon noticing the increasing interests in black music, began recording white artists who "covered" popular black songs, thereby exposing the music to white audiences. MacDonald wrote that the black disc jockeys of the 1950s "were a new breed" who played and promoted blues and rhythm and blues. He noted that black disc jockeys were found in urban markets throughout the country. They invented and developed unique phrases, language styles, perspectives and other rituals that made them cultural heroes to the growing urban populace.[17] They had names like Dr. Daddio, Big Ben Hill, The Magnificent Montague, Jocko and Daddio Daylie. Jazz, blues, and rhythm and blues characterized the kind of music they played since that was what black audiences wanted to hear. Many of these jockeys had southern accents or a hybrid style of a "cool northern accent" with black idioms tossed in. They used street language at times; at other times they rhymed phrases and interjected favorite foods, rituals, and practices of the recent migrants to make them feel at home. The black disc jockey was a "major agent of socialization for the newly urbanized Blacks. He told them what to buy, and stores at which to buy them."[18] The new members of the community identified with these disc jockeys who played their kind of music.

The Format and Payola

The popularity of their form of radio presentation, sometimes referred to as "personality," began to decline in the late 1950s. Radio stations began promoting their call letters, dial positions, and format style more often but not their disc jockeys. What factors led to the decline of personality radio? What factors have contributed to the decline in status, power, and popularity of black disc jockeys? Part of the reason can be found in the proliferation of broadcasting schools. Young men and women who have been trained as disc jockeys, are graduating in increasing numbers making it a buyer's market.

Another factor in this equation is the payola scandal that rocked the broadcasting industry in the late 1950s. Payola is the payment of unreported money to disc jockeys for including certain records on their shows. Black disc jockeys once had the power to choose their own records for broadcasts; they were able to introduce much new music to black audiences. Al Benson once remarked, "nobody has ever told me what to play on my radio shows. I picked the music and artists I liked."[19] White disc jockeys had power to decide which songs they aired as well. This situation left the jockey vulnerable to bribes. Record promoters willing to pay large sums of money to get air play for their product became very influential. As Foster observed: "The one indisputable fact was that if a DJ was prominent enough and wanted to make extra money, there was ample opportunity. It was quite possible for DJ's in a major market to add from $50 to $150 thousand dollars to their annual salary."[20] Black disc jockeys did not take as much money through payola as whites but they were involved. Spaulding made this point about black disc jockeys: "Some companies kept certain jockeys on the payroll and regarded this as a promotional expense deductible from their income tax...In exchange for the payoffs, a record company would ask for a certain number of air plays during the day, six days a week."[21]

As a result of Congressional hearings on the payola scandal, attempts by the stations' management to control it, and broadcasting industry investigations, the disc jockey's control over music selection was gradually taken away.[22]. Radio stations' management took control of the problem of payola by increasing the power of the program director; consequently record selection became a part of the managerial process. This development accomplished two goals: 1) it diminished the power of the disc jockey; and 2) it made sure that record promoters' money went through the radio station's accounts rather than in the disc jockey's pockets.

In addition to these developments, another related factor figures in the mix—the popularity of the tightly controlled music format. Denisoff noted, for example, that: "The development of the 'Boss' radio format formalized every segment of air time; dictating what was to be played when."[23] The Drake-Chenault format, invented in the mid 1950s, "compressed program elements so tightly that DJs did not have the opportunity to express their personalities."[24] Routt remarked that disc jockeys were told to "play the music and shut up." These format considerations affected black-oriented radio as well. Black disc jockeys not only lost their power to select music but could not express themselves as they had previously. Radio stations began to promote call letters, dial position, etc., rather than black disc jockeys. These factors, coupled with the increased power of the program director, contributed to the gradual erosion of the black disc jockey's status in the community. The black disc jockey lost his position as guardian of the community's culture and was replaced by music directors, sales managers, and program directors as "cultural gatekeepers."[25]

Yet another key factor contributing to the black disc jockey's decline in status, power, and prestige was the separation of the sales function from the radio personality. This development began in the 1950s and was part of the movement toward corporation radio, where management took over the sales function, programming—all facets of the business. The early black disc jockeys had been primarily salesmen. They usually worked on a commission rate that varied from 10 to 35 percent. During the late 1950s station management continued to hire black disc jockeys but created separate sales staffs who were usually all white. Eventually, corporate officers took over national, regional and local advertising accounts.[26] This development, perhaps more than any other, curtailed the black disc jockey's power, especially vis-a-vis station management. Sales managers, program directors, and station managers became the power brokers. With the disc jockey eliminated from the sales function, his power base was severely limited. The results of these developments meant that black disc jockeys' professional roles were diminished, their names taken off outdoor billboards, and their status as cultural heroes allowed to fade.

Some of today's black disc jockeys are distressed and disturbed by the developments illustrated in this study. One black disc jockey—The Mad Hatter—remarked: "The politics of the country are right wing now. But there is no White person who knows what Black people want to hear."[27] George Woods, of WDAS in Philadelphia, observed: "Personality radio began to lose popularity when the personality got bigger than the station. The station's call letters are more prominent now; the personality is put in the background. Small record companies have been hurt most by the situation. Format radio has been detrimental to the industry as a whole. DJs lack freedom of expression to choose the kind of music people want to hear. Radio station management wants to control the disc jockeys. Black radio is kinda sad; it can't use the power it has."[28] Yet another disc jockey put it this way; "listeners are being robbed and cheated. Record companies are hurting most as a result of format radio." But Barry Mayo of New York said that "Although formatted radio stations are predictable, people listen because of the music. Integrating personality and a music format is the way for the 1980s."[29] Finally, another disc jockey noted: "A type of format where the on-air personality is the key link to the audience is most useful. The on-air personality can be innovative, free form expressive and creative. The air personality can have a loyal audience—non predictability is the key."[30]

Cultural Heroes of the 1980s

George Woods is to black radio in Philadelphia as the Liberty Bell is to Independence Hall: both are symbols of freedom. For the past twenty-five years, George Woods, "The Guy With the Goods," has worked at WDAS-AM/FM, the number one station in the hearts and minds of black Philadelphians. During those years he has hosted a morning talk show from 8-11 a.m. (Monday-Friday), conducted voter registration drives, raised money for the poor, and collected donations for groups such as the United Negro College Fund. Woods is recognized by the black community as a concerned individual, interested in the welfare of those less fortunate than himself. His listeners have witnessed Woods' efforts to open new opportunities for them in education and employment. They have seen as well his determination to fight for freedom, dignity and human rights.

Woods is a cultural hero in Philadelphia. He is recognized in this manner not only for his abilities as a disc jockey, but for his commitment to the black community. One example of Woods' work came during a recent Christmas holiday, when he helped raise money to feed, clothe, and pay rent for 5,000 needy families.[31] A close associate of Dr. Martin Luther King, Jr., Woods is a firm believer in non-violent protest as a means to change society. Because of his commitment, Woods has been re-elected to the Board of Trustees of the Martin Luther King, Jr. Center for Non-Violent Change. Black Philadelphians admire those qualities in Woods and recognize his value as a role model for the community.

The Magnificent Montague is a cultural hero in the Los Angeles area. Renowned for his positive and uplifting rapport with listeners as a disc jockey, Montague is now the owner of KPLM-FM in Palm Springs, California. Although no longer an on-air personality, Montague is well-remembered and revered by those who heard him or knew of his reputation. Montague gained widespread respect because of his announcing abilities and "because I was able to get into the lives and lifestyles of my listeners."[32] Today Montague is recognized as a black man who used his talents and finances wisely, so much so that he was able to buy and operate a radio station. Montague says he "left an imprint on listeners and they still regard me as a hero."

Black Radio Today

There are 201 Black/Urban formatted radio stations in America today, representing 10 percent of all currently-used formats.[33] Contemporary Hit Radio, sometimes referred to as CHR/TOP 40 is now the most popular format, found on 16.8 percent of the nation's radio stations. The Black/Urban format has continued to enjoy popularity, however. In 1977 only 6.6 percent of American radio stations used this format. By 1982 the number had increased to 11.6 percent.[34] In addition, Black/Urban formatted stations continue to attract listeners. Since 1977 these stations have witnessed a 53 percent increase in their audience share. According to Duncan's *American Radio*, the ten best markets for Black Urban format stations are in the South. Stations using this format with the highest quarter hour listening nevertheless, are found in major urban areas. (See Tables I and II.)

To be sure, part of the increase in black formatted stations is because the number of black-owned radio stations continues to grow. In 1977 there were fifty-six; this number had increased to 125 by 1982, and in 1984 there were 131 black-owned radio stations.[35] It should be noted, however, that not all black-owned radio stations have adopted the Black/Urban format.

The black disc jockey has continued to evolve and change. Many of the changes have been forced upon him by the dynamics of the radio industry. Still, the black disc jockey has made positive changes alone, seeking new ways to communicate with his listeners, helping solve their problems, and speaking for his listeners when they had no voice. Format changes, deregulation and ownership patterns will no doubt continue to influence how the black disc jockey does his job. The black disc jockey's commitment to his community will determine how well he completes his tasks.

Table I
(Source: Jim Duncan, *American Radio*, Spring, 1984. Kalamazoo, MI)
Black/Urban
(Nat. Avg: 10.12%)

1. Columbus	37.8
(Represents share of listening in market)	
2. Memphis	36.2
3. Macon	34.9
4. Charleston, SC	33.1
5. Jackson	32.2
6. Savannah	31.1
7. New Orleans	30.7
8. Mobile	28.2
9. Fayetteville	27.9
10.Lafayette	27.4

Table II
Black/Urban

1. WRKS-F	NY	1411
(Represents quarter hour listening		
in market)		
2. WKTU-F	NY	913
3. WGCI-F	CHI	741
4. WBLS-F	NY	722
5. WUSL-F	PHILA	623
6. WBMX-F	CHI	608
7. KMJQ-F	HOU	521
8. WDAS-F	PHILA	513
9. WKYS-F	DC	471
10.KSOL-F	SF	432

Notes

[1]At the Black Exclusive Conference held in Houston, TX, June, 1981, several black disc jockeys argued that formats have taken the freedom of the DJ away. He can no longer entertain his audience with his personality but must adhere to a strict regime of playing music and reciting the time, temperature and record selected.

[2]Norman W. Spaulding. "History of Black-Oriented Radio in Chicago, 1929-1963," Ph.D. Thesis, University of Illinois, Urbana-Champaign, 1981, pp. 29-41.

[3]Bureau of the Census, (Government Printing Office, Washington: 1969), *The Statistical Abstract of the United States* pp. 21-30.

[4]Charles Keil, *Urban Blues* (Chicago, 1966) pp. 15-16.

[5]Spaulding, op. cit., pp. 122-125.

[6]Keil, op. cit., pp. 16-17.

[7]Ibid., p. 17.

[8]Christopher H. Sterling and Timothy Haight, *Mass Media* (New York, 1978). See also Eugene Foster, *Understanding Broadcasting*, (Readings, Mass., 1982) pp. 90-93.

[9]I am indebted to Norman Spaulding for this explanation and analysis. For a more detailed analysis, see chapters 3, 4, and 5 in his work "History of Black-Oriented Radio in Chicago, 1929-1963."

[10]J. Fred MacDonald, *Don't Touch That Dial*, (Chicago, 1979), pp. 327-370.

[11]Spaulding, op. cit., p. 47.

[12]Ibid, p. 72.

[13]Ibid, p. 72.

[14]Keil offers this analysis for blues singers. I have used these words to demonstrate an analogous perception of black disc jockeys.

[15]Spaulding, op. cit., pp. 78-79.

[16]Ibid., p. 80.

[17]MacDonald, op. cit., pp. 327-370.

[18]Spaulding, op. cit., pp. 115-116.

[19]Ibid., pp. 110-116.

[20]Eugene Foster, *Understanding Broadcasting* (Reading, Mass., 1982) p. 100.

[21]Spaulding, op. cit., 65-66.

[22]*Broadcasting*, August 21, 1959, p. 34.

[23]R. Serge Denisoff, "The Evolution of Pop Music Broadcasting: 1929-1972," *Popular Music and Society*, 1973, 2 (3), pp. 202-226.

[24]Ed Routt, *The Radio Format Conundrum* (New York, 1978), pp. 20-24.

[25]Spaulding, op. cit., p. 62.

[26]Ibid, pp. 47-48.

[27]Comments made during a panel discussion on the topic, "Format versus Personality Radio"

[28]Ibid.

[29]Ibid.

[30]Ibid.

[31]Harry M. Gould, Jr., "The Sound and The Soul of Black Radio, *Philadelphia Inquirer*, 8/13/83.

[32]Personal Interview, 9/27/84.

[33]James Duncan, *American Radio*, Spring, 1984, p. A30.

[34]Ibid.

[35]National Association of Broadcasters Statistics.

Radio Deregulation:
The Impact on Black Families
and Non-Profit Social Agencies

Lawrence N. Redd

In his book *The African Slave in Colonial Peru*, 1524-1650, Frederick P. Bowser states that "it was only 25 years after the epochal first voyage of Columbus that the commitment to African slavery was made and the greatest forced human migration in history began."[1] The basis for the early success of slavery in the Americas was the thirst for wealth which existed in a largely unregulated economic marketplace. Marketplace forces determined the rules of trade, and mainly on the basis of economic factors New World slavery thrived for over three hundred years. The current movement by the federal government towards deregulation also places emphasis on permitting marketplace forces to significantly influence trade policy. Although largely unnoticed by the public, the communication industry has been partially deregulated, and the impact may in some ways equal the disruption of black families which unregulated economic forces inflicted on the foreparents of African Americans.

The purpose here is to highlight and bring into focus the relationships which exist among the communication industry, particularly radio; black families, and non-profit social service organizations. The non-profit organizations with which this paper is primarily concerned are those social agencies which provide services to black families and seek to protect and improve their mental health and welfare. By describing and highlighting the relationships among non-profit social agencies, black families and the communication industry, it is hoped that a more formal coordination among the three will eventually develop. It is important also to support the advancement of a sound rationale which can assist non-profit organizations in establishing policy leading to the ownership, programming and management of commercial radio stations.

Communication and Black Families

One of the perennial struggles which black people have faced in the United States is that of establishing adequate and effective communication among themselves. The enslavers who chained and brought Africans to the Americas centuries ago understood the importance and role of communication among the oppressed. To control against rebellion and institutionalize ignorance of self, enslaved Africans were separated from members of the same tribe and regrouped with persons who spoke different languages.[2] The disruptive communication process was so thorough that most families today can trace their family heritage back only a few generations. Still, as revealed in Alex Haley's *Roots*, some black families have preserved their heritage through oral communication.[3]

For this writer, family communication was restored during the civil war, somewhere in Mississippi. A troop of Union soldiers arrived at the Warren plantation on which Rhody Warren, this writer's great-grandmother, then twelve years old, was enslaved.[4] The Union soldiers demanded the ole massa sign papers which would give Africans their freedom. When the enslaver refused Union soldiers bound the white plantation owner in rope and dragged him across the fields behind a galloping horse until he agreed to free the African families. Rhody's brothers were so caught up in the action and glad to be *free* from the old massa, they saddled some horses to ride a short distance with the Union soldiers. When night began to fall and they had not returned, Rhody walked in search for them.

Even into her nineties she vividly recalled hiding at night behind a thick grove of trees in fear of strange approaching noises which turned out to be Union soldiers who took much of the night to file by (an historical marker at New Madrid, Missouri states General Sherman's troops were in the region). But her search was in vain and never again did Rhody see or hear from her brothers. Rhody's scattered family members, like so many others, entered freedom mentally distressed and without access to communication media for the purpose of family reconstruction.

What were Rhody Warren and other broken African families free *to?* They were given no land, no money and no support system. Most did not know what to do or where to go. Said Dr. Martin Luther King, Jr.:

It was freedom to hunger! It was freedom to the winds and rains of heaven. It was freedom without a roof over their heads. It was freedom without bread to eat. It was freedom without land to cultivate. It was freedom and famine at the same time, and it is a miracle that the Negro has survived![5]

Centers for Counsel

The abyss of uncertainty into which black families entered was largely filled by non-profit institutions, mainly government and religious social service organizations that helped sustain black survival. The agencies helped blacks comprehend the new environment, understand themselves, and face life under reformed relationship policies.

Historical records duly note the enormous contributions to blacks by General Oliver O. Howard who headed the Freedmans Bureau and for whom Howard University is named; the missionary work of agencies such as the American Missionary Association that helped blacks before and after the war; and philanthropists such as Julius Rosewald of Chicago who help fund hundreds of schools for blacks throughout the South. In addition, blacks themselves often helped fill the void with agencies of their own. Many such organizations actually functioned as counseling centers in that the people who staffed and directed them engaged in a process that assisted "an individual in learning about himself, his environment, and methods for handling his roles and relationships."[6] Black self help organizations actually predate the birth of the United States.

Black Organizations and the Community

In 1772 the first black organization, a church, was established in Silver Bluff, South Carolina.[7] Increasingly, blacks used the pulpit and quasi-religious gatherings to counsel and exhort their kinspeople towards the common goal of freedom. Richard Allen and Absalom Jones, both free men, acquired organizational skills from their involvement in religious conferences and meetings sponsored by sympathetic whites and used their experiences in 1787 to establish the Free African Society in Philadelphia.[8] Their leadership laid the foundation and became a model for subsequent black organizations in the United States. In Boston, Newport, and New York similar non-profit organizations were founded as a means of improving the mental health and welfare of blacks. States Lawrence Jones:

In most instances, these benevolent or mutual aid societies were, in fact, quasi-churches and were only prevented from being identified as such because they could not agree on denominational affiliation, or else that did not occur as an option. Their charters emphasized the care of widows and orphans, stipends to sick members, provision for education of orphans and excluded persons of questionable moral character from membership.[9]

The black non-profit social organizations of the 18th and 19th century spread nationally and led to the emergence of the Niagara Movement, the National Urban League, the National Association for the Advancement of Colored People, the Association for the Study of Afro-American Life and History, the Nation of Islam, the Black Panthers, CORE, etc. Lennox S. Yearwood, in 1978, estimated that:

...there were at least 244 National Black (active) organizations in the United states with an estimated 26,720,000 membership. Church organizations predominated in number and size.[10]

Out of the extended kinship African descendants have felt for each other over the centuries has developed a strong support structure in the culture which is pervasively visible. Gunnar Myadal observed that phenomenon in his famous study of the "Negro":

In Chicago in 1937, when the total negro population of the city was less than 275,000, there were over 4,000 formal associations...In Natchez Mississippi, where the total

Negro population of that city was about 7,500, there were more than 200 Negro associations discovered in one week in 1935.[11]

In black communities throughout the United States today there exists literally thousands of active local non-profit organizations which function as counseling centers to sustain self pride, assist blacks in building good relationship skills, foster self dependence, care for the deprived, and carry on programs to raise blacks to universal standards of excellence.

Ta Wa Si Athletic Association and Communication

One such local organization is the *Ta Wa Si* Athletic Association of Grand Rapids, Michigan. Established in 1957 by black professional men, the organization became a source for personal counsel among young blacks; a protector against the winds and deeds of racism practiced against the youngsters of that city.[12] Those black men and their families literally led the rescue of an entire generation of young blacks from low expectations and helped create the present generation of effective black leadership in that city.

Frank (not his real name) was Grand Rapids' most gifted all around high school athlete and exceptionally skilled in basketball. To observe the athletic artistry of Earvin "Magic" Johnson or Michael Jordan today was to feel and see the excitement of Frank in the late 1950s. But at age 15, the local newspapers printed his name in a huge negative headline and carried a story involving an in-school incident which witnesses claimed he never committed. The newspaper attack emotionally strained Frank, his family and friends.

Dr. Joseph McMillan, now director of the National Black Family Conference, and ten other great black men such as the late Urban Leaguer, Paul Phillips (he ran second only to Jesse Owens); and Dr. Julius Franks (all-American guard at University of Michigan, 1942), organized into *Ta Wa Si* (an Indian name for Friend and Helper) and came to the rescue. They wrote letters to black families and obtained permission to counsel their children (among them this writer). They organized programs and spoke to young blacks about the importance of academic excellence. They held rap sessions, took young men on visits to college campuses and inspired them to believe it was possible to attend and graduate. They sponsored spring dances for all of the black male athletes and their dates, established personal relationships with them and organized achievement banquets each year.

Table 1
Ta Wa Si Athletic Association
Founding Members

Jay Adams	Educator
Dr. Julius Franks	Dentist
Elmer Greene	Pharmacist
Allen Jackson	Educator

Fred Johnson	Businessman
Dave King	Fireman
John Letts	Judge
Joseph McMillan	Educator
Paul Phillips	Urban League, Executive
Ruben Smart	Educator
Sam Triplett	Educator

To help finance their activities, the *Ta Wa Si* Athletic Association sponsored a series of basketball tournaments and all-star games each year. In response the community filled local school gymnasiums and kept the financial resources adequate for the organization to do its job effectively.

An important part of *Ta Wa Si*'s overall relationship with the community involved media, particularly radio. Public Service announcements were sent regularly to all of the stations in town. The announcements were effective in keeping the community informed; served to gain community support for *Ta Wa Si*, and established accountability to the community.

Communication is indispensable in that a mutually accountable relationship and process. Today, however, access to an important communication channel by non-profit organizations has been curtailed legally and future media access could disappear entirely. The situation is potentially life threatening to organizations which have played extremely valuable and supportive roles in the lives of black families.

Radio Deregulation

In April of 1981, the Federal Communications Commission removed some important regulations governing public access to commercial radio stations. The deregulation of radio by the FCC covered four general areas:

> Non-entertainment Programming
> Ascertainment of Community Needs
> Commercials
> Program Logs[13]

Two of these areas have more than the appearance of importance to non-profit social agencies: non-entertainment and program logs.

Non-entertainment

Prior to the deregulation of radio, commercial stations (AM and FM) had specific requirements in non-entertainment programming. AM stations were required to devote 8 percent of their air time to non-entertainment: Public affairs programs, news, religious programs, public service announcements, etc. FM stations were required to devote 6 percent of operating time to non-entertainment.[14]

Under deregulation stations are no longer required to provide *any* fixed amount of minimal time to non-entertainment programming.

The primary type of radio programming which non-profit social agencies are perhaps most concerned about in the non-entertainment area is the elimination of any public service announcement (PSA) requirement. With the removal of the non-entertainment requirement, commercial radio stations are no longer legally compelled to air an agency's public service spots. In order for social service agencies to obtain public interest airtime now, they must depend upon the goodwill and grace of broadcasters.

The PSA is an important part of advertising; the last step in a social agency's array of methods used to promote and publicize itself and the services it offers to the public. There is little that can be wrong and much that is right with an agency that understands its environment and clientele, perfects its needed services, and takes the necessary steps to *advertise* its services to those in the community who need them. In business the process is called marketing.[15] Without effective marketing and communication no institution can long survive in this highly technologicalized society.[16]

The PSA, although only one communication tool among many, is efficient, effective and vital to informing potential community clients, politicians, private donors, and industry about an agency. Conceptually, the PSA is to the non-profit social agency what the commercial advertisement is to private industry.[17]

Under the old policy, commercial radio did a commendable job with non-entertainment programming. Most stations made good and admirable efforts to air PSAs in their prime time hours. The FCC, however, did not place much value on PSAs in eliminating non-entertainment programming requirements. It overlooked the role and function of PSA's and focused entirely on non-entertainment programs. This is what the FCC concluded in eliminating non-entertainment programming:

...the history of governmental involvement in non-entertainment programming has been driven by one overriding concern—the concern that the citizens of the United States be well informed on *issues* affecting themselves and their communities. It is with such information that the citizenry can make intelligent, informed decisions essential for the proper functioning of a democracy.[18]

To that end the new rules require radio stations to offer programming responsive to public *issues* in their communities. However, the FCC established no uniform guidelines for stations to follow in order to demonstrate compliance. Thus the FCC did not recognize the primary use by which non-profit organizations utilize commercial radio stations: public service announcements.

Program Logs

Not only has deregulation removed PSA requirements from radio broadcasters, the new rules attempt to destroy even the process which might later be used to gather evidence to argue for future reinstitution of PSAs. The 1981 FCC deregulation ruling states that program logs are no longer required to be made available to the public for inspection. Program logs are a written record of a station's program material which it airs. Logs are printed out every day. They can be used later to determine which commercials were programmed, time and length of newscasts, titles of public service announcements, and names of public affairs programs.

Before deregulation each radio station was required to keep a random sample of daily logs in their public file which made one random composite week. Citizens could walk into a station, ask for the public file and see just what PSAs were run and where they were placed in the schedule. All programming records were open to the public.

Under "deregulation" a radio station is required to maintain a public file but not compelled to keep or show program logs publically. There is no way for the public or a scholarly researcher to compare what non-entertainment programs or PSAs a station has run and where they have been placed in the schedule. Unless one already has a set of logs and subsequently monitors a station's programming there is "no way" to check and compare whether a station has decreased the number of PSAs or programs it has aired for non-profit agencies since deregulation.

The U.S. Court of Appeals (United Church of Christ vs. Federal Communication Commission) upheld radio deregulation (May 10, 1983). The issue of placing program logs in the public file was remanded back to the FCC for lack of appropriate rationale.[19] However, commercial radio stations are still permitted by the courts to withhold program logs from public inspection or access until the case is someday resolved.

Discussion

Three things have been emphasized so far. First, communication among blacks has been under serious attack since black people were enslaved in America. Secondly, black organizations have played a valuable role in surmounting those communication barriers and functioning as centers for support and counsel. Lastly, an important means by which modern black organizations communicate with their constituents to gain support and publicize services has been seriously threatened by the policy of radio deregulation.

Ironically, radio deregulation policies dovetailed into the period in which the welfare of black families became adversely affected by Ronald Reagan's presidential policies. Although Reagan proclaimed national economical recovery, poverty among black families increased. Social agencies, including counseling services, were pushed far beyond intended clientele capacity and service capability. Exacerbating the situation were federal budget cuts in social programs. The federal reduction of social program funds increased competition for financial survival among non-profit social service organizations and concomitantly shifted portions of the governmental marketplace directly into the local public arena where agencies have discovered traditionally free radio lines to their respective communities legally removed under deregulation policies.

The strong survival of non-profit social organizations is considered by some black scholars to be the fundamental avenue to black survival in the United States. Dr. Lee P. Brown, speaking at Howard University in 1979, clearly articulated the importance of modern black social organizations to the survival of black people:

...we have had a war on poverty; we have had our model cities programs; we have seen other federally-initiated programs designed to address the plight that black people in this country must face. Yet, the programs have gone and we are still here with the same, if not worse, problems.

What this suggests is that we as people cannot depend on others for survival; rather, we, both individually and collectively, must develop our own resources. No longer can we afford to depend upon that which others give us. We must develop and support those organizations that address our needs. In effect, we must develop our own survival kit. And, as we do so, I suggest that our organizations should form a nucleus for carrying out our agenda for survival.[20]

Without good and efficient communication channels to make non-profit agency services known, people who need services may go wanting and people who can support the organizations may forget their existence or fail to comprehend their needs. A prime example was renowned Fisk University's marginally visible struggle against life threatening financial problems in the 1980s. Access to mass communication media is essential for the survival of non-profit organizations.

Conclusions and Recommendations

Radio stations throughout the United States may continue to provide free public service announcements to non-profit social service organizations. However, under deregulation there is no law to hold stations accountable if they decide to reduce or eliminate access entirely. Non-profit agencies should therefore continue to carry out positive public relations with radio stations as a means of obtaining air time and space.

The ownership and operation of commercial radio stations by non-profit social service organizations is a policy worth pursuing. Public sector control of their own station license would better insure a strong combination of commercials and public service programming, including PSA's. Such a station could help build black businesses and increase the circulation of money in black communities. Most importantly black non-profit organizations will insure control over their financial resources for survival and control communication access to clients and supporters alike.

The key to the success of such an approach resides in the formation of coalition building among non-profit organizations. The coalition would bring together a pool of financial supporters of the various organizations and expertise to execute the plans. The model for non-profit group ownership of commercial stations exists already. Howard University owns and operates a private Washington, D.C. radio station. Pluria Marshall of the National Black Media Coalition in recognizing the station's importance has asked, "If it weren't for WHUR-FM where would you get information about black communities in Metropolitan Washington, D.C.?"[21] Table 2 lists known nonprofit organizations that own and operate commercial broadcast stations.

Table 2
Nonprofit Organizations That
Own Commercial Broadcasting Stations

Station	City	License Holder
WWL Television	New Orleans	Loyola University
WWL Radio	New Orleans	(Owned by Loyola University until sold in 1989 to Keymarket Communications, Inc.)
WNDU-AM	South Bend, In.	Michiana Tele-
WNDU-FM	South Bend, In.	casting Corp. (Notre
WNDU-TV	South Bend, In.	Dame University)
WOI-TV	Ames, Iowa	Iowa State University of Science and Technology
WHUR-FM	Washington, D.C.	Howard University
WCFL-AM	Chicago	(Owned by Chicago Federation of Labor until sold in 1979 to Mutual Broadcasting)
WGPR-FM	Detroit	International Free
WGPR-TV	Detroit	and Accepted Model Masons, Inc.
KSL-TV	Salt Lake City,	Bonneville Inter-
KIRO-TV	Seattle	national (Church of
KIRO-AM	Seattle	Jesus Christ of
KSEA-FM	Seattle	Latter Day Saints)
WRFM-FM	New York City	
KMBZ-AM	Kansas City, Mo.	
KMBR-FM	Kansas City, Mo.	
KBIG-FM	Los Angeles	
WCLR-FM	Skokie, Ill.	
KOIT-FM	San Francisco	
KAAM-AM	Dallas	
KAFM-FM	Dallas	
WBAY-TV	Green Bay	(Owned by Norbertine

Fathers until sold
in 1974 to Nation-
wide Communications,
Inc.)

The management and ownership of the above listed facilities should be called upon and consulted for leadership and guidance in the area of broadcast license acquisition, financing, and station operation. The National Black Media Association in Washington, D.C. has a long and distinguished record in fighting for public interest broadcasting as well as increased minority broadcast ownership and should be consulted. The National Telecommunication Information Administration within the United States Department of Commerce directs the Minority Telecommunication Development Program aimed at increasing minority participation in radio, television and other forms of electronic media. Lastly, Broadcast Capital Fund, Inc. (BROADCAP) with offices in Washington, D.C. assists minorities seeking to own and operate broadcast stations. The program would assist a coalition in broadcast station and license acquisition and planning.

Communication has been and continues to be the weak link in the black struggle for equality. The strongest force has been the ability of black organizations to surmount the barriers which have inhibited the most fundamental aspect of being human: communication. In the new technologicalized world it has become imperative for institutions of all kinds to develop sophisticated means of staying in touch with their constituents and environments. It is no less important for black nonprofit social organizations to do the same. It is the key to black family survival.

Notes

[1]Bowser, Fredrick. The African Slave in Colonial Peru 1524-1650 (Palo Alto: Stanford University Press, 1974), p. 1.

[2]Haley, Alex. *Roots* (Garden City: Doubleday and Company, Inc., 1976), p. 151.

[3]Ibid., p. 671.

[4]Redd, Ida Bell. Personal Interview.

[5]King, Martin Luther. *Speech to National Association of Television and Radio Announcers* (Atlanta, 1967), RCA Records.

[6]Hansen, James C., Stevic, Richard R., and Warner, Richard W. *Counseling: Theory and Process* (Boston: Allyn and Bacon, Inc. 1972), p. vii.

[7]Johnson, Audrey. "The Extended Kinship for Survival in Black Organization," *Black Organizations*, ed. Lennox Yearwood (Washington, D.C.: University Press of America, 1980), p. 104.

[8]Woodson, Carter G. *History of the Negro Church* (Washington, D.C.: The Associated Press, 1921), pp. 72-73.

[9]Jones, Lawrence. "They Sought a City: The Black Church and Churchmen in the Nineteenth Century," in *The Black Experience in Religion*, ed. C. Eric Lincoln (New York: Anchor Press/Doubleday, 1979), p. 10.

[10]Yearwood, Lennox. Black Organizations (Washington, D.C.: University Press of America, 1980), p. XII.

[11]Myrdal, Gunnar. *An American Dilemma: The Negro Problem and American Democracy* (New York: Harper and Row, 1962), p. 46.

[12]Adams, Jay. Ta Wa Si Athletic Association (Grand Rapids), Personal Interview.

[13]"Deregulation of Radio," Federal Communication Commission, April 14, 1981, p. 6.

[14]Ibid., p. 4.

[15]Maddalena, Lucille A. *A Communication Manual for Non-profit Organizations* (New York: Amacom, 1981), p. 4.

[16]Ibid., p. 5.

[17]Newberg, Richard. "An Audience Study of the Black Oriented Radio Program Taking Care of Business on Michigan State University's WKAR-AM." Michigan State University, M.A. Thesis, 1971.

[18]*Federal Reporter*, Volume 46, No. 36, February 24, 1981, p. 925.

[19]"Office of United Church of Christ vs. FCC," *Federal Reporter*, 2d Series, p. 1413.

[20]Brown, Lee P. "Black Organizations: An Agenda for Survival," in *Black Organizations* (Washington, D.C.: University Press of America, 1980), p. 217.

[21]"TV Deregulation, Too Much, Too Soon," *Media Line*. National Black Media Coalition, July, 1983, p. 1.

Bill Cosby: TV Auteur?

Bishetta D. Merritt

In the 25 years Bill Cosby has been in show business, he has simultaneously entertained "adults with dry humor and captured the imaginations of children with his almost magical sense of the ridiculous."[1] From executive producer to product spokesperson, American television audiences have been exposed to Cosby for over twenty years. If the 1950s garnered the title, "decade of the westerns," the 1980s might easily be remembered as the "Cosby years." The monumental achievement and success of "The Cosby Show" and his acceptance as a product representative for companies such as Coca Cola, Jello Pudding, Ford Motor Company and Del Monte qualify him for that accolade.

Starting in 1964 with the Emmy award winning *I Spy*, Cosby's most popular series' include *The Bill Cosby Show* and *Fat Albert and the Cosby Kids*. He experienced only one minor setback in his television career when *The New Bill Cosby Show* was cancelled in 1973 followed by *Cos* in 1974. Cosby's forte as a producer was the half-hour comedy and when he ventured outside that formula, his efforts did not prove successful. The above shows, both variety programs, did not succeed and MacDonald attributes these failures to their genre.[2] A series of comedy-variety programs starring blacks premiering from 1972-74 met the same fate and did not survive the ratings test. About this same time in his career, however, commercials began to interest the actor/comedian and eventually Cosby developed into one of the most respected and believable product spokespersons in television.[3] Not only did this lucrative venture strengthen his appeal to the masses but helped him achieve more financial stability.

Cosby's audience appeal and financial security contributed to the success of his newest series, *The Cosby Show*, but are these factors, though important, the only reasons for the shows large weekly viewership? Do past situation comedies produced by Cosby share commonalities with this current program? What is the benefit of studying them collectively? And, is there an established set of criteria to measure an individuals impact on a medium as diverse as television? To begin to answer these questions three of the series were chosen for analysis—*The Bill Cosby Show, Fat Albert and the Cosby Kids (Fat Albert)* and *The Cosby Show*. These programs were selected on the basis of their common genre, content, Nielsen ratings and executive producer or executive consultant—Bill Cosby. Though *The Bill Cosby Show* aired only two years, media historian J. Fred MacDonald named it one of the most popular shows (with a black central star) of the late 1960s, basing this selection on audience approval supported by Nielsen ratings.[4] In addition, the program is syndicated and aired on cable in several markets across the country. For the above reasons, *The Bill Cosby Show* was considered a successful program. *Fat Albert* and *The Cosby Show* qualify because of their longevity on television and high ratings.

Background

Research indicates that television has been analyzed utilizing various critical methods. Some include the use of the tenets of mythology, signification, the comparison of television to the "dream-world" espoused by Freud and genre analysis.[5] Genre analysis, for example, categorizes television shows and series within a conceptual system from which the critic can draw similarities and make critical judgements. Problems surface using this method when programs within the same genre bear little meaningful resemblance. For example, *The Outcasts* and *Gunsmoke*, are both westerns, but share no other distinctions. In film, *Silverado* and *Heaven's Gate* are both westerns, yet again no further similarities exist. Whether the medium is television or film, genre analysis becomes cumbersome when the critic must differentiate within formats.[6]

Genre criticism may take another approach. The critic may elect to focus on one episode within a series. This method narrows the scope, and creates another problem, breadth of analysis. Alternatively, a critic may choose to evaluate the entire series by utilizing one element. For example, Wanders' study of "put-down" humor in *Maude*.[7] Media researchers Davis and Marc write, however, that a model exists that would allow for in-depth analysis and make the appropriate distinctions by form and type between various programs.[8] Such a system, holistic in design, is used in film criticism and would facilitate analysis of television on a number of levels. It is the "auteur" theory.

What components constitute the "auteur" approach to film criticism and how should this critical method be applied to television? Based on three concepts, this theory avoids isolating a director's work into compartments. A film undergoes evaluation as part of the director's entire creative output. Generally, excluded from inclusion in the study are first films, yet no director's films exist in a vacuum nor should be barred from scrutiny.[9] A new film, analyzed in relation to the others, is investigated by exploring the themes followed, whether the director exhibited any artistic growth, and whether the director attempted and succeeded in accomplishing his/her goal with the film. An artistic context, when established using the above standards, allows for broad indepth analysis of the particular work.[10] Secondly, each film is analyzed for the personality, style or as Sarris writes, the "signature" of a specific director. Finally, the third and "ultimate primise" concerned with the film as art—the interior meaning of a film, distinguishes one director from another. This meaning can be detected in tempo, rhythm and pacing of the film. More difficult to describe than the first two concepts, the third may be defined as the "soul" of the director. "Soul," Sarris writes may be defined as that "intangible difference between one personality and another, all other things being equal...[T]his difference is expressed by no more than a beat's hesitation in the rhythm of a film."[11] If one were to diagram the three concepts of the auteur theory, three concentric circles should be drawn with "the outer circle representing technique; the middle circle, personal style; and the inner circle, interior meaning."[12] "Auteur" status is granted according to Davis, therefore, when a director in film demonstrates technical competence, familiarity with the medium and creative growth from film to film.[13] What distinguishes one creator of film form another are those recurring characteristics of style, process and technique. Hitchcock, for example, became known for his very effective use of stairways. In addition, his blond heroines, who at times meet unpleasant ends, were often a Hitchcock trademark, along with his cameo appearances. Other directors whose film technique and competence qualify them for auteur status are John Ford and Charlie Chaplin. Their films bear the distinguishing marks of their creative genius.

Then, how does this theory apply to television or a study of Bill Cosby? The creative center of film is the director. In television the producer has that role. Cantor[14] and Marc[15] note that producers are powerful individuals in shaping television series, while Newcomb and Alley[16] consider producers the creative forces in television. As in film, television auteurs possess characteristics that are above all distinguished by the themes they follow in a group of shows supported by their artistic progress, "signature" or style, and their technique and procedural tendencies. Marc considers the most meaningful way to determine television authorship is to find the thematic continuity in a group of shows produced by the same personality. "Surprise" endings were the signature of *Twilight Zone* episodes written by Rod Serling whereas law-and-order politics dominated the series' *Adam-12* and *Dragnet* produced by Jack Webb.[17]

Setting a style that would dominate situation comedy and leave a permanent imprint on the genre were the comedies of Norman Lear. The flagship series *All in the Family*, followed closely by *Sanford and Son*, then *Maude*, *Good Times*, *One Day at a Time*, and *The Jeffersons* revolutionized sitcoms. His characters were so universal, the audience felt part of the families being presented. Though loud and augmentative, these families coaleased during stressful situations. Lear's trademarks included episodes that discussed real-life issues relating to the family, generational conflict, and frank political dialogue that contrasted to the traditional sitcom setting and structure. Instead of conversing on such topics as school grades and the necessity of purchasing a second car, the Bunkers debated racism, poverty, women's liberation, and transportation. In addition to Lear, other television producers elevated to "auteur" status are Quinn Martin, Aaron Spelling, James Brooks and Allan Burns, and Garry Marshall.[18] These persons attained their status because the shows they produced reflected their distinctive look and vision.

Bill Cosby, though not categorized as a producer with the individuals listed above, has served as executive producer and executive consultant for his successful television series' (*The Bill Cosby Show, Fat Albert,* and *The Cosby Show*). His creative technique, style, personality and "signature" are evident in each series. Therefore this paper utilizes the criteria ascribed to the auteur method of analysis to determine whether Cosby (and his work) qualify him as a television "auteur."

Cosby as Auteur

The Bill Cosby Show, Fat Albert and *The Cosby Show* share several common characteristics. Each of the series was a trendbreaker in its time, each included characters surrounded by family and friends, and each specialized in plots with universal themes and multidimensional characters. For the purposes of this paper, the terms trendbreaker, universal themes and multidimensional characters require definition. The Cosby shows were *trend-breakers* because each series either presented a different view of blacks in situation comedies by breaking previously held stereotypes, or created an innovative method to handle content in an established genre. Chet Kincaid (*The Bill Cosby Show*) defied the image of the typical "clenched fist" black man depicted on television in the 1960s, by exuding his blackness in more subtle, nonverbal ways. *Fat Albert* was the first cartoon show to include value-laden messages instead of the slapstick humor used in cartoons to that time. *The Cosby Show* discontinued using mechanical plots, disrespectful children, and generational conflict and presented the two-parent black family where both partners worked as professionals.

To ensure that *universal themes* were depicted (situations presented where the entire television audience could identify; those slice-of-life scenarios), Cosby hired professionals to serve as consultants and to review scripts. Gordon Berry assumed that role for *Fat Albert* and Alvin Poussaint for *The Cosby Show*. "My job is to ensure all the situations presented in the program are possible in real-life families and that the content focuses on what one can rather than cannot accomplish," asserts Poussaint.[19] The three series, seeking to tell an American story, appealed to as ethnically broad an audience as possible.[20] Cosby has been quoted as saying, "I don't think you can bring the races together by joking about the differences between them. I'd rather talk about the similarities, about what's universal in their experiences."[21]

Multidimensional characters are those that reveal their resourcefulness, intelligence, sensitivity *and* frailties and weaknesses. Not one character is all good or all bad. All characters possess angelic and mischievous traits. Characters on the Cosby shows portrayed a wide range of personality differences, qualifying them for multidimensional status.

Trendbreaker

Cosby, the first black person to co-star in a network dramatic series (*I Spy*), created Chet Kincaid, the featured character in *The Bill Cosby Show*, very differently from the way other blacks were depicted on television during the late 1960s. Although a middle-class professional, living in an integrated environment, Cosby's Kincaid was strikingly different from Diahann Carroll's Julia who shared many of the same characteristics. Unlike *Julia*, a program criticized for the shallowness of its central character and saccharine dialogue, *The Bill Cosby Show*, evolved into a series extracted from the black experience.[22] The characters' blackness subtly integrated into the plots and dialogue, created a unique black man for that era. Kincaid listened to black music, had pictures of Martin Luther King, H. Rap Brown and prints by black artist Charles White hanging on the walls of his home. He worked with less privileged children, wore dashikis, and ordered "soul" food in black restaurants. Starting with the opening music by Quincy Jones, *The Bill Cosby Show* created a black ambiance totally missing in *Julia*, says MacDonald.[23]

Kincaid did not use stereotypical language and mannerisms, but let the non-verbal props chosen to complete the scenes help to reflect his cultural identity. A physical education teacher living in San Francisco and moonlighting to earn more money, Chet contradicted another black image of that period—the riotous rebellious black. In the series Cosby portrayed a black man who had not deserted his roots, but moved effectively in all circles. He tutored students in history, recruited athletes for his track team, attempted to settle arguments between his aunt and uncle, had friends over to watch basketball and encouraged another to stop smoking. The program did not rely on old stereotypes or the tendency to present blacks in roles that avoided any association with black life and culture like *The Leslie Uggams Show* and *Julia*.[24]

Fat Albert also broke tradition when the half-hour cartoon about friends from a Philadelphia neighborhood began airing on CBS in 1972. Cosby rejected slap-stick comedy and violence, therefore strenuous behind-the-scenes work was necessary to convince CBS executives the series would garner an audience which would appreciate the program and its educational storylines.[25] Used as a vehicle to teach social values, judgment and personal responsibility, the show precipitated the major realignment of Saturday morning programming at CBS, as well as presented its black characters in a positive light. The Cosby kids, though black and living in a poor neighborhood did not display offensive behavior. They were innocent children, making the best of life and learning from experiences.[26]

After the success of *Fat Albert*, CBS added other children's shows to its Saturday morning line-up (*Valley of the Dinosaurs*, *Shazam*, for example) that also communicated value-laden messages. Most of these cartoons and childrens' programs were eventually cancelled, but *Fat Albert* continued on the network until the early 1980s and then moved into syndication. Other networks, inspired by the popularity and appeal of *Fat Albert*, introduced their own set of message shows for children. Included were *The Big Blue*

Marble, Zoom, and *Kids are People.* Program content initiated in the episodes of *Fat Albert* and adopted by the above shows became the primary subject matter of children's programs.[27]

Breaking tradition a third time, *The Cosby Show* rejected the use of contrived plots, gag lines, and generational putdowns (the latter a characteristic of Norman Lear comedies). "The over utilized characteristics of previous black-oriented comedies with stereotyped black adults (*Good Times, Sanford and Son*) or wise-cracking black children (*Diff'ent Strokes, Webster*) with white parents were also missing," according to television critic Tom Shales.[28] The Huxtables—Clair, Cliff and the Children (Sondra, Denise, Theo, Vannessa and Rudy), exposed audiences to a two-parent, successful, upper middle-class, cohesive black family without the self-deprecation of series' like *The Jeffersons* or *Good Times. The Cosby Show* avoided this brand of humor and other negative characteristics (isolated, matriarchal, violent, and conflict prone), observed in black television families of the 1970s.[29]

As in *The Bill Cosby Show,* the black experience on *The Cosby Show* emerged through subtle references. Black artist Varnette Honeywoods' pictures hang on the walls along with posters of Frederick Douglass and signs to "end-apartheid." The children dance and listen to black music while discussing whether to attend black schools like Howard University or Talledega College. Storylines develop, according to critic Sally Smith, from life's small humorous moments that viewers recognize, not contrived situations that offer cliff-hangers before each commercial.[30]

Not only was *The Cosby Show* instrumental in the revitalization of situation comedies but it helped NBC become the number one rated network for the first time in thirty years.[31] During the series' first season, ABC and CBS unsuccessfully counter-programmed the show, and then during the second season, created clones (*Charlie & Co.* and *Growing Pains*), and reshuffled the lineups in an attempt to offset its' popularity. Interestingly enough, Cosby had to fight the same battle he encountered with *Fat Albert* to get the Huxtable family on the air. Additionally, ABC and CBS rejected the program anticipating the continued unpopularity of situation comedies.[32]

In one way or another each series set a standard in the treatment of black people or black situations by not acquiescing to old stereotypes of behavior or subject matter. Television programming was affected by the trends set by *Fat Albert* and *The Cosby Show.* Derivatives of these series fill the programming schedules of American television (*Electric Co., Kids Break, Smurfs, Growing Pains* and *227*).

Characters Surrounded by Family and Friends
In addition to the role of trendbreaker, a second distinguishing feature of the Cosby programs was the presentation of characters surrounded by family and friends. Never isolated from the larger community, the characters in the Cosby shows do not exist in a vacuum but have families that provide support, continuity, and generational links to the past and present. Characters

frequently mention ancestors whose lives have been inspirational or who passed along family remedies or keepsakes. The audiences for *The Bill Cosby Show* were introduced to Chet Kincaid's mother, siblings and extended family. Fat Albert, Bill, Rudy, Mushmouth, Russell and the other Cosby kids regularly spent time with their parents. However rare the moments, specific episodes high-lighted these parent-child relationships. The Huxtable family circle, enriched not only by paternal and maternal grandparents, enjoyed the pleasure of friends who visited their New York brownstone. This particular characteristic, often absent from previous black television families became an integral element in *The Cosby Show*. Video audiences were rarely introduced to the extended families or ancestors of the Evans' of *Good Times* or those of Louise and George Jefferson. From inception, the Cosby programs included family members. Kincaid lived next door to his sister, while Rudy's (*The Cosby Show*) friend Peter visited her regularly from his home across the street. With *Good Times* and *The Jeffersons*, for example, audiences only caught glimpses of family members.

Universal Themes and Multidimensional Characters

A third characteristic shared by the Cosby shows are their dependence on plots utilizing universal themes and characters with multidimensional personalities. Audiences, through identification, relate to the experiences unfolding before them on the television screen. This process is nothing new to television. However, Cosby's characters and the situations in which they appear depict people with a distinct ethnic background coupled with universal appeal.[34]

Chet Kincaid of *The Bill Cosby Show* had experiences that placed him in varied situations and settings that contribute to the development and portrayal of a well-rounded character. Not confined to his apartment or classroom, Chet moved about San Francisco shopping for groceries, visiting his sister, and auditioning for a commercial. These activities placed him in contact with his students' parents, old classmates and people in his neighborhood. Occasionally guest stars appeared on the program as members of the Holmes High School staff or as romantic interest for Kincaid (Cicely Tyson).

Situations depicted him stuck in an elevator overnight at his high school, exhausted after sleepless nights caused by a barking dog in his neighborhood, and frustrated after delivering papers for his sick nephew to all the wrong homes. Kincaid was pictured as a colleague, friend, teacher, and member of a close supportive family unit. Audiences experienced his failures and successes in coping with life's everyday occurrences and saw themselves or what they'd like to be reflected in Kincaid. A teacher in New Fairfield, Connecticut assigned the program to her students for homework. They were required to watch the show every Sunday night. Impressed with the type of teacher Cosby portrayed and the ideals he represented, she felt the show set an example modern teachers should be required to follow when communicating to students.[35]

Drawing from his experiences growing up in Philadelphia, Cosby created *Fat Albert* as an extension of his childhood. Cosby's voice, in its many variations, became the one most frequently used by the characters. Plots featured Fat Albert and the kids playing, going to school, and sharing experiences that provided the back-drops for the inclusion of pro-social messages. These messages, fused with entertainment, offered the young audiences the opportunity to be exposed to values and concepts applicable to their age and experience in life.[36]

The main center of action was the junk yard and the club house, but occasionally the children wandered home where their parents offered discipline and counsel. Major characters included Fat Albert and the Kids joined by different persons whose problems or personalities helped introduce the message for that particular episode. The Brown Hornet, the children's favorite television hero, Mudfoot, an elderly gentleman from the neighborhood, and Bill Cosby who appeared between scenes to focus the messages, completed the cast. In certain episodes Mudfoot gave his particular form of advice while the Brown Hornet's adventures served as vehicles to introduce additional subject matter.

Fat Albert, generally cast as the "good angel," provided the strength and backbone of the gang, while Rudy often cast as the "bad angel," became his foil while the others fell somewhere in between. All the children developed skills, learned, and expanded their levels' of knowledge and understanding as the series developed. Even Fat Albert lost his halo once when he drove his father's car without permission, and Rudy gained one when he saved a friend from drowning. The multidimensionality of the Cosby Kids was reflected in the range of personalities represented by each child and in the manner in which they accepted, internalized and matured emotionally from the problem-solving tasks they shared and the lessons they learned in each episode.

Just as Chet Kincaid and the Cosby Kids portrayed their frailties and personality traits, the Huxtables followed this Cosby tradition by depicting imperfect, but likeable people in realistic situations. Borrowing heavily from experiences with his real-life family (as he did with his childhood with *Fat Albert*), Cosby helped create plots audiences easily recognized.[37] Norment considers the storylines ones with which viewers of the eighties could easily identify. Episodes presented the overworked mother; the unmechanical husband who insisted on making home repairs; the teen daughter who frustrated her parents by dating boys with earrings; the pre-teen who one moment was frightened by a horror movie and the next discovered boys; and the son who hated homework, exams and cleaning his room. One or all of these situations conceivably occurred in real families. With the age of the siblings, spanning primary school to college, children easily identified with their counterparts in the series.[38] For example, a *Washington Post* article from November 1986 included interviews of five families with different incomes, ethnic backgrounds and composition, who all acknowledged they related to a situation or character on *The Cosby Show*. Cliff goes to the refrigerator and takes out an empty carton of orange juice. Jim McEachien, director of operations for the distribution division of National Public Radio and father of three was quoted as saying, "That happens every day." "Someone goes to the frig and takes out an empty orange juice carton that someone's put back in."[39] Harvard Psychiatrist Robert Coles asserts, "I hear white working class families quoting 'The Cosby Show' as though it were the last church sermon they heard...It's a pastoral quality."[40]

The personalities of each family member, revealed people who were resourceful, intelligent, sensitive, and yet had human frailties. The Huxtables, though imperfect, showed fear, pain, rejection, and betrayal, qualifying each of them as multidimensional people. Children and parents in the television audience share the same problems, have similar faults and personality quirks, and could conceivably see themselves in each episode of the program, comments media analyst Mary Helen Williams.[41] Cosby succeeded in presenting universal themes, multidimensional characters, and added to the trend of narrowcasting to capture specific audiences by "broadcasting" to appeal to a mass audience.[42]

The Cosby "Signature"

The Cosby "signature" developed from his use of raceless humor in his role as comic storyteller. This trait, central to each of his series from *I Spy* to *The Cosby Show*, and evident in his act as a stand-up comedian, became the Cosby trademark. Once Cosby began appearing on television in *I Spy* he vetoed the use of racial messages in the dialogue and, when he became an executive producer, this technique was maintained. Cosby solidified this concept of raceless humor in his television series' by his presence, and influence.[43] Scriptwriters were challenged to satisfy Cosby's image of how the individual characters should be created, the plots developed and the humor fused into the dialogue of the episodes. The writing staffs, therefore, translated Cosby's ideas into stories crafted around his comedic style.

Cosby created this style based on situations and storytelling, not racial jokes. When he first appeared in clubs, Cosby imitated Dick Gregory's brand of humor. He soon discovered "there was room for only one Dick Gregory" and created a mode of comedy he could master.[44] His "color-blind" humor, therefore, developed as an outgrowth of this realization. Cosby's "humor for everyone" cast him as a humorist commenting from a personal point of view on the experiences of life, rather than a comedian. Often compared to Mark Twain, Cosby created stories that grasped the funny side of life yet echoed a sutle seriousness based in reality.[45]

Cosby structured his work similarly to jazz musicians playing a melody. A joke translated into a musical tune with a beginning, middle, and an end. Cosby assumed the soloist role and his cord changes evolved into punch lines that made people laugh. Once he mastered the melody, improvisation followed and the same story developed taking many turns before it ended.[46]

For Cosby, a very simple story could be embellished by simply changing the "melody" to accommodate the audience or situation.

Breaking the mold of verbal insults and "put down" humor utilized by sitcoms like *Sanford and Son* and *The Jeffersons*, Cosby also included in his comedy style the communication mode defined in black verbal behavior as narrative sequencing. Dating back to an African past, this method of storytelling takes the form of a concrete narrative and relates general abstract, observations about life, people and love. The storyteller uses his voice and body movements to bring the story to life.[47] Cosby's brand of raceless humor, influenced by this linguistic style in the black community and his exposure to the words of Mark Twain, his love of jazz, his childhood in Philadelphia and his life as a father, became his signature. Cosby's allegiance to his code of raceless humor did not waver, even when critics labeled Alexander Scott of *I Spy* as "Second banana" to Robert Culp's Kelly Robinson; Chet Kincaid, a black man trying to play white, and, The Huxtables, *Leave it to Beaver* in blackface.[48]

Conclusion

Acquiring auteur status indicated a producer has communicated successfully with the audience, created innovative themes that challenged tradition, advanced the medium through artistic and technical competence and demonstrated the ability to sustain a "signature" from series to series. Auteurs are the creators of programming history and have the power to significantly influence and restructure programming aired by the networks. For, in television, success very often breeds imitation. In considering the discussion on the preceding pages and the definition of an auteur in the above sentences, one question remains: Does Bill Cosby merit the title, television auteur?

Cosby was a ground breaker. His technical competence and familiarity with television, evident by the success and longevity of his series', influenced the medium. *Fat Albert* and *The Cosby Show* significantly altered television programming. Value-laden cartoons laced with humor grace the Saturday morning network offerings as a direct result of *Fat Albert and the Cosby Kids*. Further, situation comedies, thought to be a dying genre by network decision makers were salvaged when *The Cosby Show* aired and reversed that trend. *The Bill Cosby Show* presented a different, more realistic image of the black male than the accepted portrayal utilized frequently in television during the 60s.

Cosby went against the stereotype and did not create blacks as sterile white reproductions like *Julia* or place them in abject poverty performing odd jobs for survival (*Good Times*). His characters were accepted or rejected because they depicted real people not "types." The people and situations he created for television emanated from his own experience, not through reading the pages of eighteenth century literature or viewing old tapes of *Amos 'n Andy*.

As a creative artist, Cosby's forte was the half-hour comedy. His application of universal themes and multidimensional characters created situations common to audiences of all ages and races. In addition, Cosby subtly introduced unique elements of black culture to his audiences. With *The Cosby Show*, a standard was set by which all television portrayals of black characters and culture will be compared.

Cosby's creative technique and "signature" of raceless humor, apparent in each series, have their base in the black communication mode of narrative sequencing. Never a comedian who found humor in verbal insults or the "put down," Cosby maintained his standard by never acquiescing to the criticism his series' garnered concerning their authenticity or "blackness." Cosby stated, "I want to share the happiness within our people. I want to show that we have the same kind of wants and needs as other American families. I'm going to take this show [*The Cosby Show*] and make it last as long as I can to show black people that they have something to be proud of."[49]

The Bill Cosby Show presented a different image of the black male while *Fat Albert* and *The Cosby Show* significantly influenced television programming and its audiences image of the black family. Cosby's personal style is stamped on all his products. His creative technique and "signature" are reflected in each series, and his shows influenced the medium, thus qualifying him as a television auteur.

Notes

[1]Cynthia Griffin and George Hill, "Bill Cosby: In Our Living Rooms for 20 Years," *Ebony Images: Black Americans and Television* (Los Angeles: Daystar Publications, 1986), p. 97.

[2]J. Fred MacDonald, *Blacks and White TV: Afro-Americans in Television Since 1948* (Chicago: Nelson-Hall, 1983), p. 189.

[3]William Greider, "On Television, Race no Longer Divides Us," *The Washington Post*, 12 April 1978, p. A12.

[4]MacDonald, p. 114.

[5]Robert Sklar, *Prime-time America: Life on and Behind the Television Screen* (New York: Oxford University Press, 1980). See also Robert R. Smith, *Beyond the Wasteland: The Criticism of Broadcasting* (Annandale, Virginia: Speech Communication Association, 1980).

[6]Donald David, "Auteur Film Criticism as a Vehicle for Television Criticism," *Feedback* 26 (1984), 14.

[7]Philip Wander, "Was Anyone Afraid of Maude Finlay," *Understanding Television: Essays on Television as a Social and Cultural Force*, Robert Adler, Ed. (New York: Praeger, 1981), 225-230.

[8]Donald Davis, p. 15. see also David Marc, "TV Auteurism," *American Film* (1981), 52-53.

[9]Andrew Sarris, "Notes on the Auteur Theory in 1962," *Film Theory and Criticism*, Gerald Mast and Marshall Cohn, Eds., (New York: Oxford University Press, 1974), p. 511.

[10]Donald Davis, p. 14.

[11-12]Andrew Sarris, p. 512-513.

[13]Donald Davis, p. 15

[14]Muriel Cantor, *The Hollywood TV Producer* (New York: Basic Books, 1971), p. 8.

[15]David Marc, p. 53.

[16]Horace Newcomb and Robert Alley, *The Producer's Medium: Conversations with Creators of American TV* (New York: Oxford University Press, 1983).

[17]David Marc, p. 52.

[18]Horace Newcomb and Robert Alley. see also Donald Davis, pp. 16-17. David Marc, pp. 54-55.

[19]Alvin Poussaint, personal interview, March 1, 1985, Cambridge, Massachusetts.

[20]Ann Feltman, "Laughing and Learning with Bill Cosby," *Parent's Magazine* (1974), 48.

[21]Bill Cosby, personal interview by Larry Linderman, *Playboy* (1985), 75-92.

[22-23]J. Fred MacDonald, p. 118.

[24]Ibid., pp. 117, 119.

[25]Audrey Wright, "Cosby on Comedy: What it's Like Being Number One!" *Right On! Special*, 1985, p. 40.

[26]J. Fred MacDonald, p. 195.

[27]Ibid, p. 196.

[28]Tom Shales, "NBC's Cosby, the Pick of the Fall Crop," *Washington Post*, 20 September 1984, sec. C, p. 6.

[29]Gordon Berry, "Research Perspectives on the Portrayals of Afro-American Families on Television, *Black Families and the Medium of Television*, Jackson, Ed. (Ann Arbor: The University of Michigan, 1982), pp. 47-59. See also Barry Greenberg and Kimberly Neuendorf, "Black Family Interactions on TV," *Life on Television*, Barry Greenberg, Ed. (New Jersey: Ablex, 1980), pp. 173-181. Pilar Baptista-Fernanadez and Barry Greenberg, "The Context, Characteristics and Communication Behaviors of Blacks on Television," *Life on Television*, Barry Greenberg, Ed. (New Jersey: Ablex, 1980), pp. 13-21.

[30]Sally Smith, "Cosby Puts His Stamp on a TV Hit," *New York Times*, 18 November, 1984.

[31]Harry Waters, "Cosby's Fast Track," *Newsweek*, September 2, 1985, p. 51. see also Jeff Jarvis, "TV and Family," *Elle*, September 1987, p. 152-153. Richard Zoglin, "Cosby, Inc." *Time*, 28 September 1987, p. 60.

[32]Audrey Wright, p. 40.

[33]Bill Davidson, "I must be Doing Something Right," *McCall's*, May 1985, p. 147.

[34]Sally Smith, see also Tom shales, p. 1C. Harry Waters, p. 54.

[35]Muriel Davidson, "Command Performance," *Good Housekeeping*, June 1971, p. 50. see also Muriel Davidson, "Bill Cosby: The Man, His Work, His World," *Good Housekeeping*, March 1970, p. 26.

[36]Ann Feltmann, p. 47.

[37]Alvin Poussaint, personal interview. also Lynn Norment, "The Cosby Show: The Real-Life Drama Behind Hit TV Show About a Black Family," *Ebony*, April 1985, p. 28.

[38]Lynn Norment, p. 30.

[39]"Thursday Night at the Huxtables," *The Washington Post*, 6 November 1986, p. D1.

40Richard Zoglin, p. 56.

41Mary Helen Williams, "How to Make Cosby Even Better," *TV Guide*, 22 March 1986, p. 5.

42Paula Matabane, personal interview, March 7, 1986, Howard University, Washington, D.C.

43Richard Zoglin, p. 58, 60.

44"Right," *Newsweek*, 17 June 1963, p. 89.

45"Color-Blind Comic," *Newsweek*, 20 May 1968, pp. 92-93. see also Lawrence Christon, "Bill Cosby—A Family Style," *Calendar*, 2 May 1982, p. 57. Ross Daniels, "Inside Cosby," *US*, 6 May 1985, p. 43.

46Bill Cosby, personal interview by Lawrence Linderman, p. 89.

47Geneva Smitherman, *Talkin and Testifying: The Language of Black America* (Boston: Hougton Mifflin Company, 1977), pp. 147-166.

48Melvin Moore, "Blackface in Prime Time," *Small Voices and Great Trumpets: Minorities and the Media*, Bernard Rubin Ed. (New York: Praeger, 1980), p. 130. see also Muriel Davidson, p. 26. John Leonard, "Leave it to Cosby," *New York*, 22 October 1984, p. 154.

49Bill Cosby, 1985 quoted by Lynn Norment, p. 30. see also Cynthia Griffin and George Hill, p. 105. Richard Zoglin, p. 60.

The Anti-Heroic Hero
in Frank Yerby's Historical Novels

James L. Hill

A completely new venture, no matter how perceptive the individual may be, usually contains some unknown or unexpected happenings. When Frank Yerby elected to become a popular fiction writer in 1945, he could not have foreseen his meteoric rise to success, nor the subsequent controversy surrounding his career. Neither did he foresee the ungainly position that writing popular fiction would create for him. This abrupt change in his career pitted him squarely between two literary worlds, one whose overt racial ideology he flatly rejected and the other which generally ignored him because of the genre of fiction he had chosen to write. In spite of, or perhaps because of, the consequences this change effected, however, Yerby developed a sense of mission in his fiction which evolved eventually into his philosophical response to isolation within American literary culture.

In fact, Yerby's cognizance of his isolation from important aspects of American literary culture has significantly informed his fiction. His sense of isolation—working at a vocation in which his literary efforts were misunderstood or underrated—generated his most persistent theme. Contrary to some of Yerby's claims, his great theme is not evil, man against himself, man's relationship to God, or the warfare of the sexes, although these themes are prevalent in his novels. Rather, his great theme is the exploration of the turbulent life of an outcast who fights his way into an alien culture. As one Yerby critic has said:

> Significantly, Frank Yerby, a Georgia-born Negro exile from America, has concentrated on the theme of the outcast who, as in Existentialist literature, pits his will against a hostile universe. By intelligence and courage, he proves himself superior to a society which rejects him because he is of alien, inferior, or illegitimate birth.[1]

Indeed Yerby's concentration on this theme has obvious contemporary implications. "Alienation, once seen as the consequence of a cruel (but changeable) economic order," says Kenneth Keniston, "has become for many the central fact of human existence, characterizing man's 'thrown-ness' into a world in which he has no inherent place."[2] Rather than treating this theme in contemporary settings, however, Yerby examines alienation, the paradoxes of human existence and the elusive promises of a full life in societies and civilizations of the past.

Like many works of the popular fiction genre, Yerby's costume novels adhere to a proven fiction formula, which he introduced in *The Foxes of Harrow* (1946), his first novel. None of his thirty-two successive novels has varied significantly from this pattern. Generally, the pattern includes: (1) a tall or short handsome protagonist, usually blond or redheaded, who is alienated from society by misfortunes of birth or personal convictions; (2) a villainous antagonist who provides the major opposition for the protagonist; (3) a loyal companion who understands and aids the protagonist; (4) several beautiful women who possess different feminine attributes but are all attracted to the protagonist; (5) one or more minority groups—Blacks, poor Whites, slaves, serfs, etc., who are oppressed by society; and (6) a significant historical focus—important historical events or issues.

Unlike the traditional romance hero who acts honorably in war and in love, the protagonists of Yerby's costume romances are not all brave men who achieve honor, fame and happiness. They are men or women whose visions are constantly in conflict with society. Struggling to secure a place for themselves in an alien culture, these outcasts suffer tremendously, they often remain alienated, and they usually win only Pyrrhic victories. They are sometimes forced to make decisions which result in their ruin or in injury to their families; and even when they make the right decisions, the choice is usually one of the lesser of two evils. In fact, Yerby's protagonists become rebel-victims of the societies into which they gain entrance. Sometimes ruthless, amoral and non-religious, they are anti-heroes who represent no social force or movement of a society but are concerned mainly with their own personal quest for identity in it.

In his study of heroes, Harold Lubin gives both a historical and generalized view of the anti-hero. Interpreting the modern emergence of the anti-hero as a reflection of the bitter aftermath of World War I, he sees anti-heroism as an impassioned rejection of old concepts—glory, honor and the holiness of war. Lubin provides perhaps the most flexible definition of the anti-hero:

> The anti-hero takes many forms. Sometimes he is a mockery of the old hero forms, a poor slob fumbling his way through life exposing the incongruity of the heroic stance in a non-heroic world. One thinks of an earlier version of such an anti-hero, Voltaire's Candide. The anti-hero may be heroic—even noble—in behavior, but this heroism is quixotic or desperate. He is a rebel, an outsider, like the Romantic hero, but he does not have the tyrant God of the Romantic hero to rebel against. There is only an abstract fate that toys with men as they wiggle desperately, like ants on a burning log—Hemingway's image—to avoid their ultimate fate—death.[3]

More descriptive of the Yerby anti-hero, however, are the characteristics of the unheroic hero in the picaresque novel. In his delineation of the characteristics of picaresque fiction, Ulrich Wicks describes the picaro as an unheroic protagonist who is:

"...a pragmatic, unprincipled, resilient, solitary figure who manages to survive in his chaotic landscape, but who in ups and downs can also put that world very much on the defensive. The picaro is a protean figure who cannot only serve many masters but play different roles, and his essential characteristic is inconsistency—of life roles, of self-identity...Through experience, too, the picaro develops a kind of internal gyroscope, what might be called a picaresque equilibrium—yet another paradox, as the inside-outside situation of the picaro socially is one."[4]

While both of these definitions may characterize other works of fiction, they are descriptive of Yerby's uses of the anti-heroic mode in that they both emphasize: (1) the impossibility of the traditional heroic ideal, (2) some variation on the theme of man's alienation in life and (3) a definite quest for self-identity in a world where achievement of individuality is at best difficult.

Even though Frank Yerby's novels incorporate a modern realistic perspective, they are, nonetheless, modifications of the conventional picaresque novel. Like the anti-romantic picaresque fiction of earlier centuries, Yerby's costume novels are implicitly satirical of the heroic ideal and contain two poles of interests—one, the protagonist and his adventures; the other, the manners of the society that the protagonist pillories.[5] Adhering to the pattern of the picaro, Yerby's protagonists are alienated by circumstances of birth or their past; they seek to establish themselves in an alien culture; and they always expect to accomplish their goals. Usually, however, they find very little that is permanent; for, either failing to know or disregarding the traditions of the societies they enter, these protagonists find themselves enmeshed in a series of conflicts and paradoxes. In the Yerby costume romance, the protagonist is similar to the archetypal American picaro whom Frederick Karl describes:

The American picaro ideally depends on no one; he hopes, in fact, to make the system bend to himself. He may or may not be rebellious. He is certainly different, and his quest is the mark of his individuality. His situation is usually paradoxical. To get what others seems to have (he can never be sure what it is), he tries to fit himself into ways that have worked for them. Put another way, he attempts all methods he deems necessary in order to obtain the goods of this world—and he pursues the means wherever they take him and regardless of the consequences.[6]

Like this American picaro, Yerby's protagonist denies the impossible and refuses to give up the pursuit of his goals. Consequently, he is always susceptible to the blows which fate will inevitably deal him. Even when he does achieve his desired goal, he often finds that he has won only a Pyrrhic victory.

Another trait of the Yerby anti-hero is that he is sometimes a ruthless opportunist. Rejecting the circumstances of his past life, he enters an alien culture as an outcast, and in that culture, he becomes both victimizer and victim. This anti-hero is an ambivalent character who both identifies with and rebels against society, in the manner of the contemporary anti-heroes of modern fiction. Or, in the case of most of the anti-heroes in Yerby's short fiction, they are oppressed and denied a respectable status in society, and they remain victims of oppression. Characteristically, the picaresque anti-hero in Yerby's costume novels does not represent any movement or cause in society; his primary concern is with his individual quest.[7]

Like the prototypical Existentialist hero, the Yerby anti-hero pits himself against the hostile forces of his environment. In his pursuit of the goal which will give meaning to his life, he reveals in actuality a life which lacks any real substance. Yerby's protagonist, however, differs from the Existentialist hero. He does maintain a sense of purpose and knows exactly what he wants or does not want. Usually, his identification with society is the avenue to his realization of the goal he seeks; but at the same time, he rebels against the restrictive morality and mores of that society, often remaining a marginal man. In addition, his disappointment with the goal he achieves in society frequently proves a source of further alienation.

Unlike the conventional romance hero, the protagonist in Yerby's novels is not always patriotic or heroic. He often engages in perilous adventures, but he finds neither glory or honor in them. Most Yerby protagonists, for example, express their disdain or hatred of war even though they fight heroically. Additionally, the Yerby anti-hero does not conform to any particular societal code. He is a visionary who, in his rise to success, victimizes all who stand between him and his goal; however, in the process of realizing his visions, he becomes himself a victim of society. He inherits the burden of the traditions of society and finds himself oscillating between tradition and individualism, alienation and opportunism, rebellion and acceptance. Constantly buffeted by fate in his pursuit of an elusive goal, he usually comes to accept in old age what he would have earlier refused. These distinct aspects of the characterization of the Yerby anti-heroic protagonist are recurrent in most of his novels. Essentially, they reveal the nature of the main genre pattern and the three patterns of characterization in his fiction: (1) mock-romance, (2) societal alienation, (3) amoral codes of behavior and (4) self-determined fate. In Yerby's fiction, some or all of these four distinct patterns constitute and illustrate his uses of the anti-heroic mode.

1. Yerby's Use of Mock-Romance

In his costume novels, Yerby incorporates many of the commonplace properties of the romance, but these properties become a tool. They are subsidiary to his main purpose, which is ultimately to present a philosophical or historical point of view. The protagonists in his novels are picaros who undertake exciting adventures, destroy their opposition physically or psychologically, dominate women and win recognition in an alien culture. Yerby described these romance elements of his novels in 1959 in a *Harper's Magazine* article entitled "How and Why I Write the Costume Novel." Accordingly, the Yerby protagonist is a "charming scoundrel, preferably with a dark secret in his past."[8] Apropos of romance conventions, he is attractive and daring, though often diabolically mysterious. He is an initiator of action who never resigns himself to his inevitable fate. The heroine of his novels, unless a protagonist, is less picaresque; she is usually a beautiful woman who is more inclined toward the romantic than is the protagonist. Sometimes she is the portrait of the female who is "at first unloved" but who will wait for years "to win our Johnathan."[9] Not only are the romance elements an essential part of the successful Yerby fiction formula, but according to him, they have always been a part of most successful popular novels.[10] Yet, the union of the picaresque and romance in his novels has an alternative purpose; there is implicit parody of the romance. As Ulrich Wicks has observed, "...the picaresque fictional world often parodies the social norm and the ideal harmony as well by including within itself anti-societies of rogues...."[11]

To solidify his position in society, Stephen Fox in *The Foxes of Harrow* (1946) joins the Confederate Army even though he knows that the South cannot match the superior manpower of the Union Army and that the South will gain very little in the war. Similarly, both Kit Gerado in *The Golden Hawk* (1948) and Ariston in *Goat Song* (1967) oppose war; but each is forced to participate in it to acquire citizenship. In *Pride's Castle* (1949) and *Captain Rebel* (1956), Pride Dawson and Tyler Meredith are embittered Southerners who join neither the Union or Confederate Armies; they both become pirate gun runners during the Civil War. Small but intelligent, Pietro Donati in *Saracen Blade* (1952) is a knighterrant in the Crusades of the thirteenth century, but one whose war tactics are unknightly because he uses deception and weapons that society considers unfair. Although initially meek, Alaric Teudisson in *An Odor of Sanctity* (1965) becomes a most feared warrior; however, war for him is not a question of honor or bravery but one of survival. In *The Dahomean* (1971), Nyasanu goes to war because of tradition and becomes a hero accidentally and foolhardily. Yet, he discovers that there is no glory in the actions of man, the cruelest of animals.

Like all satire, Yerby's parody of the romance vents the author's criticism. Yerby, who is philosophically opposed to war, is especially critical of it in his novels about war. In *Devil's Laughter* (1953), for example, Jean Marin views the French Revolution as a "tremendous parade of ideals which never in human history have worked, and never will, because man is forever greedy, grasping, vile, his heroism a comedy of errors, his dying robbed even of tragedy by its uselessness...."[12] Or, in the case of John Farrow in *The Voyage Unplanned* (1974), his extreme suffering motivates again and again his aversion to war. While there are innumerable incidents of violence and brutality in Yerby's novels, the anti-war attitude is always present. In some of his novels, this attitude is extended to other kinds of societal violence. It is especially prominent in the novels of the South where Yerby criticizes such traditions as the code of dueling and the brutal practices of white terrorist groups.

Another characteristic of the romance which Yerby mocks is the love-adventure theme. Usually, the conventional romance hero selects the one woman with whom he will live happily ever after, but Yerby's picaros are sometimes involved with as many as three females. Each male protagonist exemplifies the author's philosophy that no man can be satisfied in all his needs by just one woman. Commenting on this anti-romance element in his novels, Yerby said: "...the action of the costume novel's plot is carried forward by our hero's failure to realize that in any man's life there are literally dozens, if not hundreds, of women who will do just as well...."[13] In contrast to the male-female relationships in conventional romances, the liaisons in Yerby's costumes novels do not always end happily. When the protagonist wins the lady of his choice, he usually discovers "a most uninteresting variety of hell...."[14] Whereas the conventional romance hero is never disillusioned,[15] Yerby's protagonists often find unhappiness in marriage, or after achieving their goals. In *The Garfield Honor* (1961), for example, Roak Garfield succeeds in becoming one of the wealthiest men in Texas; but he alienates his wife and becomes responsible for the death of the woman he loves.

Strategically, the romance trappings in Yerby's costume novels constitute a part of the entertainment purpose of his fiction. Far from being the essence of his novels, however, the romance properties provide mostly pattern, color and appeal in his fiction. His heroes are not always sturdy, hardy and honest as romance heroes traditionally are,[16] for Yerby endows his characters with human qualities of fear, weakness, prejudice and stupidity. Offsetting the romance elements in each novel is the author's parody inspired by his modern realistic attitude. By creating protagonists with less magnanimity than that possessed by conventional romance heroes, he satirizes the norm of the romance. "Caught up in a chaotic world...in which he is on an eternal journey of encounters that allow him to be alternatively both victim of the world and its exploiter,"[17] the Yerby protagonist succeeds so dismally that his life is much less than romantic.

2. Societal Alienation As A Theme In Yerby's Fiction

Yerby emphasizes the fact that alienation has been a disintegrative force in earlier societies. Whether they are victims of circumstances of birth, class or caste, most protagonists in his novels begin as outcasts. Each strives to gain recognition in an alien culture, where he subsequently discovers another kind of alienation.

In *The Foxes of Harrow* (1946), Stephen Fox is an Irish gambler and immigrant who wins recognition among New Orleans aristocrats, but he can never totally accept their traditional Southern views. Laird Fournois in *The Vixens* (1947) is a Southerner who fights with the Union Army; when he returns to the South, he joins forces with those politically opposed to Southern traditions. Kit Gerado in *The Golden Hawk* (1948) is a man without a country. An ex-Confederate soldier, Pride Dawson in *Pride's Castle* (1949) must win recognition among the industrial tycoons of the North; and Ross Pary in *Floodtide* (1950) works to gain respect among the Mississippi planters but is disillusioned in that society. In *The Saracen Blade* (1952) Pietro Donati is the son of a blacksmith in the caste structure of thirteenth-century feudal society. Fancy Williamson is a South Carolina hillbilly and a former show wagon dancer who never quite lives down her past among Southern gentry in *A Woman Called Fancy* (1951). The son of a wealthy French merchant, Jean Marin in *The Devil's Laughter* (1953) is a revolutionist who works to destroy an entrenched eighteenth-century French aristocracy. In *Benton's Row* (1954), Tom Benton is a fugitive from justice in Texas, and in *Captain Rebel* (1956), Tyler Meredith is a Southerner who neither takes sides during the Civil War nor accepts the barbarism of the South after the war.

Although they may vary slightly, similar portrayals of the outsider characterize other Yerby novels. Guy Falks in *Fairoaks* (1957) is a displaced Southern aristocrat who strives to regain his status among Mississippi plantation owners. Duncan Childers in *The Serpent and the Staff* (1958) climbs from the cellar of New Orleans society to prominence as a physician, but he remains an outsider because he chooses to heal the poor. In *Jarrett's Jade* (1959), Scottish immigrant James Jarrett is a nobleman born into poverty and he seeks his fortune in America. Both Alaric Teudisson in *An Odor of Sanctity* (1965) and Ariston in *Goat Song* (1967) are foreigners who enter other cultures where they must win recognition. Peter Reynolds in *The Old Gods Laugh* (1964) is an American correspondent in the turbulent Caribbean, and Harry Forbes in *Speak Now* (1969) is a black American self-exiled in France. A French-born American, John Farrow in *The Voyage Unplanned* (1974) is an American intelligence agent during World War II who develops strong Jewish sympathies.

3. Amoral Codes of Behavior in Yerby's Fiction

Since the picaros in Yerby's novels usually begin as outsiders in an alien society, they desire to win a place in that society. Yerby's protagonists, however, govern themselves not by societal rules but by their own codes of conduct. Thus, even after they have carved their niche in society, they live continually on the fringes of that society's standards. Philosophically, these protagonists illustrate Yerby's conviction that one does not achieve success by conforming to societal ethics but by possessing strength and intelligence and the willingness to use these in pursuit of desired ends. His protagonists operate on the assumption that "every man who isn't a fool makes his own rules, constructs his own morality."[18] However, since the protagonist's successful achievement of his goal depends on the extent to which he is willing to conform to some traditions of that alien culture, it is usually his conformity, or role-playing, which leads to his becoming a victim. He is a rebel in society, not only in his own personal code but in his refusal to subscribe totally to the views of that society. Therefore, Yerby's portrayal of the rebel-victim of society illustrates, if nothing else, his contention that "Morality is a set of rules set up by society to protect itself."[19]

In most of Yerby's novels, the amoral codes to which his picaresque anti-heroes adhere are readily observable. Typically, the protagonists are almost always charming scoundrels who live by codes of behavior in conflict with those of society. Irish immigrant Stephen Fox in *The Foxes of Harrow* (1946) wins a fortune in land from a German planter, kills him in a duel and assists the planter's widow and children in moving to Philadelphia. He adds to his fortune by cheating his future father-in-law and swindling the flatboatman who transports merchandise on the Mississippi River. In *The Golden Hawk* (1948), Kit Gerado amasses his wealth by sea privacy. Pride Dawson in *Pride's Castle* (1949) marries the daughter of a robber baron to obtain his first million, and after he loses it, he swindles his business associates to gain the second million. Guy Falks in *Fairoaks* (1957) acquires his wealth as a slave runner; Tyler Meredith in *Captain Rebel* (1956) becomes rich by running guns to the Confederate and Union Armies during the Civil War; and James Jarrett in *Jarrett's Jade* (1959) makes his money running liquor in Georgia. In *Benton's Row* (1945), Tom Benton, a fugitive outlaw, invades a traveling minister's Louisiana farm, seduces his wife and steals her and the farm. Hired by Mexican General Valles to build a road in Mexico, Engineer Roger Blake steals the general's wife in "The General's Road."[20] In *Goat Song* (1967) Ariston almost rapes his mother, kills the girl who informs on him and becomes responsible for the death of his mother and father. A prostitute in the New Orleans Red Light District, heroine Fanny Turner in *The Girl from Storyville* (1972) marries an aging Louisiana planter to achieve respectability. Other Yerby protagonists adhere to similar codes of behavior. Always ambitious, they demonstrate that it is by selfish use of individual attributes that one succeeds, not by being virtuous or altruistic.

4. Will Versus Fate In Yerby's Fiction

Yerby subscribes to the view that man must be a self-reliant individual, one who in actuality determines his own outcome in life. With neither a God nor a system of ethics on which he can depend, Yerby concludes, man must depend on his own capabilities. In the spirit of social Darwinism, therefore, the individual must rely on his own strength and intelligence and his willingness to use these attributes in the achievement of desired goals in society. In his pursuit of his goal, he assumes any role that the world forces upon him, disregarding both ethics and societal mores. Otherwise, the individual suffers for his weaknesses, stupidity or defenselessness. This philosophy is, according to Yerby, "a new theory of law: the guilt of the victim. That sheep have no rights. That when they tempt the lion by being sheep, it is they, not he, who sin!"[21] Yerby illustrates, however, that man is susceptible to the blows of an abstract fate which is referred to variously as chance, luck, God and destiny.

Thus, the individual struggles constantly against a blind fate; but if God, fate or chance is indifferent to man's desires or actions, the individual's struggle is ultimately with himself. For the protagonists in Yerby's novels, therefore, the struggle in life becomes a matter of exercising one's individual will. It is the fighter, not the docile individual, who gains respect in society.[22] The success of each of Yerby's protagonists depends on the effectiveness with which they use their strength and intelligence, even though their lives may be affected by numerous incidents and coincidences. In essence, the Yerby protagonist knows "that a man's salvation is always within himself; that, and the sown dragon's teeth of his own destruction. He can will either...."[23]

In *Floodtide* (1950), for example, Ross Pary allows himself to become an unwilling partner in the crimes of the psychotic Morgan Brittany. He is fascinated by the voluptuous but cruel Morgan, and because of his curious attraction for her, he watches her destroy his brother, his sister, his best friend and her husband and several slaves. Similarly, Alaric Teudisson in *An Odor of Sanctity* (1956) suffers throughout his adult life because of his inability to rid himself of his feelings for Clothilde. In love with her since his adolescence, he becomes a victim of her exploits, allowing her to destroy his brother, divert him from marrying Zoe and trap him into marriage to her. John Farrow in *The Voyage Unplanned* (1974) develops an undying love for Simon Levy, a Jewish woman in the French Resistance movement, and he allows his memory of her to destroy his marriage.

In some novels, Yerby sets his protagonists within cultures in which a belief in fate is indigenous. Greece and Dahomey, for example, are the cultures treated in *Goat Song* (1967) and *The Dahomean* (1971). Within these cultures, there is the belief that some unknown force, divine and all-powerful, controls the events in the lives of men. As might be expected, these novels appear more credible than other novels in which Yerby simply imposes fate. The characters in these novels do not determine what they do; therefore, the reader does not hold them responsible for their actions. In *Goat Song*, (1967), the events in Ariston's life are acceptable because one knows that his predestined fate is to be banished from his country. In the first part of the novel, his attempt to steal a goat leads to his falling in love with Phryne, his watching a mob of women stone and butcher her, his murdering the woman leader of the mob and his killing the man who discovers his act of murder: all of these predetermined actions contribute to his leaving Sparta. Similarly, in *The Dahomean* (1971), Nyasanu's fate is clouded when his jealous brother destroys his fate-watcher tree. His fate is subsequently revealed as the destiny to live two lives, one in Dahomey and one in a foreign land; and the events of the novel move the protagonist toward the fulfillment of his destiny. Because Nyasanu saves his king's life, the king gives him a wife, who becomes responsible finally for his being sold into slavery in America.

In some ways, the anti-heroes in Yerby's costume fiction resemble other contemporary anti-heroes who wrestle to overcome forces within their environment and within themselves. Unlike many twentieth-century anti-heroes who struggle to achieve their individuality, Yerby's historical protagonists experience little difficulty in maintaining their identity. Even though his characters are victims of a blind fate that toys with the lives of men, they never lose their sense of purpose and they maintain visions of their original goals. Only in old age does the Yerby protagonist give up his dream; for by then he has come to realize that "Life dulls all things, destroys all things finally, batters down our youth into age, our strength into fatigue, our hope into hopelessness, until we finally come to accept death."[24]

These four discernible patterns in Yerby's novels constitute the anti-heroic perspective in his fiction. Both the fictional patterns and the traits of characterization reveal the philosophical notions undergirding the semi-romance of his novels. The unheroic hero denotes not only Yerby's skepticism about the heroic ideals of the traditional romance, but also the modern realistic perspective he incorporates in his costume fiction. Alienation, his novels suggest, is one of the ever-present disintegrative forces of society, whether past or present. Almost all of Yerby's protagonists illustrate his philosophical view that man's actions in society have been governed by his own strength and intelligence and his use of these, not by false ethics or principles. Finally, Yerby creates amoral characters because he believes that they, not the glorifications of historians, represent the actual images of mankind.

Notes

[1]Darwin T. Turner, "Frank Yerby as Debunker," *Massachusetts Review* (Summer, 1968), 570.

[2]Kenneth Keniston, "Alienation and the Decline of Utopia," *American Scholar*, 29 (Spring, 1960), 161.

[3]Harold Lubin, *Heroes and Anti-Heroes* (San Francisco, 1968), p. 311.

[4]Ulrick Wicks, "The Nature of the Picaresque Narrative: A Modal Approach," *PMLA*, 89 (March, 1974), 245.

[5]Frank Chandler, *The Literature of Roguerry*, Vol. I, (Boston, 1907), p. 5.

[6]Frederick R. Karl, "Picaresque and the American Experience," *Yale Review*, 57 (Winter, 1968), 200.

[7]Roger B. Rollins, *Hero/Anti-Hero* (New York, 1973), p. XVII.

[8]Yerby, "How and Why I Write the Costume Novel," *Harper's*, 219 (October, 1959), 146.

[9]Ibid., p. 147

[10]Ibid., p. 146.

[11]Wicks, "The Nature of the Picaresque Narrative," 245.

[12]*The Devil's Laughter* (New York, 1953), p. 206. Subsequent Yerby novels will be cited by titles only.

[13]"How and Why I Write the Costume Novel," p. 147.

[14]Ibid., p. 147

[15]Gillian Beer, *The Romance*, (London, 1970), p. 40.

[16]Brander Matthews, *The Historical Novel and Other* Essays (New York, 1901), p. 44.

[17]Wicks, "The Nature of the Picaresque Narrative," 242.

[18]*The Girl for Storyville*, p. 334.

[19]Ibid., p. 336.

[20]An unpublished Yerby short story, "The General's Road."

154 Perspectives of Black Popular Culture

Griffin's Way (New York, 1962), p. 118.
[22]Ibid., p. 118.
[23]*Gillian*, (New York, 1960), p. 176.
[24]*The Devil's Laughter*, p. 227.

Black America and the Black South African Literary Consciousness

Emmanuel S. Nelson

Literary influence appears to be most frequent and most fruitful at the times of emergence of national literatures...[when] authors may seek [from foreign sources] that which they can adopt or transmute for their own consciousness, time or nation.

——Joseph Shaw

Models come from your encountering a work in which you recognize a kinship, and that helps you.

——Galway Kinnel

Although Janheinz Jahn's *Neo-African Literature* (1968) has established a sound theoretical foundation for comparative studies in African diaspora literatures, the comparative approach still remains marginalized in the African, Afro-Carribbean and Afro-American critical practice. Critics, in general, are engaged more extensively in the tasks of establishing, defining and analyzing national and regional black literary traditions than in constructing coherent frameworks to study those traditions in comparative contexts. Such a tendency, sadly, has served to de-emphasize the cultural links, the spiritual affinities and the unifying racial memories that connect the peoples of the African diaspora. There are some encouraging signs, however. Recent publication of works such as Henry Louis Gates' *Black Literature and Literary Theory* and Bonnie Barthold's *Black Time*—works which seek to establish meaningful lateral connections among the various national literatures that articulate the Black Experience—suggest a slowly growing interest in comparative critical practice.

My paper has an explicit comparative objective; it attempts to examine the significance of black America in the context of black South African literary consciousness. More specifically, it examines the impact of the revolutionary literature and culture of black America on the artistic imaginations and ideological stances of four representative black south African writers. Since the list of black writers in Africa's Deep South is too long and includes many prolific writers, such as Peter Abrahams, Alex LaGuma, John Dube, Ezekiel Mphahlele, Richard Rive, James Matthews, Oswald Mtshali, Sidney Sepamla, Wally Serote, Keorapetse Kgositsile, Stanley Motjuwadi, Mafika Gwala, among others, I have limited my discussion to four artists. Included are two writers from the first generation of committed and articulate South African black writers—Peter Abrahams and Ezekiel Mphahlele—and two writers of the new generation of artists who sensibilities have been shaped by the brutalities and uncertainties of the post-Sharpeville era: Wally Serote and Keorapetse Kgositsile. The selection of these writers over the others is based primarily on three considerations: the representative nature of their works, their stature within the South African literary tradition and the international recognition of their works.

The receptivity of the black South African writers to Afro-American influence is at least partly due to their perception of significant similarities between their own experience—historical as well as contemporary—and that of American blacks. Both groups share a racial heritage; both bear the burdens of their colonial inheritance; both are familiar with the dehumanizing realities of a racist society; both have long histories of violent contact with whites; and both face a compelling need to affirm their blackness in the face of raw white assault. Mphahlele eloquently articulates the response of many black South Africans to Afro-Americans:

Nowhere in Africa does one find such a strong fellow-feeling towards the American black as there exists among the Africans of South Africa. How else could it be? The African in South Africa and the Afro-American have both suffered from and endured white arrogance and their history written in in blood: it is a history of pillage and plunder; fire and murder; dispossession and humiliation (*The African Image* 96).

But one should also acknowledge the vast differences between the two groups. They differ in their numerical strength: less than twelve percent of the United States population is African in origin, whereas nearly three-fourths of the South African population is black. The sheer numerical superiority of the black South Africans enhances the racial and economic insecurities of the whites who respond with brutal methods of repression to maintain their privileged status. And substantial differences in the structures of American and South African political systems render the conditions of blacks in the two countries radically different. American democracy, despite its imperfections, has always provided space for dissent and in the last three decades has demonstrated remarkable legislative flexibility to accommodate the legitimate demands of its minority citizens. But enshrined in the Constitution of the Republic of South Africa is a Nazi-style racist ideology; the reactionary nature of the South African judiciary and legislative bodies stifles political dissent and renders almost impossible any meaningful movement toward progressive, non-violent change. The prevailing political conditions in both countries account for the differences in the socioeconomic situations of black Americans and black South Africans. For example, in contrast to black South Africans, their counterparts in the United States are a powerful group: they are largely literate; they enjoy, relatively speaking, a high standard of living; they have a substantial middle-class that is influential and articulate; they have thousands of elected public officials and hundreds who hold key positions in the American power structure; and they have, especially because of their spectacular successes in the sports arena and in the entertainment industry, become a dominant force in international culture. Also, absent in black America are the tribal fragmentations and accompanying inter-tribal hostilities and suspicions which continue to debilitate black political resistance in South Africa. The relative cohesiveness of black Americans has enabled them to make major gains in their civil rights struggle.

The similarities which the politically aware black South African perceives between himself and his American counterparts are likely to generate in him at least a vague sense of emotional identification. However, what captures his imagination is the crucial difference that exists: the considerable political clout and cultural power that blacks are perceived to enjoy in the United States. The coherently orchestrated militancy which black Americans displayed during the sixties and the quiet assertiveness they have shown more recently appeal to the black South African consciousness. The largely successful Afro-American struggle for civil rights provides the black South Africans with an exemplary model for personal and collective liberation. The militant assertiveness of the modern Afro-American consciousness inspires the black South African whose fundamental dilemmas are not unlike those of his trans-Atlantic counterparts. Of course, as one might expect, the influence of black America is more extensive on those detribalized urban black South Africans who have some level of literacy and who possess a self-conscious awareness of the political implications of their blackness. The Afro-American influence is particularly strong on those who are politically active; hence its manifestation is most prominent in the black South African political arena where its function is largely inspirational. Since many of the black South African artists are urban, racially aware and politically informed individuals, they constitute the group that is most likely to be receptive to black American influence.

Before we can grasp the impact of Black America on the consciousness of individual writers, we need to understand the substantial interaction between black America and black South Africa that has taken place in last few decades. Though personal contacts have often been limited to an occasional black American missionary, to intellectuals and artists at international conferences, and to students and teachers from South Africa on American campuses, indirect contact between the two groups is surprisingly extensive.

The means of such contacts have largely been American books, magazines, movies and music. Despite the government's strict enforcement of its censorship statutes, South African blacks, especially on university campuses, have access to a fairly wide range of Afro-American texts. Although the South African educational system is decidedly and deliberately Eurocentric in its focus, an interested reader can find at least some of the books by Langston Hughes, Richard Wright and James Baldwin. While some American magazines, such as *Ebony* that celebrate black achievement are banned, South Africans do have access to a wide range of popular periodicals form the United States, many of which include at least some coverage of Afro-American life. Movies and television shows are yet another source of contact that has introduced a variety of black American celebrities—from Mr. T. to Eddie Murphy to Whoppi Goldberg—to South African audiences. But an even more significant Afro-American cultural importation is music: jazz and the blues. American jazz idiom has not only been superbly adapted by many South African musicians, such as Hugh Masekela, Letta Mbulu, Jonas Gwangwa and Caiphus Semenya, but it has also become an identifiable element of a good deal of the post-Sharpeville urban black poetry.

The most enduring and nourishing form of Afro-American influence, however, is ideological. Almost since the beginning of the twentieth century black American political thought has exerted a demonstrable influence on black South Africa; since then American blacks have served as a political reference group for South African activists. The National Association for the Advancement of Colored People (NAACP), for example, initially served as a model for South African blacks attempting to organize themselves politically. John Dube, a co-founder of the subsequently outlawed African National Congress (ANC), was profoundly influenced by the political philosophy of Booker T. Washington (*Soweto Poetry* 162). In the mid-fifties the landmark Supreme Court decision in the Brown vs. The Board of Education case, which led to the desegregation of public school systems, as well as the widely publicized and ultimately successful Montgomery bus boycott under the leadership of the Rev. Martin Luther King generated considerable interest among South African blacks. During the sixties the South African media substantially—perhaps inadvertently—enhanced black awareness of the civil rights struggles in the United States. It is likely that the newspaper and television reports, though censored, of the increasingly violent black revolt in America had an emotional impact on black South Africans.

"But never had social and political ideas originating in black America been subject to as wide and searching scrutiny as the ideas emanating in the 'Black Power' aftermath of the civil rights movement" (Gerhart 275). Eldridge Cleaver's *Soul on Ice*, Stokely Carmichael and Charles Hamilton's *Black Power*, the works of James Cone and other black American theologians gave further impetus to the substance as well as the style of black South African nationalism (Gerhart 275). Among organizations that borrowed ideas and strategies from the American Black Power movement are South African Student Organization, Black People's Convention and numerous outlawed cells of the African National Congress. Many young black nationalist leaders, such as Steve Biko, began to articulate their racial outrage in rhetoric that was almost identical to that of the American Black Power activists. Characteristically Afro-American expressions such as "Uncle Tom" and "Black Is Beautiful" began to appear with insistent regularity in the speeches and writings of many young and angry black South Africans.

A particularly important element of this radical rhetoric imported form the United States is the word *black* itself. As Gail Gerhart argues in *Black Power in South Africa*, the importation of this word led to a "terminological revolution" (277). A term that became popular among Afro-Americans during the sixties, it was made fashionable by the Black Power rhetoric of racial self-affirmation and cultural assertiveness. It was a word that had traditionally carried a cluster of negative connotations in the Western context; but it was redeemed and made wholesome by a supreme act of linguistic and cultural reappropriation. And it was used to refer not simply to a color but to a condition; it did not merely suggest a biological inheritance but a political reality. This broad definition proved particularly useful in South Africa where it became an inclusive signifier for the Africans, the "Coloureds" and the Indians, as an affirming word to counter the negation implied in the official South African designation of "non-White." By forging a "conceptual regrouping" (281) of the three divided and dispossessed groups into a single, broad category, the word *black* helped generate—at least in a small measure—a sense of political solidarity among them.

It is in the context of such significant connections between black America and black South Africa that one has to examine the Afro-American influence on individual black South African artists. All of the four writers to be discussed—Peter Abrahams, Ezekiel Mphahlele, Wally Serote and Keorapetse Kgositsile—evince some degree of responsiveness to black American cultural influence. This influence, however, tends to be primarily psychological; direct literary influence, though it does occur, is generally minor.

Peter Abrahams, one of the first writers from Africa to gain international attention, acknowledges the liberating effect of Afro-American literature on his own private quest for a healing sense of self in a savagely racist culture. In his poignant autobiography, *Tell Freedom*, Abrahams speaks of his excitement when he first heard Paul Robeson's rich voice on a phonograph at the Bantu Men's Social Centre in Johannesburg (224). It was there he also discovered Afro-American literature. Works such as *The Souls of Black Folk, Up from Slavery, Along This Way, The Black Christ*, and *The New Negro* helped him forge a sense of affinity with those across the Atlantic who, like him, "were black, dispossessed, and denied" (224-25). To W.E.B. DuBois he attributes his discovery of "a key to the understanding" (226) of his black reality. Langston Hughes' poetry inspires him; Claude McKay's famous sonnet "If We Must Die" stirs him "to aggressiveness pride" (229); Georgia Douglas Johnson enables him to celebrate "the blackness of [his] mother and sister" (230); and Jean Toomer moves him "to the verge of tears" (230). He becomes "a nationalist, a colour nationalist through the writings of men and women who lived a world away" (230). He declares, "To them I owe a great debt for crystalizing my vague yearnings to write and for showing me the long dream was possible" (230).

Black American literature not only helps Abrahams discover himself and to formulate a valid political philosophy but it also substantially influences his early writing. As Mphahlele comments, *Dark Testament*,

Abrahams' first collection of short sketches and stories, is "indeed also a testament of his Afro-American literary legacy" (*The African Image* 97). Abrahams' first collection of poems, *A Blackman Speaks of Freedom!*, reveals that he has not only mastered the jazz synocapations of Langston Hughes' poetry but that he has also, with considerrable success, learned to employ Hughes' famous device of 'naming' and his imagistic technique of 'saturation' (Chapman 203). His early novels, especially *Songs of the City* and *Mine Boy*, show the unmistakable impact of Richard Wright's naturalistic techniques.

Ezekiel Mphahlele's familiarity with Afro-American literature and culture is even more extensive than that of Abrahams'. He first visited the United States in 1960 when he came to Philadelphia to attend a conference of the American Society of Culture. He holds a Ph.D. in English from the University of Denver; he has taught courses in creative writing and in Black literatures both at Denver and at the University of Pennsylvania.

He has numerous literary ties with the United States. For example, in his recent autobiography *Africa My Music*, he talks about his "discovery" of Richard Wright's *Uncle Tom's Cabin*: "I smelled our own poverty in his Southern setting. The long searing black song of Wright's people sounded like ours" (18). It is Wright, says Mphahlele, who inspried him to use writing "as a way of dealing with my anger and indignation" (18). Mphahlele began to correspond with Langston Hughes in 1954; Hughes sent him a copy of his anthology of short stories, *The Ways of White Folks*, and a collection of his poems, *The Weary Blues*. In a "gentle and almost unobtrusive manner," declares Mphahlele, "Langston's short fiction and poetry did things to me" (19). Yet another Afro-American writer whom he greatly admires is Gwendolyn Brooks; in fact, the title of his essays, *Voices in the Whirlwind*, which he dedicates to Brooks, comes from one of her poems.

Mphahlele's enthusiasm for American music is even greater. In *Exiles and Homecomings* he states,

Jazz: that was once a favorite pastime of mine in the United States. Even today my scrapbooks of those years still contain a wealth of oddments, newspaper clippings, photographs, and obituaries of outstanding black musicians. The music, the blues idiom, had so much to say that was close to the bone, the pulse of my own experience and that of my people (254).

He has a special liking for Billy Holliday's blues. Nina Simone's lyrics, he says, "sink deep and chill my marrow" (135), while Dinah Washington's music "bores into me like a corkscrew" (137).

Despite his extensive familiarity with Afro-American literature and culture, his works reveal little direct influence. This absence of any palpable black American impact may be attributed to the fact that Mphahlele senses a certain personal disconnection from the Afro-American experience. He candidly admits in *Chirundu*,

I could identify intellectually and emotionally with the black American's condition, but I could not in any tangible, particular way *feel* his history (vii).

Africa, to him, is still the "home" and it is Africa that dominates his political awareness and shapes his literary sensibility.

Like Mphahlele, Wally Serote—a major figure in the Soweto Renaissance—has interesting American connections. He holds a degree in fine arts from Columbia University and, with support from the African Studies Center of the Boston University, has travelled extensively in the United States. His informed interest in Afro-American experience is evident in some of his interviews and works. In a conversation with Michael Chapman, Serote states that his familiarity with the Afro-American struggle has sharpened his racial awareness and has made urgent his personal need to come to terms with his South African roots (114). In his praise song titled "The Seed and the Saints" he includes his Afro-American heroes:

> I have been a look after
> black seed; by black saints and prophets
> by Sobukwe Mandela Sisulu
> Fanon Malcolm X George Jackson (*Tsetlo*, 29).

While he is inspired by the model of Afro-American resistance, it is Afro-American music that influences his poetry. The patterns of repetition, refrain and staccato syncopation in poems such as "Jo'burg City" clearly reveal the influence of jazz. Even more telling is the influence of Negro spirituals in his poem, "Hell, Well, Heaven":

> I do not know where I have been
> But brother
> I know I'm coming.
> I do not know where I have been,
> But brother
> I know I heard the call.
> Hell! Where I was i cried silently
> Yet I sat there until now.
> I do not know where I have been
> But brother
> I know I'm Coming (*Soweto Poetry* 158).

Serote's interest in the blues is evident in his novel *To Every Birth Its Blood*. The blues shapes the thematic as well as the narrative structures of the novel. Clearly one of the greatest contributions of Afro-Americans to world culture, the blues is an art form that has evolved out of the Africans' nightmarish experience in America. A uniquely Afro-American creative expression, the blues is a musical articulation of private anguish. Ralph Ellison defines the term most eloquently:

The blues is an impulse to keep the painful details and episodes of a brutal experience alive in one's aching consciousness, to finger its jagged grain, and to transcend it, not by the consolation of philosophy but by squeezing from its near-tragic, near-comic lyricism. As a form the blues is an autobiographical chronicle of personal catastrophe expressed lyrically (78-79).

To Every Birth Its Blood, set in the turbulent Alexandra Township outside Johannesburg, deals with lives broken by apartheid. Serote uses the blues to define the protagonist's feelings of anguish and to reinforce the theme of alienation that is central to the novel. Interwoven into narrative are bits of the blues songs that poignantly underscore the protagonist's personal pain. The novel is replete with references to numerous black American singers: John Coltrane, Jimmy Garrison, McCoy Tyner, Nina Simone, Roy Haynes, Miles Davis, Gladys Knight. Their music articulates the protagonist's own emotions; he feels a ready affinity with the chaos and despair out of which the music emerges to give shape to pain. The music has "taught" him "so much" (79) and it has been "revealing so many things" (196) that he did not know.

In addition to emphasizing the theme of despair and alienation, the blues shapes the structure of the novel as well. In fact, *To Every Birth Its Blood* can indeed be viewed as an extended blues song. For example, the novel, like the blues, is narrated in the first person and it is cast in the autobiographical-confessional mode. The narratorial stance of the central character, like that of the blues artist, is one of tragi-comic detachment. Just as a blues singer, the narrator explores his painful condition and shares the details of his anguish with the audience. A blues song, while it gives aesthetic shape to the singer's suffering, never ends on an unrealistic note of falsely romantic optimism; on the contrary, it concludes on a note of victory by bringing pain under control by boldly confronting it. Like a classic piece of the blues, Serote's novel ends on a note of triumph: the blood-stained baby emerging out of the womb triumphantly affirms life in the midst of death and asserts continuity in the face of chaos.

Perhaps the South African writer who identifies most strongly with the Afro-American experience is Keorapetse Kgositsile. Born in Johannesburg in 1938, Kgositsile first arrived in the United States in the early sixties. He attended Pennsylvania's Lincoln University, a predominantly black institution, and subsequently enrolled at Columbia University. His sense of personal and political identification with black Americans was probably enhanced by the fact that he was in the United States during the sixties and, therefore, was able to witness the civil rights struggles. His personal friendships with Afro-American writers such as Gwendolyn Brooks, Don Lee and Amiri Baraka also must have heightened his feeling of solidarity with black America.

Black Americans, in turn, have reciprocated Kgositsile's admiration. His volume of poetry, *Spirits Unchained*, was published by the black-owned Broadside Press founded by Dudley Randall; the book won the prestigious

Conrad Kent Rivers Prize from *Black World*. His subsequent books, too, were published by black-owned presses in the United States. And his poems are frequently anthologized in volumes of Afro-American verse.

Kgositsile's enthusiasm for the militant Afro-American literature of the sixties—especially for the works of Larry Neal, Nikki Giovanni, Amiri Baraka and others—is evident in the "agit-prop" quality of his poetry as well as prose and in his easy command of the hip rhythms of black American English. The following passage, taken from Kgositsile's introduction to his collection of poems titled *For Melba*, could have been easily written by Amiri Baraka or Hewey Newton:

Brother, manhood is not about being supercool and how many dizzy chicks have their noses wide open behind whatever game you're running. It ain't about how many chicks you can lay in a week either. Most of us have been that route and it's shaky like a bitch! Sister, a bitch under a huge Afro is still a bitch and the longest African-print dress couldn't cover up that fact either (3).

The extent of his awareness of experiential connections between Africans and Afro-New World blacks is evident in his strategy of juxtaposing the African and Afro-American references; for example, he speaks of "Patrice and Malcolm," "Meadowland and Harlem Streets," "Sophiatown and Harlem," "Watts and Sharpeville," "Don Lee and Maizi Kunene," "Ayi Kwei and Gwendolyn Brooks," "Malcolm and the brothers in Robben Island." Such a strategy not only underscores Kgositsile's own broad pan-African political consciousness but it also reflects the poet's attempt to bridge the trans-Atlantic chasm by sharply focusing on the shared dispossession and the common resistance of blacks everywhere.

The fierce, earthy and angry tone of much of Kgositsile's poetry makes it almost indistinguishable from the works of many of his Afro-American contemporaries. His use of words such as "fuck," "bullshit," "motherfucker," "faggot," "asshole"—terms generally alien to African poetry in English— is also symptomatic of the influence of what J. F. Povey calls "the obligatory scatology of some black American writing" (52).

While it is obvious that many black South African writers evince at least some measure of responsiveness to the Afro-American model, I do not wish to suggest that all of them have an uncritical admiration for black America. Mphahlele, for example, finds the tendency among some Afro-Americans to romanticize Africa "irritating" and refers to such individuals as "a huge trans-Atlantic joke" (*The African Image* 102). He believes that many black Americans are incapable of connecting with Africa in any meaningful way and he confesses his own inability to *feel* the Afro-American history. He also expects little concrete assistance form Afro-Americans in the liberationist struggle of blacks in South Africa. Pascal Gwala, a prominent figure in the Soweto literary scene, expresses resentment of black American influence on black South Africa; he calls such influence "imperialist" (*Soweto Poetry* 174). Serote tries to trivialize the influence of black America on his works by asserting that the only Americanisms in his works are words such as "bullshit" and "motherfucker" (*Soweto Poetry* 114). He also dismisses his extensive travels in the United States as "a waste of time" (*Soweto Poetry* 114).

This unwillingness on the part of Serote to explore in any detailed manner the Afro-American influence on his personality and works is evident among quite a few, especially younger, black South African artists. This reluctance is understandable, since influence many sometimes imply paucity of creative originality. Such an anxiety, though understandable, is unfounded; after all, event he greatest writers have freely acknowledged their indebtedness—psychological as well as intellectual—to other writers. The reluctance may also reflect certain nationalist sensitivity: As Ali Mazrui points out, it is "in the nature of nationalism to be inhibited in acknowledging a debt to foreign inspiration" (119). Of course, what appears to be an unwillingness to admit influence could be merely unawareness: the writer being influenced may not be always consciously aware of it. The influence of the blues on Serote's *To Every Birth Its Blood* is more likely to be an unconscious than a conscious process.

While the degree of Afro-American influence on the general *Weltanshuung* of the four writers examined varies, there are certain sharp similarities in their basic responses to black America. All of them recognize a striking parallel between their own experience and that of their counterparts in the United States. All four writers are inspired by the Afro-American model of political resistance and they view black Americans as an effectively organized and militantly assertive minority group. The influence of black America on some of the writers (e.g., Ezekiel Mphahlele) is primarily psychological, while on some others (e.g., Abrahams, Serote, Kgositsile) it is literary as well. All of them cite individual black Americans—musicians, writers, political activists—whom they admire: Malcolm X, Langston Hughes, Richard Wright, Gwendolyn Brooks, Ray Charles, John Coltrane, Charlie Parker, Sterling Brown, Amiri Baraka, Claude McKay, Georgia Douglas Johnson, Booker T. Washington, W.E.B. DuBois, Billy Holliday, among others. What is worth noting is the fact that many of these black Americans are/were activists with a radical and uncompromising commitment to racial justice. Hence it is clear that the trait that black South Africans most frequently associate with and admire in Afro-Americans is their assertive resistance to oppression. It is the power that blacks are perceived to command in American culture and society that most strongly inspires the political consciousness of black South Africans and influences their literary sensibility.

Acknowledgment

I wish to thank the SUNY-Cortland Faculty Research Program for a generous grant during the summer of 1988 that made research for this paper possible.

Works Cited

Abrahams, Peter. *Tell Freedom*. New York: Knopf, 1954.

Chapman, Michael. Ed. *Soweto Poetry*. Johannesburg: McGraw-Hill, 1982.

Gerhart, Gail M. *Black Power in South Africa*. Berkeley: University of California Press, 1978.

Kgositsile, Keorapetse. *For Melba*. New York: Third World Press, 1969.

Monganyi, Chabani N. *Exiles and Homecomings*. Johannesburg: Raven Press, 1983.

Mphahlele, Ezekiel. *Africa My Music*. Johannesburg: Raven Press, 1986.

_____ *The African Image*. New York: Praeger, 1974.

_____ *Chirundu*. Westport: Lawrence Hill & Co., 1979.

_____ *Voices in the Whirlwind and Other Essays*. New York: Hill & Wang, 1972.

Povey, J. F. "Intentions in African Poetry: Keorapetse Kgositsile's 'My Name Is Africa.' " Typescript at Ryder College Library, New Jersey.

Serote, Wally, *To Every Birth Its Blood*. London: Heinemann, 1981.

_____ *Tsetlo*. Johannesburg: Ad. Donker, 1974.

The Weight of Sambo's Woes

Joseph Bodziock

In 1853 an unsympathetic reviewer from *Graham's Magazine* declared that he was weary of reading the narratives of American slaves. "The whole literary atmosphere has become tainted," the reviewer insisted, with "those literary nigritudes—little tadpoles of the press—which run to editions of hundreds of thousands" (215). The numbers were no exaggeration, and more narratives were yet to come. The plaint of the *Graham's* reviewer, beyond its literary and racial elitism, revealed two fundamental and remarkable truths: that at an opportune moment in American history, black Americans had raised their literary voices from a whisper to a roar, and that white Americans—throughout their history so deeply troubled by the presence of blacks and blackness—had nonetheless chosen to listen, so much so that the reviewer could complain that "The shelves of the booksellers groan under the weight of Sambo's woes, done up in covers" (209). It was indeed a noteworthy day in our history when a literary reviewer could complain about a glut of black American literature.

Autobiographical narratives written by American slaves had existed since the latter half of the 18th century, beginning with Briton Hammon's 1760 narrative. With Olaudah Equiano's 1789 narrative—an early best-seller—the writers began to attack the institution of slavery, culminating in the unbridled and unapologetic attacks that would mark the narratives written in the thirty years before the advent of the Civil War.

The two remarkable aspects of the narratives' popularity are their longevity and the number of editions that they sold. The ante-bellum narratives were popular for nearly thirty years, and if we include well-read early narratives, such as that of Equiano, the narratives captivated readers for over seventy years. Equiano's narrative, in fact, was still selling well fifty years after its initial publication, having gone through at least ten editions by 1837 (Nichols 150).

Other narratives did as well or better. Douglass's 1845 narrative, for example, became the greatest seller in narrative history, going through seven editions in four years, and eventually being translated into most European languages. Three years after its initial publication Douglass's narrative had run through nine editions in England; by 1850 it had sold 30,000 copies (Starling 36). The reception for his narrative was strong enough that in 1855 Douglass, stung by critics who questioned his decision to leave out certain details from his 1845 text, published *My Bondage and My Freedom*, the most richly textured of all the narratives, which was "enthusiastically reviewed," and "netted its author a splendid financial return" (Nichols 151). Josiah Henson's work (1858) reached 6,000 copies by 1852, and as the apocryphal tale circulated that Henson was the model for Stowe's Uncle Tom, Henson and his publishers prepared a "Stowe Edition." That narrative included an introduction by Stowe, and in 1858 it had gathered advance orders of 5,000 copies. A later (1878) edition of Henson's life claimed that 100,000 copies of that Stowe edition had been sold (Nichols 150). All told approximately 32 narratives became popular sellers (Starling 37).[1]

What is curious about the popularity of the narratives is that in America whites from the North, who shared nothing historically, socially, economically, or ontologically with the Southern slaves, were the virtually exclusive readers of the texts. A number of factors can account for the popularity of the narratives, including a burning concern over the problem of slavery and a curiosity over the "exotic" life of the slave. But the narratives were autobiography, and as such the white readers had to confront more than history; they had to confront something they had never really confronted before: a black self. Before the ante-bellum narratives few black-authored texts even existed, and what black characters readers experienced in literature had inevitably been created by, and thus mediated by, white authors. With the slave narratives, blacks were in positions of textual power, both as authors and protagonists. American whites, who as a whole had grave doubts about the intellectual capacity of blacks and who cared little for what has come to be known as the "black experience," were suddenly asked to accept the role of black authorship, and care about the vicissitudes of the life of American blacks. And as the popularity of the narratives testifies, they did. What enabled white readers to identify with individuals who for so long had been regarded at best with indifference or condescension, and at worst dread?

The vast majority of the narratives were sponsored, edited, and published by whites, usually abolitionists or the abolitionist-minded, and often those whites were able to provide the means with which a reader could accept the significance of a black life. Many of the longer, book-length narratives, with which this essay is concerned, were accompanied by numerous texts— letters, testimonials, prefaces, introductions, an occasional book review— which often gushed with praise over the *character* of the individual who wrote the narrative. Part of their purpose was practical, stemming from the need to persuade a skeptical white readership to trust the narrator as an historian. These documents helped authenticate the narrative texts as the real products of real slaves.

However, these documents also served a purpose that traditionally had been crucial in American literature: They mediated between the black authors and the white readers. The authenticating documents provided the comfort of a familiar guiding hand; they not only authenticated but literally framed the narrator's vision of the world and his self. If one read everything in the order presented, the reader would commonly encounter white authentication and interpretation before seeing the first word of the black author's text. The reader would have been given a frame of reference within which the narrative text could be placed before the text was even read. The narrators became enclosed by, if not infused with, a white way of seeing that could guide a reader towards a particular way of responding to the text and the narrative self. Readers familiar with white writers writing about slaves and slavery would have been comfortable with this textual hierarchy, would have perhaps been more inclined to accept the veracity of a text, and perhaps would have been more receptive to the idea of an individuated black self, since a fundamental hierarchy still persisted.

And that self had nothing to do with a discrete black self or discrete black culture. As far as the abolitionists were concerned, white Americans did not read the narratives to find out about black culture. White Americans wanted to discover a people aspiring to the truisms of white American mythology. The abolitionists, as Merton Dillon points out, were quite underwhelmed by notions of a discrete culture for American blacks:

Abolitionists had little appreciation for what a later age would call "black culture." They took for granted that blacks would share the common American culture. Their observation led them to believe that Blacks had similar expectations. (73)

The authenticating documents certainly portrayed black character in a far more positive light. But they also sketched that character according to a system of values and beliefs which white Americans honored and which had been incorporated as part of the cultural mythology of white America. The men and women who wrote these documents wrote them from the prospect that if white Americans were going to accept the realities of manumission and blacks as part of the culture, white Americans had to believe blacks revered what they themselves revered. If by virtue of writing autobiography the narrators were not meant to live an entirely unexamined life, they nevertheless had to examine it with someone peering over their shoulders, someone with his or her own ideas about what marked appropriate historical character and behavior.

In his 1855 narrative, *My Bondage and My Freedom*, Frederick Douglass offers a good example of the abolitionists' need to mediate between black character and white audience. Douglass knew quite well that he was one of the most, if not the most, significant and celebrated black member of the abolitionist movement. Throughout a good portion of his career as antislavery writer and lecturer he maintained an iconic status among fugitive slaves, one who eventually became, in one critic's words, a "popular idol."[2] Merton Dillon points out that the abolitionists "especially dwelt on the genius of Frederick Douglass" (69). The ever-garrulous William Lloyd Garrison, in his preface to Douglass's 1845 narrative, commented that Douglass had been "consecrated...to the great work of breaking the rod of the oppressor, and letting the oppressed go free" (ix-x).

Yet his relationship with his white abolitionist compatriots was often ambivalent, marked with tension, even antagonism, as his struggle for autonomy at times brought him into conflict with whites seeking to re-create Douglass in their own image.

Douglass tersely expressed his own awareness of his quasi-mythic standing among the abolitionists, remarking that while on an abolitionist lecture circuit, after Douglass narrated his life, "Mr. Garrison followed me, taking me as his text" (358). Douglass knew not only that his life was an exemplum—his phrasing even hints at a life of Biblical proportions—but that he himself was, to white abolitionists, a rhetorical structure, a grammar written by Garrison to be interpreted by Garrison.

That mediation ultimately led to a conflict between himself and his white abolitionist companions concerning the division of labor on the lecture circuit:

During the first three or four months, my speeches were almost exclusively made up of narrations of my own personal experience as a slave. "Let us have the facts," said the people. So also said Friend George Foster, who always wished to pin me down to my simple narrative. "Give us the facts," said Collins, "We will take care of the philosophy." It was impossible for me to repeat the same old story month after month, and to keep my interest in it. It was new to the people...but it was an old story to me; and to go through with it night after night, was a task altogether too mechanical for my nature. "Tell your story, Frederick," would whisper my then revered friend, William Lloyd Garrison....[3] I could not always obey, for I was now reading and thinking. New views of the subject were presented to my mind. It did not entirely satisfy me to *narrate* wrongs; I felt like *denouncing* them. (361-2)

Douglass's need to display a rounded humanity was countered by his companions' need to persuade Douglass into his "proper" role and character—at least as far as the audience was concerned—which Douglass resisted:

[I] was growing, and needed room. "People won't believe you ever was a slave, Frederick, if you keep on this way," said...Foster. ["]Be yourself," said Collins, "and tell your story."..."Better have a little of the plantation manner of speech than not; tis not best that you seem too learned." These...friends...were not altogether wrong in their advice; and still I must speak just the word that seemed to *me* the word to be spoken *by* me. (362)

The publishers, sponsors, and editors who provided authenticating material also assumed the philosophical role, and left the story-telling to the narrators. In part this was nothing more than good business sense. The abolition of slavery demanded an active response from Northerners; they needed to be aroused. As William Andrews rightly points out, "experienced abolitionists recognized that first-person narration, with its promise of intimate glimpses into the mind and heart of a runaway slave, would be much more compelling to the uncommitted mass of readers than the outcry and polemics of the anti-slavery press" (9).

But as a consequence the authenticating documents often implicated the writers as naïfs: They were skilled enough to tell a coherent tale, but not clever enough to be artful—not clever enough to fashion history into a fiction. Their minds were apparently not nimble enough to deal with anything but the facts they had in hand. Readers were constantly enjoined by the prefaces, reviews, letters, and even narrative text not to attend too much to the writer himself, thus diminishing the authorial presence and command of the writer. The narratives, as Edwin Scranton observed in his introduction to Austin Steward's 1856 narrative, were "plain, unvarnished" tales (vi). Henry Bibb published one of the more romantically adventurous narratives in 1850, but the *New York Tribune* praised him for offering an "artless record," and *The Chronotype* agreed, citing Bibb for his "perfect artlessness" (206, 207). William Wells Brown (1850) inspired Edmund Quincy to marvel at his ability to write with "simplicity and calmness" (v).

The narrators also occasionally vouched for their own modest skills and intentions, and were quite willing to advocate authorial innocence. Moses Roper (1838) assured his readers that "the facts related here do not come before the reader unsubstantiated by collateral evidence, nor highly colored to the disadvantage of cruel taskmaster" (7). Charles Ball (1837) claimed that as a writer he desired to make the narrative "as simple, and the style of the story as plain, as the laws of the language would permit" (xi). The reader could be certain that in his narrative "the reader will find nothing but an unadorned detail of acts, and the impressions those acts produced on the mind of him upon whom they operated" (xii).

Such modesty and disinterestedness on the part of the narrators can at times tax a reader's credibility and become laden with irony. When compared to the quality and strong self-interest evident in some narratives, the disclaimers stand as little more than rhetorical posture—a concession, perhaps, to editorial desires. Ball, for example, is incurably fond of tales rife with gothic grue and perverse sexual undercurrents that would seem to contradict his claims of restraint. Austin Steward could write several hundred pages worth of an "unvarnished, but truthful narrative" about his "humble and uneventful life," a bit odd given that the vast majority of the narratives were typically much shorter.

Frederick Douglass also agrees, with painful modesty, to the task of writing *My Bondage and My Freedom*:

I have . . . felt that it was best for those having histories worth the writing—or supposed to be so—to commit such work to hands other than their own. To write of one's self, in such a manner as not to incur the imputation of weakness, vanity, and egotism, is a work within the ability of but few; and I have little reason to believe that I belong to that fortunate few. (vi)

Presumably, then, we are to regard *My Bondage* as an essential, rather than superfluous text, and are to be assured that Douglass had a legitimate rationale for writing a life. Douglass's modest text, however, is nearly 500 pages long. Moreover, it was his second autobiography in ten years. (He would publish two more after the Civil War.) Finally, it is one of the rare narratives titled in the first person, as he purposely calls attention to his particular self, rather than to the life of a representative slave.

To an extent the narrators had to pose as naïfs. For one reason, many narrators were *not* skilled writers. More significantly a white readership had little or no awareness of black consciousness. Narrative artlessness was a rhetorical trope that guarded against damaging accusations of fabrication and misrepresentation.[4] For the narrator, as William Andrews notes, "the very reception of his narrative as truth depended on the degree to which his artfulness could hide his art" (5).[5]

Artlessness implies that the writer's conscious, manipulative presence has been removed, or at least weakened, in favor of the textual events. This is a curious enough conceit as it is, since in autobiography textual events and author are indistinguishable on the surface. Artlessness also means that the individuated black self, in the person of the writer, recedes into the background. What the reader is encouraged to confront in the text, as with any exemplary autobiography of the time, is a cultural product—a set of character conventions that confirm or articulate the highest values of a culture. The black as writer, then, was expected to have the primary role of black as historical character, a role where character could be treated as an abstraction and easily manipulated.

Once the "fact" was established that the narrators were too innocent and unsophisticated to fabricate tales about slavery, a reader could then believe the truth of the character presented in the narrative itself. The authenticating documents provided the guidelines with which to perceive that character, and a lofty character it was indeed. What one encounters is a paradox: The authors may have been innocent, but the texts they wrote were often marketed in terms of historical romance that embellished history with a dramatic flair sure to bring a reader's blood to boil.

This would seem to contradict notions of unadorned texts steering clear of the shoals of literariness. But the abolitionists managed to get around this point by first of all insisting that the nature of a slave's existence was so fraught with peril that it was *in fact* an adequate analogy for what readers experienced in romances. An unadorned tale of slavery, then, could in truth be a tale of high adventure—such were the genuine woes of a slave's life.

Those who sponsored the narratives were, as the shrewd marketers they were, simply taking advantage of a prevailing cultural attitude that developed about he fugitive slaves. By the 1850s, "The fugitive slave and his rescuer had become folk heroes" (Dillon 192). The sponsors were prompt to compare the narratives to the best romantic fiction of the day, and so signalled the readers to take certain expectations into the texts of the narratives. For example, Lucius Matlack, assessing the state of the slave narratives in his introduction to Henry Bibb's narrative, admires the narratives as "startling incidents *authenticated, far excelling fiction* [my emphasis] in their touching pathos" (i). These narrative writers, apparently no worse the wear from the hardships suffered during slavery, escape, and assimilation into a new culture, were, to Matlack, even capable of "gushing fountains of poetic thought" (i). In this preface to Douglass's 1845 narrative Garrison pointed out that his favorite passage in the narrative was this one containing Douglass's reflections upon ships he watched in the Chesapeake:

You are loosed from your moorings, and are free; I am fast in my chains, and am a slave! You move merrily before the gentle gale, and I sadly before the bloody whip! You are freedom's swift-winged angels, that fly round the world; I am confined in bands of iron! O that I were free! O, that I were on one of your gallant decks, and under your protecting wing! Alas! betwixt me and you, the turbid waters roll (67).

The passage, which goes on for some length in that rhetorical vein, is unabashedly sentimental and overwrought. Yet to Garrison the passage was "thrilling" and caused him to ponder "who can read that passage, and be insensible to its pathos and sublimity" (xv). The pinnacle of the narrative for him was not its factualness, but a moment of high sentimental romance.

Yet how could an intelligent reader accept the artlessness of a writer who could generate such a passage? If readers accepted the conventions of overblown sentimentalism to begin with, that was part of a tacit agreement that literature, in its highest form, structured and articulated the finer and more sublime feelings of human beings. Romance may not have been rooted in earthly reality, but true to its neo-platonic underpinnings, it was rooted in a reality of a higher order. Narrators might blatantly write carefully posed scenes filled with complex oratory, but if such poesy gushed from a heartfelt expression of genuine inner torment or joy, then indeed the texts could be artless—the *feelings* were not contrived, even if the language were.

Many were the narratives described as "thrilling," or with some such synonymous phrasing, to assure the reader that therein lay a tale to quicken one's heart and breath. Matlack, ever reserved and circumspect, guaranteed that Bibb's tale was a "thrilling narrative" that would stand as a "monument more enduring than marble." (i). His story, in fact, "must stir the blood of every reader who has the pulsations of a man," according to Douglass's paper *The North Star*, which further praised Bibb's tale as "one of the most...thrilling narratives of slavery ever laid before the American people" (206). Similar kudos were offered for Thomas Jones's narrative (1857)—which was, of course, one of "thrilling interest"—and Harriet Jacobs narrative (1861), for which, as Lydia Maria Child promised in her introduction, "those who know her will not be disposed to doubt her veracity, though some incidents in her story are more romantic than fiction" (xi).

Indeed the narratives did have many of the staples of popular romantic literature—sex, violence, dramatic action and adventure—with the bonus of all of it being true. The narrators were not inventing the cruelties and deviancies of slavery, but were presenting a history that dovetailed neatly with the more prurient interests of the audience.[6] As docu-dramatists of contemporary television might claim (and perhaps did as the miniseries *Roots* aired), this was history the way it was meant to be.

What was happening, then, was that the agonies of slavery and the slave narrators were being abstracted in the authenticating documents. Equating a slave's tale with romance removed it from the world of harsh, unyielding reality, and enabled a reader to maintain, perhaps, the same distance from the cruelties of the slave's world as from the cruelties in a piece of sentimentalist fiction. In *Anatomy of Criticism,* Northrop Frye defines romanticism in terms that explain not only the context of sentimental romance at large, but that also offer an insight into what was perhaps the subconscious cultural rationale for embracing the slave narratives with romance:

Romance...is characterized by the acceptance of pity and fear, which in ordinary life relate to pain, as forms of pleasure. It turns fear at a distance, or terror, into the adventurous; fear at contact, or horror, into the marvellous...It turns pity at a distance, or concern, into the theme of chivalrous rescue; pity at contact, or tenderness, into a languid or relaxed charm...(37)

Romance indulges in distance, and romantic history and autobiography embody a fundamentally optimistic discourse. The message in the authenticating documents was that white readers could consider the problem of slavery without needing to approach too near it. If a guileless narrator presented what was essentially a romantic view of history and self, then neither the narratives, nor slavery itself, belied the "truth" of white cultural mythology; in fact, the struggle for truth was being played out in the arena of the South.

These documents were giving readers permission to extend their literary and cultural pre-disposition into the texts and impose them upon the narrators' autobiographical selves. *The New York Tribune,* writing about Bibb's narrative, acknowledged that the book had "the attraction of a romance," though it saw "no romance in his sufferings" (206), an intriguing pairing that suggests what was difficult in Bibb's life could still comfortably, and without apparent irony, be encased in the conventions of romance in the reviewer's mind. Writing also about Bibb, *The True Wesleyan* praised his tale highly, citing the narrative's capacity to confuse fact and sentimental convention as a reason for success:

But it is not in the execution that the interest lies; it is in the thrilling incidents so well told. We have never been a great reader of novels,...yet we have read enough to know the almost resistless power which a well-executed tale, when once we commence reading, exerts over the mind, until we reach the end; and did we not know the author, and know from the best of proof that the book is a true narrative, on reading it we should pronounce it a novel. the reader may rely upon its truth, and yet he will find it so full of touching incidents, daring adventures, and hair-breadth escapes, that he will find his attention held spell-bound, from the time he begins until he has finished the little volume. We feel the work cannot fail to meet with an extensive sale. (206)

The True Wesleyan reassures the reader that he or she will not be blazing new attitudinal trails by reading Bibb's life. Implicit in the *Wesleyan's* remarks is that Bibb had forsaken an autonomous autobiographical self in favor of convention. Note that the reviewer lauds the work not for its execution—an expression of personal style and imagination—but for its incidents. The *Wesleyan*, then, recapitulates the same process attempted by Douglass's white abolitionist cohorts, as it reduces Bibb the author, the individual, to a status of invisibility.

Those whites who authenticated the narratives further guaranteed the comforting romance of the narratives by presenting the narrators as gloriously heroic figures cut from a broad romantic cloth. The narrators were kin to those historical figures who brought conflicts to resounding and successful conclusions. As was pointed out in the preface of the tale of Aunt Sally (1858), a third person narrative written by a relative, "Robinson Crusoe and the Arabian Nights would seem lifeless and uninteresting by the side of hundreds of true and simple narratives which might be written of slave life in our Southern States" (iii). Rarely, however, do the narrators themselves ponder their own greatness. That is an observation to which mostly whites seemed privy. It was white authority which placed the imprimatur of great character upon the narrators.

For example, Henry "Box" Brown (1849), who escaped to the North by having himself shipped to Philadelphia in a box, wrote a "heart-rending tale" displaying character "worthy of a Spartan." In the same preface to Brown's narrative, the writer mentions the escape of William and Ellen Craft, and suggests that their story "will yet be made the groundwork for a future Scott to build a more intensely interesting tale upon than 'the author of Waverly' ever put forth" (v, vi, vii).[7] Edmund Quincy assured William Wells Brown, in a letter prefacing Brown's narrative, that some of the scenes "are not unworthy of De Foe [sic] himself" (vi). A reader of Venture Smith's 1798 narrative, one of the few narratives of Northern slavery, was informed that he or she "may here see a Franklin or a Washington" (3). William Lloyd Garrison, finding few limits to the possibilities of Douglass, compared him to Moses, the Irish statesman Daniel O'Connell, and Patrick Henry. For Douglass such heroic contexts became an eerie reality in this personal history. He was originally named Frederick Augustus Washington Bailey, and was given the name "Douglass" by a northerner referring to an heroic Scottish chief from Scott's "Lady of the Lake." Douglass makes no comment on such, but we can speculate about the sources of Augustus and Washington.

Ephraim Peabody spoke, perhaps, for all who perceived the narratives within these heroic contexts when he noted that the narratives continued an honored mythic tradition—a tradition particular to white Western civilization:

There are those who fear lest the elements of poetry and romance should fade out of the tame and monotonous social life of modern times. There is no danger of it while there are any slaves left to seek for freedom, and to tell the story of their efforts to obtain it. There is that in the lives of men who have sufficient force of mind and heart to enable them to struggle up from hopeless bondage to the position of freemen, beside which the ordinary characters of romance are dull and tame. They encounter a whole Iliad of woes...in recovering for themselves those rights of which they have been deprived from birth. Or if the Iliad should be thought not to present a parallel case, we know not where one who wished to write a modern Odyssey could find a better subject than in the adventures of a fugitive slave. What a combination of qualities and deeds and sufferings most fitted to attract human sympathy...! (62)

Even one narrator, Josiah Henson, willingly perpetuated this heroic ideal in his own tale, as he suggested that the fundamental conflict between master, male slave, and female slave could at times resemble chivalric romance:

The miseries which I saw many of the women suffer often oppressed me with a load of sorrow. No white knight, rescuing white fair ones from cruel oppression, ever felt the throbbing of a chivalrous heart more intensely than I, a black knight, did, in running down a chicken in an out-of-the way place to hide till dark, and then carry it to some poor overworked black fair one...I felt good, moral, heroic...This...was all the chivalry of which my circumstances and condition in life admitted. I love the sentiment in its splendid environment of castles, and tilts, and gallantry, but having fallen on other times, I love it also in the homely guise of Sambo as Paladin, Dinah as outraged maiden, and old Riley [Henson's master] as grim oppressor. (21-3)

For Henson, the context and manifestations of romance may change, but the central terms of romance prevail. Yet the manifestations of this romance convey a certain wry irony to Henson's example, perhaps skewering, with gentleness, the heroic conceit.

White abolitionists were not the only ones responsible for these broad delineations. James M'Cune Smith, the black abolitionist who introduced *My Bondage*, issued a resounding rhetorical assessment of the virtues of Frederick Douglass. "He is a Representative American man—a type of his countrymen," wrote Smith. "Frederick Douglas [has] passed through every gradation of rank comprised in our national make-up, and bears upon his person and upon his soul every thing that is American. And he has not only full sympathy with every thing American; his proclivity or bent, delighting to outstrip 'all creation' " (xxv-vi). For Smith, then, Douglass personifies a democratic ideal; he is an exemplary model for the values of self-reliance and social mobility that American whites cherished as part of their national character.

In the eyes of Smith, what makes Douglass the supreme example of black achievement in America is precisely his ability to transcend delimiting notions of negritude and so implicitly demonstrate an "innate" black impulse to become one with an homogeneous culture. Slavery thus would seem more horrific, as it would then be binding ideological brethren to a state of moral and social debasement. The narrators could call on their white readers to help abolish the evil of slavery and so free the slaves not only from bondage, but also free the slaves to allow their democratic ambitions to flourish. Narrators such as Samuel Ringgold Ward (1855), Austin Steward, and Josiah Henson, who called for an autonomous black society apart from white society, would only help their cause more if they could demonstrate that American values were valorized within their systems.

We cannot, however, really know how deeply Smith or Douglass or any of the narrators believed this. Neither Smith, nor Douglass, nor most narrators, nor most white abolitionists were naive enough to believe that white Americans would cheerfully embrace blacks as fully enfranchised members of mainstream society—certainly not in a North which feared that abolition would instigate a massive black exodus to the North. White Americans mistrusted blacks, and believed them to be quite adept at deceiving, at wearing masks. How much, then, would readers be inclined to believe about the black characters being presented to them?

Ultimately these more noble perceptions of black character improved radically upon the sort of clownishness or mindless servility that often marked black character in much of the contemporary literature, both apologist and abolitionist. Yet these heroic constructs do not represent a genuine release of black character, or autobiographical selves, from the boundaries of white desires. The terms for comparison hinge upon the autobiograhical selves being "consumed" by a grander, more stylized, and identifiably white context. Like the concept of romance itself, such heroic splendor abstracted the narrators, equating them with figures who had long since been transmuted into symbols of white western grandeur.

Notes

¹Other best-sellers included Solomon Northup's 1853 narrative, which sold 27,000 copies in two years (Bontemps xviii). Charles Ball's narrative was one of the few challenged for its authenticity, but such a challenge did little to hinder its sales— six editions of the text were issued between 1837 and 1859 (Nichols 150). Moses Roper's narrative enjoyed eleven printings, including an edition in Celtic (Starling 36). In one year four editions of William Wells Brown's narrative were issued; by 1849 his work had sold its 10,000th copy, and in that same year it was published in England and sold 11,000 copies. Even apologists for slavery joined in a small way: In 1861 the spurious narrative of one Harrison Berry, a Georgia slave, was published in defense of the peculiar institution.

²An interesting example of Douglass's fame is that at one point during his tenure as bright star of abolitionism he was paid tribute with a popular song entitled "The Fugitive's Song," written for and dedicated to him. The song was graced with an intriguing cover sheet. The illustration depicted a highly romanticized version of Douglass escaping slavery—romanticized beyond any truth. Despite what the cover may have suggested, Douglass did not escape by wandering barefoot through the wilderness with nothing more than a cudgel and a sack of food; he never even attempted

such an escape. The song's cover sheet simply described the iconography of the fugitive slave as abolitionists, and as the American public, preferred to imagine it, and revealed the impulse to guide fugitives, Douglass among them, into that iconography.

[3]Between 1845, when Douglass published his first narrative, and 1855 the friendship between Douglass and Garrison cooled considerably. The two came to disagree over the appropriate political approach to slavery. At first Douglass agreed with Garrison that the Constitution justified slavery, and so those who opposed slavery were obliged not to participate in the mechanisms of American government. Douglass, however, reconsidered and challenged Garrison's position, which resulted in the falling-out between the two.

[4]A skilled narrator also raised damaging questions about the genuine maleficence of slavery. An artful narrator, by virtue of his skill, could be viewed as the exception that proved the rule that blacks on the whole were helpless and needed slavery. On the other hand, apologists for slavery could ask the question whether talent like this could really have been produced out of an institution as malevolent as abolitionists liked to claim.

[5]All of those involved with the publication of the narratives were quite successful at this task—very few narratives were challenged by apologists as being false, testifying for both the accuracy and restraint of the narrators, as well as the scrupulousness of the editors and abolitionists who published the narratives.

[6]Violence was a constant in the narratives, since violence was often the means for enforcing slavery, and a fairly common means of punishment, retribution, or defense. Some narrators, such as Charles Ball, show a penchant for dwelling upon the more gruesome characteristics of violence—not an entirely unusual trope in writings about slavery. Even white abolitionists were not loath to advantage themselves of such exciting possibilities for their anti-slavery polemics. *American Slavery As It Is* (1839), the abolitionists' stunning indictment of slavery, is for long textual stretches a litany of atrocities committed against slaves.

Sex appeared in the form of concubinage and breeding of slaves, sometimes even drifting into sadism in numerous scenes of slaves being bound and laid out naked to be whipped. Much of the power of Harriet Jacobs' narrative, for example, derives from its frightening and fascinating portrayal of the disturbed sexual psyche of her white master and the socio-sexual tension of being an enslaved black women in a society governed by white men who fundamentally created and commanded an artificial society.

[7]Indeed, in 1861 William Craft published the story of he and his wife in *Running a Thousand Miles to Freedom*. Ellen, a very light-skinned black, disguised herself as a young Southern gentleman and openly journeyed to the North accompanied by her husband William, who acted as the "gentleman's" personal servant. (A young Southern woman accompanied by a male slave would have been suspicious.) To avoid giving herself away, she disguised the smoothness of her face with a poultice for a "tooth-ache," and avoided speaking by having William indicate that she suffered from a throat ailment. They also circumvented her inability to read or write by wrapping her arm and claiming she suffered form rheumatism. Even before William ever wrote their story, they had become legendary among abolitionists and escaped slaves.

Works Cited

Slave Narratives

American Anti-Slavery Society. *American Slavery As It Is: Testimony of a Thousand Witnesses.* Ed. Theodore Weld. New York, 1839. New York: Arno Press, 1968.

American Reform Tract and Book Society. *Aunt Sally; or, The Cross the Way of Freedom.* Cincinnati, 1858. Miami: Mnemosyne Pub. Co., 1969.

Ball, Charles. *Slavery in the United States: A Narrative of the Life and Adventures of Charles Ball, a Black Man.* New York: 1837. New York: Kraus Reprint Co., 1969.

Berry, Harrison. *Slavery and Abolitionism, As Viewed by a Georgia Slave.* Atlanta, 1861. Whiteman, v. 7.

Bibb, Henry. *Narrative of the Life and Adventures of Henry Bibb.* New York, 1850. Whiteman, v. 7.

Brent, Linda (Harriet Jacobs). *Incidents in the Life of a Slave Girl.* 1861. New York: Harvest/HBJ, 1973.

Brown, Henry "Box." *Narrative of Henry Box Brown.* Boston, 1849. Whiteman, v. 7.

Brown, William Wells. *Narrative of the Life of William Wells Brown.* London, 1850.

Clarke, Lewis. *Narratives of the Sufferings of Lewis and Milton Clarke.* Boston, 1846. New York: Arno Press, 1969.

Craft, William. *Running a Thousand Miles to Freedom.* 1860. Bontemps 270-331.

Douglass, Frederick. *Narrative of the Life of Frederick Douglass.* Boston, 1845. New York: Anchor Books, 1973.

——— *My Bondage and My Freedom.* New York, 1855. New York: Dover Publications, 1969.

Equiano, Olaudah. *The Life of Olaudah Equiano, or Gustavus Vassa, the African.* London, 1789. Bontemps. 1-192.

Henson, Josiah. *Father Henson's Story of His Own Life.* Boston, 1858. New York: Corinth Books, 1962.

Jones, Thomas H. *The Experiences of Thomas H. Jones.* Worcester, 1857. Whiteman, v. 2.

Northup, Solomon. *Twelve Years a Slave.* 1853. Baton Rouge: LSU Press, 1976.

Pennington, James W. C. *The Fugitive Blacksmith.* 1849. Bontemps. 196-267.

Randolph, Peter. *Sketches of Slave Life.* 2nd ed. Boston, 1855. Whiteman, v. 2.

Roper, Moses. *A Narrative of the Adventures and Escape of Moses Roper.* Philadelphia, 1838. Whiteman, v. 2.

Smith, Venture. *A Narrative of the Life and Adventures of Venture, a Native of Africa.* New London, 1798. In *Five Black Lives.* 1-34.

Steward, Austin. *Twenty-Two Years a Slave.* 1856. New York: Negro Universities P, 1968.

Ward, Samuel Ringgold. *Autobiography of a Fugitive Negro.* London, 1855. New York: Arno Press, 1968.

Other Primary Sources and Texts Containing Primary Sources

Bontemps, Arna, ed. *Great Slave Narratives.* Boston: Beacon press, 1969.

Five Black Lives. Middletown (CT): Wesleyan UP, 1971.

Peabody, Ephraim. "Narratives of Fugitive Slaves." *Christian Examiner* XLVII: 61-93.

Whiteman, Maxwell, ed. *Afro-American History Series.* Wilmington (DE): Scholarly Resources Inc., n.d.

Criticism, Theory and History

Andrews, William L. "The First Century of Afro-American Autobiography: Theory and Explication." *Studies in Black American Literature.* 4-42.

Dillon, Merton l. *The Abolitionists: The Growth of a Dissenting Minority.* DeKalb: Northern Illinois UP, 1974.

Frye, Northrop. *Anatomy of Criticism: Four Essays.* Princeton: Princeton UP, 1973.

Nichols, Charles H. "Who Read the Slave Narratives?" *Phylon* 20 (Summer, 1959), 149-62.

Nye, Russel B. *Society and Culture in America 1830-1860.* New York: Harper and Row, 1974.

Starling, Marion Wilson. *The Slave Narrative: Its Place in American History.* Boston: G. K. Hall and Co., 1981.

Contributors

Joseph Bodziock is assistant professor of English at the University of Maryland—Eastern Shore.

Floyd Coleman, Ph.D., is Professor and Chairman of the Department of Art, College of Fine Arts, Howard University, Washington, D.C.

Ronald Dorris is Assistant Professor of American Studies at the U. of Notre Dame. His writings have appeared in *Griot, Western Humanities Review, Quarterly West, McNeese Review, Genetic Dancers, The Western Journal of Black Studies*, and *Proteus*.

Katrina Hazzard-Gordon is the founder and artistic director of the Diaspora Dance Theatre and Research Group. She is also the author of *Jookin: The Rise of Social Dance Formations in African-American Culture* (Temple University Press, 1990), and is the Henry Rutgers Research Fellow and Assistant Professor of Sociology at Rutgers, Camden.

James L. Hill is Professor of English and Dean of the School of Arts and Sciences at Albany State College, Albany, Georgia. A 1976 graduate of the University of Iowa where he received the doctorate degree in American Civilization/African-American Studies, Dr. Hill has done extensive research on the fiction of Frank Garvin Yerby. Additionally, he is the general editor of the Peter Lang series *Studies in African and African-American Culture*; and he has published in a variety of journals, including the *Arizona English Bulletin, Black Books Bulletin, Umoja*, and the *Journal of Negro History*.

Vashti Crutcher Lewis is Assistant Director of The Center For Black Studies and an Assistant Professor of English at Northern Illinois University. Her manuscripts on the use of the near-white female in novels by Black women have appeared in leading literary journals on Black culture and criticism, and her research on africanisms in Toni Morrison's *Sula* appears in *Wild Women in the Whirlwind*. She holds a Ph.D in American Studies from The University of Iowa.

D.H. Melhem is a poet, critic, teacher, and writing consultant. An adjunct professor at the Union for Experimenting Colleges and Universities, she is the author of three books of poetry, numerous essays, and two books of criticism published by the University Press of Kentucky: *Heroism in the New Black Poetry: Introductions and Interviews* (1990) and *Gwendolyn Brooks: Poetry and the Heroic Voice* (1987). She also contributed the "Gwendolyn Brooks" section to *The Heath Anthology of American Literature* (D.C. Heath, 1990) and the foreword and afterword to George E. Kent's *A Life of Gwendolyn Brooks* (University Press of Kentucky, 1990).

Contributors   181

Bishetta D. Merritt is chairperson of the Radio, Television, and Film Department at Howard University. Her research interests include African-Americans and mass media, television criticism and political communications.

Emmanuel S. Nelson is Associate Professor of English at SUNY-Cortland. Editor of *Connections: Essays on Black Literatures* (Canberra: Aboriginal Studies Press, 1988), he has published numerous articles on contemporary American and Australian literatures.

Joyce Pettis teaches in the Department of English at North Carolina State University. She has published articles on several Black women writers including Margaret Walker and Toni Morrison. She is currently writing *The Fractured Psyche: Journey Toward Spiritual Wholeness in the Fiction of Paule Marshall*.

Lawrence N. Redd is a communication arts and sciences specialist at Michigan State University. Dr. Redd's research interests include radio, music, and educational telecommunication. He is the author of *Rock Is Rhythm and Blues*, has published in a variety of journals and produced over one hundred radio and television programs, films and musical recordings.

Harry A. Reed is Associate Professor of History at Michigan State University. His principal interests are embodied in two monographs that he is working on currently: one, on 19th Century Free Black Community Controversy and the other on Black Female Novelists and Idea of Black Culture Nationalism.

Philip M. Royster is Professor of Ethnic Studies at Bowling Green State University, Bowling Green, OH. His essays on African-American literature, culture, and language appear in various places including *Obsidian II, Black American Literature Forum, Obsidian, CLA Journal, Umoja, First World,* and *Black Books Bulletin*. A study of scapegoat relationships in the novels of Toni Morrison is forthcoming and a study of musicians as rescuers in African-American fiction is in preparation. He has published two collections of poetry, *The Back Door* (Third World Press) and *Songs and Dances* (Lotus Press). He is a master drummer who, since 1958, has studied, performed, recorded, and lectured concerning traditional African, Afro-Cuban and Afro-American drumming and drum cultures.

Audrey Lawson Vinson, is Associate Professor of English, Alabama A. and M. University, is co-author, with Bessie W. Jones, of *The World of Toni Morrison*. She has published and lectured on subjects which include William Faulkner, Ernest J. Gaines and Toni Morrison.

Gilbert Williams is a faculty member in the Department of Telecommunication at Michigan State University. His research interests include mass media history, African American images in mass media and radio/TV and cable programming.

Ben C. Wilson is an Associate Professor at Western Michigan University. He has been the recipient of 17 grants and has been a consultant for high school textbooks authors. Dr. Wilson has also authored a number of articles and manuscripts as well as developed 15 educational audio-visual modules that deal with African-American heritage in Michigan.